NOTIONS AND FACTS
Collected Criticism and Research

MARY LASCELLES

OXFORD
AT THE CLARENDON PRESS
1972

Oxford University Press, Ely House, London W. 1

GLASGOW NEW YORK TORONTO MELBOURNE WELLINGTON
CAPE TOWN IBADAN NAIROBI DAR ES SALAAM LUSAKA ADDIS ABABA
DELHI BOMBAY CALCUTTA MADRAS KARACHI LAHORE DACCA
KUALA LUMPUR SINGAPORE HONG KONG TOKYO

© OXFORD UNIVERSITY PRESS 1972

73-18885
PRINTED IN GREAT BRITAIN
AT THE UNIVERSITY PRESS, OXFORD
BY VIVIAN RIDLER
PRINTER TO THE UNIVERSITY

TO
CLAIRE LAMONT

PREFACE

THE revision of essays, lectures, and other pieces of writing gathered from a span of more than twenty years must raise at least one problem: how to take account of what has been learnt since they were written without seeming to have been wise before the event. There was, for example, the recovered manuscript of *The Vanity of Human Wishes* to be reckoned with; but this entailed little change in 'Johnson and Juvenal'. The Scott lectures, on the other hand, brought a hospitable invitation to examine the manuscript of *Redgauntlet*; this led to the writing of the essay on Scott's revision of Wandering Willie's Tale; and that in turn made thorough revision of the lectures necessary—to avoid repetition, I must remove what I had said about the Tale, and put something else in its place.

In these two pieces, therefore, I acknowledge a revision more radical than the verbal polishing which seemed enough for the rest. In all, there had to be some reconsideration of references. The reader would have been vexed by citation of more than one edition of *Rasselas*, for example, although there had formerly been a reason for this. I have endeavoured throughout to refer to editions which are both reputable and available.

Of the two new pieces, one (the 'Postscript') was written in response to an invitation to amplify my review of a particular edition of *King Lear*. The other I wrote partly to please myself.

Throughout, I have had much help. Many obligations are acknowledged in the notes to the several pieces; one, in the Dedication. I owe much to the good offices of the Librarian of the English Faculty Library and her staff. But to have enjoyed the sociability of an academic community for much of a lifetime is a cumulative benefit—one not easy to estimate or express.

ACKNOWLEDGEMENTS

MY thanks for permission to reprint are due to: Mrs. F. P. Wilson ('The Rider on the Winged Horse' from *Elizabethan and Jacobean Studies* presented to her husband, ed. Herbert Davis and Helen Gardner, Clarendon Press, Oxford, 1959, 1969); Mrs. John Butt ('Scott and the Art of Revision' from *Imagined Worlds*, essays collected in memory of her husband, ed. Maynard Mack and Ian Gregor, Methuen, 1968); and Dr. L. F. Powell ('Johnson and Boswell on their Travels' from *Johnson, Boswell, and their Circle*, essays in honour of his eighty-fourth birthday, ed. Mary Lascelles, James L. Clifford, John Hardy, and J. D. Fleeman, Clarendon Press, Oxford, 1965).

The following have likewise appeared elsewhere: 'Shakespeare's Comic Insight' and 'Obituary of R. W. Chapman' (*Proceedings of the British Academy*, xlviii (1962) and xlvii (1961), O.U.P.); 'Johnson and Juvenal' (*New Light on Dr. Johnson*, ed. F. W. Hilles, Yale University Press, 1959); 'Shakespeare's Pastoral Comedy' (*More Talking of Shakespeare*, ed. John Garrett, Longmans, 1959); 'Sir Dagonet in Arthur's Show' (*Shakespeare-Jahrbuch*, ed. Wolfgang Clemen, 96 (1960), Quelle & Meyer, Heidelberg); '*Rasselas* Reconsidered' (*Essays and Studies 1951*, collected for the English Association); Review of *The Letters of Samuel Johnson*, 'Johnson's Last Allusion to Mary Queen of Scots', Review of *King Lear*, and '*Rasselas*: a Rejoinder' (*Review of English Studies*, N.S. v, no. 17 (Jan. 1954), viii, no. 29 (Feb. 1957), xviii, no. 71 (Aug. 1967), and xxi, no. 81 (Feb. 1970), Clarendon Press, Oxford); 'The Sir Walter Scott Lectures for 1960' (*University of Edinburgh Journal* (spring 1961), Oliver & Boyd, Edinburgh); 'A Physician in a Great City' (*Transactions of the Johnson Society of Lichfield* (1951)). I acknowledge with thanks permission to reprint these.

CONTENTS

A Note on References	xi

※　※　※

The Rider on the Winged Horse (1959)	1

※　※　※

Shakespeare's Pastoral Comedy (1959)	29
Shakespeare's Comic Insight (Annual Shakespeare Lecture, British Academy, 1962)	47
Review of *King Lear*, ed. G. I. Duthie (In the New Cambridge Shakespeare (1967))	65
Implications of *King Lear*: a Postscript (1971)	72
Sir Dagonet in Arthur's Show (1960)	81

※　※　※

'A Physician in a Great City' (Presidential Address, Johnson Society of Lichfield, 1951)	91
Rasselas Reconsidered (1951)	102
Rasselas: a Rejoinder (1970)	120
Johnson's Last Allusion to Mary Queen of Scots (1957)	130
Johnson and Juvenal (1959)	137
Johnson and Boswell on their Travels (1965)	155
Review of *The Letters of Samuel Johnson*, edited by R. W. Chapman (1954)	170

※　※　※

The Sir Walter Scott Lectures for 1960	
I. Scott and Shakespeare	179
II. Scott and the Sense of Time	195

CONTENTS

Scott and the Art of Revision (1968)   213

Jane Austen and Walter Scott:
a Minor Point of Comparison (1971)   230

✶   ✶   ✶

Robert William Chapman
(Obituary for the British Academy, 1961)   247

✶   ✶   ✶

Index   259

PLATES

I. Proofs of the first edition of *Redgauntlet*,
vol. i, pp. 240 and 241   *facing p.* 216

II. Scott's manuscript of *Redgauntlet*, vol. i, fol. 58   ,,   217

A NOTE ON REFERENCES

IN referring to those authors who appear most frequently in the following collection, I have endeavoured to consult the reader's convenience. Thus, all quotations from *Rasselas* are alike referred to Geoffrey Tillotson's edition, although the pieces in which they occur preceded it.

In quoting from Jane Austen's novels, I have continued to give page-references to R. W. Chapman's edition, followed by the number of the chapter as it would appear in any other modern edition.

There is, unfortunately, no authoritative collected edition of Scott's writings—not even of the novels; though one of the *Journal* is in preparation, and will be used (ed. W. E. K. Anderson, Oxford 1972). I have therefore, in quoting from the novels, given volume- and page-reference to the first edition, followed by the chapter-number as it would appear wherever chapters are numbered continuously. (This precluded the 'Magnum' edition, despite its closer association with Scott.) For such other prose as Lockhart included in it, I have turned to his edition of the *Collected Prose Works*; elsewhere, to the periodicals in which the several pieces originally appeared. For his letters, H. J. C. Grierson's edition (1932–7).

Shakespeare references are to Peter Alexander's edition (one vol., Collins, 1951).

Johnson references are as follows: *Letters*, ed. R. W. Chapman (Oxford, 1952); *Lives of the Poets*, ed. G. B. Hill (Oxford, 1905); Boswell's *Life of Johnson*, ed. G. B. Hill, revised L. F. Powell (Oxford 1934–50, second edition of vol. v, 1964).

> Nec fonte labra prolui caballino,
> nec in bicipiti somniasse Parnaso
> memini, ut repente sic poeta prodirem.
> Heliconidasque pallidamque Pirenen
> illis remitto, quorum imagines lambunt
> hederae sequaces: ipse semipaganus
> ad sacra vatum carmen adfero nostrum.
> quis expedivit psittaco suum 'chaere'
> picamque docuit nostra verba conari?
> magister artis ingenique largitor
> venter, negatas artifex sequi voces;
> quod si dolosi spes refulserit nummi,
> corvos poetas et poetridas picas
> cantare credas Pegaseium nectar.

If, among these disclaimers of poetic ambition, there linger any echoes of Bellerophon's tragic fall, they will not be heard again until editions of Greek authors begin to come from the Italian presses in the 1480s. But the repercussions of Persius' Prologue are quite another story. The Satires were known and esteemed in the Middle Ages;[1] and these lines, with their ostensible profession of unworthiness, were evidently regarded as a pattern exordium. It may indeed be said that *not sleeping on Parnassus* became an indispensable piece of literary good manners. Not every one who repeated this formula, however, had an ear for its intonation. Presently, therefore—in England, not later than the beginning of the fifteenth century—irony, with its mingled colours, enters the story: the persons become agents of happenings which they neither intend nor expect. To Chaucer, Persius' intention is of course clearly audible; he captures the import of the whole passage in a glancing allusion, and clinches it with a comparable disclaimer of rhetorical skill:

> I sleep never on the mount of Pernaso,
> Ne lerned Marcus Tullius Cithero . . .[2]

And, if there is irony in prefixing these lines to a tale in which poetical and rhetorical art are happily allied, we may be sure it is deliberate.

[1] J. E. Sandys, *History of Classical Scholarship*, 1921; E. R. Curtius, *European Literature and the Latin Middle Ages*, trans. W. R. Trask, 1953.
[2] Chaucer, *Works*, ed. Skeat, 1894, iv. 482 (Prologue to the Franklin's Tale).

A small circumstance serves to measure the quickness of response on which Chaucer might reckon: the Ellesmere scribe wrote in the margin against the Franklin's apology the first two lines of Persius' Prologue—perhaps from memory, for he is not word-perfect. Later variations on this theme, however, call in question more than verbal accuracy. What are we to make of John Walton's *Prefatio Translatoris* to his version of Boethius?

> Hyt leketh not me to labour nor muse
> Upon these olde poyses derke
> For cristen fayth such thynges moste refuse
> As witneseth Jerom the noble clerke
> Hyt shulde be no cristen mannes worke
> Tho false goddes names to renew . . .
> And certen I have tasted wonder lyte
> As of the welles of calyope
> No wonder though I sympelly endyte
> Yel wyl I nofte un to Tessiphone
> Ne to her susters that in hel be
> Besekynge after craft of eloquence
> But pray to God of hys benignitie
> My spirit to enspyre with hys influence.[1]

If indeed he knew Persius, and had not met his disclaimer already reduced to a commonplace, may we accept Dr. Curtius' pleasant suggestion that to a medieval clerk Persius' *semipaganus* might signify only half a pagan?[2] This would certainly open the way to a *half-Christian* distrust of the Muses, accepted as implicit in any such disclaimer as his. A hundred years later Gavin Douglas, having praised Virgil for drinking deep of Helicon,[3] professes his own independence of such sources:

> Calliope nor payane goddis wyld
> May do to me no thing bot harme, I wene . . .[4]

Lydgate may have been intermediary between Persius and such allusions as these; his variations on the theme of the Prologue are

---

[1] *The Boke of Comfort called in Latyn Boecius de Consolatione Philosophiae*: . . . 1525. Walton (who wrote in 1410) says, moreover, that he knows himself inferior to Chaucer and Gower.   [2] Op. cit., p. 233.
[3] For the confusion of Helicon with Hippocrene, see p. 10, below.
[4] *Works*, ed. Small, 1874, ii. 5 and 17-18 (*Proloug of the First Buik of Eneados*).

notable. He appeals, for example, to Clio who dwells with her sisters

> ... by Elicon the welle,
> Rennyng ful clere with st[r]emys cristallyn,
> And callyd is the welle Caballyn
> That sprang by touche of the Pegasee ... [1]

Indeed, he seems to have known all fourteen lines of the Prologue, and valued them as a collection of mythological allusions—on which he drew no fewer than four times.[2] Can he have guessed that the word *caballinus* was chosen to suggest a decidedly underbred horse? Its sound was pleasing, its rhyme serviceable; what more could a poet ask than that a fountain should be both caballyn and crystallyn?

Alike as commonplace and allusion, this disclaimer of the Muses' aid long retains one constant characteristic—its personal application: with whatever variations of tone, serious or sardonic, the poet must be understood as referring to himself—as it were, in his professional capacity. Whence it follows that such a passage is most likely to occur in prologue or dedication, or else in some part of a longer work which gives occasion for a reaffirmation of poetic purpose. The implications, however, of this denial of the Muses could be extended. 'Avoid Parnassus', whether this signifies self-admonition or a warning offered to a fellow poet, may mean: 'Withdraw from a barren region.' Thus, to Maynard, at odds with Richelieu, it affords a figure of speech for stinted patronage.

> Descens de la double montagne

is one expression of a favourite theme for epigrammatic complaint;

> Le feu de la Prose & des Vers
> Ne fait plus bouillir la marmite ... [3]

So is the more famous epigram which ends:

> Malherbe, en cét âge brutal,
> Pegase est un cheual qui porte
> Les grands hommes à l'Hospital.[4]

---

[1] *Troy Book*, ed. Bergen (E.E.T.S.), 1906, p. 2.
[2] Besides the *Troy Book*, these contain allusions of this kind: *The Complaint of the Black Knight*; the *Fall of Princes*; the *Life of St. Albon*. There is sufficient reason for believing that each allusion is Lydgate's own addition to his source.
[3] François de Maynard, *Œuvres poétiques*, ed. Garrisson, Paris 1885–8, iii. 109–10.
[4] Ibid., iii. 102–3.

From here, a ready way opens downwards to the use of Pegasus as a figure of speech in satire of poetic pretension; and Boileau takes it.[1] This is the mood of Butler's satire, and this the employment to which he puts the winged horse—for example, in his Character of *A Small Poet*: '... To what Purpose did the Antients feign *Pegasus* to have Wings, if he must be confined to the Road and Stages like a Pack-Horse, or be forced to be obedient to Hedges and Ditches?[2] But I doubt whether outright satire was ever the characteristic English response to this myth. To the systematic French mind we must often seem like children who strike out an odd notion by chance and, on hearing others laugh, set up for humorists. Thus, Corbett, a generation earlier, had eased the passage from satiric observation to grave reflection with this gently ironic allusion:

> Away, my Muse, from this base subiect, know
> Thy Pegasus nere strooke his foote soe low.[3]

And these mingled colours had appeared in Thomas Randolph's warning to a friend not to look for 'the Pegasian spring' either by 'the Oxes ford' or 'the bridge through which low Cham doth run'.[4] One more English illustration may be cited for its odd simplicity. *Queen Tragedy Restor'd* is a little piece of drollery for the stage: the Queen, sick almost to death, is rescued from the coma into which quack physicians have thrown her by a pageant, in which Shakespeare rises and speaks:

> At the Behest of *Sol's* bright Charioteer
> Patron of those choice Spirits, who with youthful
> Ardour mount fiery-footed *Pegasus*,
> *Bellerophon's* proud Steed, lo *Shakespear* comes![5]

Despite the pitiable failure of the verse to wake Shakespearian echoes—despite much that is deliberately ludicrous in the context—these four clumsy lines surely imply recognition of the splendour

---

[1] e.g. in *L'Art poétique*, Chants I and III; *Discours au roi*, etc.
[2] Samuel Butler, *Genuine Remains*, ed. R. Thyer, 1759, ii. 115. See also p. 119.
[3] Richard Corbett, *Iter boreale*, ll. 99–100; *Poems*, ed. J. A. W. Bennett and H. R. Trevor-Roper, 1955, p. 34. Corbett is passing from gibes at tapsters to thoughts stirred by the fall of Richard III.
[4] Thomas Randolph, *Poems*, ed. Thorn-Drury, 1929, p. 97.
[5] I know this 'Dramatick Entertainment' only in the anonymous edition of 1749.

still latent in that outworn figure of speech which was once part of a poetic myth.

It is pleasant to turn back towards some of the numerous references to the Muses in Italy of the fourteenth and fifteenth centuries, and to observe acknowledgement rather than disclaimer as the customary approach. (Disclaimer itself, when it appears, will be softened and brightened by the suavity of Italian poetic manners, until it shines with a lustre not unlike that of acknowledgement.) Among these references are to be found passages which Chaucer knew, and to which he paid his tribute of imitation—for example, the invocation at the opening of the *Teseida*, and the valediction:

> O sorelle Castalie, che nel monte
> Elicona contente dimorate
> dintorno al sacro gorgonëo fonte
> sottesso l'ombra delle frondi amate
> da Febo, delle quali ancor la fronte
> spero d'ornarmi sol che 'l concediate,
> le sante orecchi a' miei prieghi porgete
> e quelli udite come voi dovete.

—and, after a closing reference to the Muses:

> E però che i porti disïati
> in si lungo peleggio giá tegnamo,
> da varii venti in essi trasportati,
> le vaghe nostre vele qui caliamo,
> e le ghirlande e i don meritati,
> con l'ancore fermati, qui spettiamo,
> lodando l'Orsa che con la sua luce
> qui n'ha condotti, a noi essendo duce.[1]

Chaucer, as his commentators have remarked, gathers images from both these widely separated stanzas, glancing also at a passage, or passages from the *Divine Comedy*, when he frames the invocation to his *Anelida and Arcite*:

> Be favorable eek, thou Polymnia,
> On Parnaso that, with thy sustres glade,

[1] Boccaccio, *Opere*, iii. ed. A. Roncaglia, Bari 1941; *Teseida*, i. 1, and xii. 86. Propertius likewise had linked his reference to the Muses with this simile of the storm-beaten vessel making into port—whether by coincidence merely, or a natural train of figurative thought.

By Elicon, not fer from Cirrea,
Singest with vois memorial in the shade,
Under the laurer which that may not fade,
And do that I my ship to haven winne . . .[1]

He could, indeed, have found similar *Helicon* references in the prose of Dante and Boccaccio.[2] I venture to call in question the inference often drawn from such passages that these poets *confused* Helicon with Hippocrene.[3] The springs associated with Pegasus, or with the Muses, or (as the tale grew) with both, were so numerous; the relationships between the mythical beings were so intricate; and both had so long a record of figurative service, that some such explanation as this seems preferable. To the great Italian poets—and to some few others, surely, who had taken them for masters— one function of myth was to serve as plaything for a craftsman, and *the pleasure of the thing* consisted in a bold and happy redisposition of the figures, whether in pictorial or verbal composition. Where words compose the pattern, the changes will be rung on names and the epithets from which they are framed, or with which they are compounded—with a strong preference, in a literate society, for the oblique and allusive formation, such as Dante's 'diva Pegasea'[4] or Boccaccio's 'antrum Gorgoneum'.[5] This latter, with deliberate artifice, recalls Pegasus' birth from the death-pangs of Medusa, the dint of his hoof in the rock, and the stream that issued from it, with the sole purpose of designating the source of poetic inspiration. I cannot believe that Boccaccio used the phrase 'monte Elicona' in his invocation, and 'l'Elicone / fonte' in a later passage of the *Teseida*,[6] for no better reason than confusion of mind. Here, rather, is the buoyancy of a poet who regards himself as natural heir to the

---

[1] Chaucer, *Works*, ed. Skeat, i. 365–6.
[2] e.g. Dante, *De Vulgari Eloquentia*, ii. 4; Boccaccio, *De Genealogia Deorum*, xiv, *passim*.
[3] e.g. John Livingston Lowes, 'Chaucer and Dante', in *Modern Philology*, Apr. 1917. His list of sources of misinformation would be conclusive if Chaucer, Dante, or Boccaccio had been writing a manual of information. Since, however, they were writing poetry, it may surely be urged that these sources, if they recollected them, gave them licence, if they needed it, for poetic play.
[4] *Paradiso*, xviii. 82.   [5] *De Genealogia Deorum*, xiv. 20.
[6] xi. 63. This, an elaborate verbal picture, has for subject Apollo and the Muses depicted on a shield.

treasures of ancient myth. Amongst his remoter followers, the case may well be different.

This, if it is a just interpretation, should be borne in mind when approaching a particular fifteenth-century reference which may prove important in the development of the association between Pegasus and the poet. I mean the opening to the tenth canto of the fourth book, in Nicolo delli Agostini's continuation of Boiardo's *Orlando Innamorato*. Reinach drew attention to it,[1] and suggested that here at last was that mysterious turn in the development of the myth so often attributed to Boiardo.

> Non perchio creda al Eliconeo fõte
> Tuffar el Griffo mio ne le sacre onde
> Et con rime fiorite, terse, & pronte
> Cingermi al capo de le aurate fronde
> Ne con Apollo al bel Pegaso monte
> Seder con le sue muse alte, & feconde
> Che essendo come io sõ di poco p̃ggio
> Salir non spero a si sublime seggio.
>
> Ma sol per dar diletto al Signor mio
> Et qualunque mi stara ascoltare
> Seguo dou'io lasciai con tal desio
> Che piu non si potrebbe imaginare
> Sẽza altra inuocatiõ de Euterpe, & Clio
> Perch'io so ben che lui mi pol aitare
> Et far mia naue gir con prosper uento
> Nel desiato porto a saluamento.[2]

That it is in the continuation rather than the poem that we should look for the modern conception of Pegasus I am indeed convinced, for in the *Orlando Innamorato* itself I have found no reference but to *grifoni e pegasei* as beasts of the chase[3]—and the plural alone would discredit any attempt to link this passage with the myth of the Muses' horse. Nevertheless, Reinach was (I believe) hampered by

[1] Loc. cit., p. 229. Though I shall have occasion to disagree with his conclusions, I should certainly not have found the passage without the help of his mentioning it.
[2] Boiardo, *Orlando Innamorato*, Venice 1539. My choice of an edition to quote may, I am afraid, be arbitrary, but I have made a comparison with others to ensure that it shall not be misleading.
[3] Matteo Maria Boiardo, *Orlando Innamorato*, ed. A. Scaglione, Turin 1951, ii. 569 (Book iii, Canto 5, stanza 37).

not having seen the stanzas and by attributing the word *Pegaso*, on the advice of a friend, to a printer's error: a misprint for *Parnaso*. This seems questionable. Not only is Pegasus present in the editions of 1538 and 1539; he persists in those of 1553, 1584, and 1602—which exemplify Domenichi's revision;[1] and no edition giving Parnassus has (so far as I know) been found. Lodovico Domenichi, moreover, makes himself responsible for more than merely verbal improvements; elsewhere in the poem he corrects mythological allusions with some rigour. Yet, while carefully supplying the adjectival form *Pegaseo*, he appears satisfied with the meaning. May we not say that to the sixteenth-century editor it presented no difficulty, because the poet was by now airborne? Of this at least I am sure: Agostini's passage, whether he wrote *Parnaso* or *Pegaseo*, observes a traditional pattern, though newly diversified. From the first to the fifteenth century, these refrains have been heard in alternation: 'Sleep on Parnassus? Not I.'—'Be favourable to me, you who dwell on Parnassus or by the sacred spring.' Agostini preserves the pleasantry in the disclaimer, the true modesty in the acknowledgement, while giving to both a fresh and agreeable turn: 'Sleep on Parnassus? Converse with the Muses? No, no—it is enough that I write to please *you*.' This is the mood in which Sidney—whether prompted by Agostini or another, or else without any prompting at all—recalled Persius' prologue in his seventy-fourth sonnet:

> I never dranke of *Aganippe* well,
> Nor never did in shade of *Tempe* sit:
> And Muses scorne with vulgar braines to dwell,
> Poore Lay-man I, for sacred rites unfit—

that last line surely the perfect equivalent of Persius' *semipaganus*. This sonnet, one of several playful assertions that the heart's devotion is of more avail than any help the Muses can give, may (for all we can now tell) have been formerly designed to stand first in the sequence.

From Agostini's continuation onwards,[2] we are frequently aware of that tone—of pleasantry no longer sardonic, of personal applica-

---

[1] These five Venetian editions, all I have been able to examine, contain within the two stanzas I have quoted numerous verbal variants.

[2] Said to have been published in 1495. The earliest extant edition appears to be 1506.

THE RIDER ON THE WINGED HORSE

tion without bravado—which belongs above all to letters, or verse exchanged between friends. Thus, Ariosto (in a verse epistle concerned with the education of his friend's son) complains that, at the time when *he* was fit for the melody of Pegasus (*pegáseo melo*), his father compelled him to read law.[1] And it is with a like pleasant freedom that Gabriel Harvey offers advice to Spenser: '... perhappes it will advaunce the wynges of your Imagination a degree higher: at the least if any thing can be added to the loftinesse of his conceite, whom gentle *Mistresse Rosalinde*, once reported to have all the *Intelligences* at commaundement, and an other time, Christened her *Segnior Pegaso*.'[2] But the happiest of these allusions is Milton's, in a letter to Diodati: 'Multa solicite quæris, etiam quid cogitem. Audi, Theodote, verum in aurem ut ne rubeam, & sinito paulisper apud te grandia loquar; quid cogitem quæris? ita me bonus Deus, immortalitatem. Quid agam vero? πτεροφυῶ, & volare meditor: sed tenellis admodum adhuc pennis evehit se noster Pegasus, humile sapiamus.'[3] Of such intimate communication as this, commendatory verse can be no more than a shadow; but, as a shadow may show whence the light falls, so the sonnet addressed to William Drummond by Sir David Murray of Gorthy, a poet of Prince Henry's household, illustrates the employment of this emblem in formal exchanges of courtesy:

> The sister *Nymphes* who haunt the *Thespian* Springs,
> Ne're did their Gifts more liberally bequeath
> To them who on their Hills suck'd sacred Breath,
> Than vnto thee, by which thou sweetly sings.
> Ne're did *Apollo* raise on *Pegase* Wings
> A *Muse* more neare himselfe, more farre from Earth,
> Than thine...

These lines, together with the representation of a winged horse on the title-page of the 1614 *Poems*,[4] provoke a hitherto unspoken question: what did Pegasus mean to the common reader?

---

[1] *Satires*, vii. 154–9.
[2] *Three proper wittie familiar letters, lately passed betweene two Universitie men . . .* ; text from Spenser, *Poems*, ed. E. de Selincourt, 1912, p. 625.
[3] Columbia edition, xii. 26.
[4] Drummond, *Poetical Works*, ed. L. E. Kastner, 1913. For the sonnet, see i. 95; for a facsimile of the title-page of the edition (supposedly) of 1614, see plate 6, facing i, p. liv.

It is here that the mythographers must be taken into the reckoning; both because they had something to do with the development of this myth, and because they conditioned the response on which the poets counted. Poetic allusion requires of the reader some knowledge of the matter referred to; and, while I can nowise believe that Milton, for example, pored over dictionaries and handbooks of myth,[1] yet it is evident that he would have been obliged to frame his mythological allusions very differently for an age (like ours) in which the schoolboy's mind is not furnished with the information such books contain. The mythographies, however—ancient, medieval, modern—demand the scope rather of book than essay, even for the tracing of a single myth. They have, fortunately, received attention;[2] yet only an attempt (such as this) to find the answer to a particular question will show how intricate are their relationships —how frequently, for example, successive editions or translations of some one work will introduce significant variations into a single story, or how remote the antecedents of these variations are likely to be. I propose, therefore, to take my stand on two notable works, each (I believe) illustrating a distinct and important development; each, certainly, well known and influential. Boccaccio's *De Genealogia Deorum*[3] may be regarded as the culmination of the medieval tradition in mythography, and Comes's *Mythologiae*[4] as outstanding among modern compilations. The watershed between them is formed by the labours of those printers who made available texts (often with scholia) of ancient authors, in the last three decades of the fifteenth, and first three of the sixteenth century, enabling the lesser man's work to supersede that of the greater, and making even Boccaccio's editor and translator more knowledgeable than their author.

If Boccaccio may be accepted as representative of the medieval scholar poet, then it will appear that Bellerophon was known to the

---

[1] See D. T. Starnes and E. W. Talbert, *Classical Myth and Legend in Renaissance Dictionaries*, University of North Carolina Press 1955.

[2] e.g. J. Seznec, *La Survivance des dieux antiques*, Studies of the Warburg Institute, vol. xi, 1940.

[3] First printed in Venice, 1472. I shall have occasion to use the Basle edition of 1532, but will note any significant variation from the first edition.

[4] Natalis Comitis (i.e. Natale Conti), *Mythologiae*, published in Venice, 1551. I shall have occasion to use the Paris edition of 1583, but will note where it differs from that of Venice 1567, the earliest I have been able to obtain.

Middle Ages[1] as the triumphant hero of a romance of adventure: the man in whom virtue was rewarded; who, though falsely accused, compelled to carry his own death warrant and sent on a forlorn hope, won safety and acclaim with the help of his magic horse. I have indeed found references to Bellerophon's fall in both of the works attributed to Hyginus the Mythographer: according to that known as the *Fabulae*[2] he fell in the Aleian fields, but was still to attain a happy ending; according to the even more dubious *Poeticon Astronomicon*[3] he attempted the flight to heaven, but, looking down, was seized with terror, fell, and perished. All this is a far cry from Homer. A medieval reader, however, could encounter the Homeric version of Bellerophon's end among the pseudo-Aristotelian *Problemata* (xxx. 1), or in Cicero's *Tusculan Disputations* (iii. 63)—or in their derivatives. In this thirtieth *Problem*, Bellerophon is cited among mythical heroes distinguished for their melancholy, and also for eminence in philosophy, politics, poetry, or art; and two and a half lines from the *Iliad*, recounting his disfavour with the gods and wanderings in the Aleian fields, are quoted. In the third *Disputation*, extravagance in grief is censured, Bellerophon, with other mythical figures, instanced, and two lines, the account of his wanderings, quoted. (Both quotations are in Latin.) This allusion is not without reverberations. Petrarch, in the investigation of his own melancholy which he puts into the mouth of St. Augustine (in *De Secreto*), quotes these latter two lines.[4] An indistinct version of the *Problem*, with the Homeric lines loosely translated into French, is discoverable in *Le Miroir des Melancholicques*—'En ceste question est dispute pourquoy les Melācholicques sont ingenieux'.[5] It reverberates also in that valley of echoes, Burton's *Anatomy of Melancholy*:

[1] I have endeavoured to verify this supposition by resort to the sources and analogues of the *De Genealogia*—notably, the Vatican mythographies, *Scriptores rerum mythicarum*, ed. Bode, Celle 1834.
[2] The title given to this collection by its editor, J. Micyllus, in whose text of 1535 (Basle) it survives. (*Aleios* is his correction of *alienos*.)
[3] First printed at Ferrara, 1475. I have used the text of the 1535 volume, in which it is bound up with the *Fabulae* and other matter, but have compared it with that of the first edition.
[4] In the text of 1489, *Aleis* has become *alienis*, as in the text of Hyginus corrected by Mycillus. In the Italian translation *El Secreto*, Siena 1517, the epithet has become *amoenis*—which suggests forgetfulness of the original story.
[5] This purports to be a translation from the Greek, by Meury Riflant, Paris 1543.

16   THE RIDER ON THE WINGED HORSE

'Why melancholy men are witty, which Aristotle hath long since maintained in his Problems, and that all learned men, famous Philosophers, and Law-givers, *ad unum fere omnes Melancholici*, have still beene melancholy; is a Probleme much controverted.'[1]

These are but fitful and fragmentary recollections of an older, tragic story, such as could hardly be pieced together by a reader who knew nothing else of Bellerophon than the record of triumphant adventures which Boccaccio derived from some four centuries of mythographical tradition. It is with the amplified text of the *De Genealogia* published in 1532 by Jacobus Micyllus at Basle that the old pattern begins to reappear:

> Asclepiades sic tradit: Superbientem eum, ex rerum felici successu, tentasse cum Pegaso in caelum quoq̃ subuolare, quam audaciam cum Iuppiter odisset, immisisse Œstrum Pegaso, à quo agitatus excussit Bellerophontem, ceciditq̃ in campum Lyciæ, qui post ab eodem Aleius dictus est, eo quod cæcus in eo errasset Bellerophontes donec periret.[2]

Presently, in the translation and commentary of Betussi, we recognize that the story could no longer stop short at the victory over some monster: two passages of the *Elucidario poetico*, those under the names of Bellerophon and Pegasus,[3] recount the fall. Pegasus made the spring of Hippocrene, sacred to the Muses: 'Dapoi chinando egli il capo in pirene fonte dolce, Bellerofonte vi sallì sopra volendo volare in cielo, alla fine cadette, ma pegaso giungendo al cielo fu posto tra le stelle.'[4]

It is to Comes, amplified by Linocier and others,[5] that we must turn for such an account of Bellerophon as the diffusion of Greek texts had made possible; full, circumstantial, with references to

[1] 1621, p. 263. Burton seems to have forgotten the poet.
[2] Micyllus' end-note to Boccaccio's account of Bellerophon, p. 346.
[3] In sixteenth-century dictionaries, the entries under these two names are sometimes at variance. For example, in the 1596 edition of the *Dictionarium historicum, geographicum, poeticum*, attributed to Charles Estienne, one (Pegasus) accords with Hyginus, the other (Bellerophon) with Micyllus' note.
[4] Giuseppe Betussi, *Della Geneologia degli dei di Giovanni Boccaccio, Elucidario*, p. 61; first published 1545; but I quote from the edition of 1644 (Venice)—the earliest I have seen.
[5] G. Linocier, Paris 1583. For the labours of other editors, culminating in this edition, see F. L. Schoell, 'Les Mythologistes italiens de la renaissance et la Poésie Elisabéthaine', *Revue de Littérature Comparée* (1924), p. 10.

Homer and Pausanias, but coloured by a new morality, apparent in the very telling of the story:

> Sed Bellerophon, quale est ingenium plerisque mortalium, tãta rerum gestarum felicitate nimium elatus in cœlum quoque ascendere super equo Pegaso voluit: quam arrogãtiam Iupiter omnis temeritatis grauissimus vindex deprimendam esse ratus, œstrum illi equo immisit, quare Bellerophon præceps in terram deturbatur. Cum in Aleiam Ciliciæ planitiem is cecidisset, cæcúsque factus fuisset, *tamdiu errauit per illam planitiem, quamdiu vixit, donec inedia denique fuit assumptus ac victus penuria, cùm nullam neque domum, neque hominem reperisset:* at Pegasus nũc sublimis, nunc depressus per aëra volans, in cœlum denique rediit in Iouis præsepe, quæ stellæ sunt ita vocatæ.[1]

'Quale est ingenium plerisque mortalium'—this is upon us even before we reach the systematic allegorization of the myth; but it is in the full allegory, medieval and modern and the development from one to the other, that we may hope to discover a source for the tragic vision of the poet in his association with Pegasus.

The pattern of allegorical interpretation (traceable from Boccaccio, and even from his sources, to Comes) is threefold. The strands in the plait may be sufficiently distinguished thus: the simplest is that of natural philosophy—for example, Pegasus is explained in terms of air currents. Political philosophy, rooted in the euhemerist tradition, makes Bellerophon's exploits into well-planned campaigns, and Pegasus into a naval vessel—or, as Philemon Holland says (with an eye to Plutarch, Amyot, and the Queen's navy), a pinnace.[2] Thus interpreted, Bellerophon may adventure with Perseus as his fellow knight-errant, or else be equated with him.[3] Since the distinction between this interpretation and that of moral philosophy is not so sharp as that which divides both from natural philosophy, the acts of either hero may afford matter for discourse on man's political or moral attributes. It is this moral

---

[1] Op. cit., pp. 955–6. *. . .* not in 1567.

[2] Plutarch (*Moralia*) made the Chimaera a pirate; Amyot, in a note to his translation (Paris 1572), inferred pursuit by means of *un vaisseau fort leger*, and Holland names it.

[3] Boccaccio equates them; Raoul Lefèvre, in his Troy romance, makes them companions. Various arguments have been offered in explanation.

allegory that contains the pith of my argument. Boccaccio is here encumbered with an intractable medieval accretion: the description of Pegasus as a monster (hardly less grotesque than the Chimaera) in the *De Imagine Mundi* then attributed to St. Anselm.¹ This work must be responsible for the monstrous Pegasus of Henryson and Barclay.² Notwithstanding this impediment, Boccaccio expounds the meaning of Pegasus and his riders according to tradition. The flying horse is fame—that is, good repute, earned by deeds neither lucky nor foolhardy, but well judged. He made the spring signifying that poetic utterance by which great deeds are celebrated; hence it is said to be dedicated to the Muses. The theme, more than once repeated, is: fame, in the keeping of the poets.³ The sources are the medieval mythographies, without discrimination. For the interpretation of Bellerophon, however, Boccaccio turns specifically to Fulgentius, and quotes him word for word: Bellerophon is wise deliberation (*bona consultatio*), appropriately mounted on Pegasus, after whom the eternal spring (of wisdom) is named. 'Sapientia enim bonæ cōsultationis æternus fons est.' And so we return to the association with the Muses.⁴

This interpretation of horse and rider as fame, and the qualities that earn fame, has been too little regarded; but it is not difficult to illustrate. Lydgate, after his customary disclaimer of poetic skill, reflects that the celebration of his hero, St. Albon, does not require it:

> The golden trompet of the house of fame
> With full swyfte wynges of the pegasee
> Hath [blowe] full farre the knyghtly mannes name.⁵

In Hawes's *Pastime of Pleasure*, an allegorical figure, who is not called Fame but leads the dreamer where fame may be won, approaches surrounded with tongues of flame and riding upon a palfrey

---

¹ The author was Honorius Augustodunensis—see Migne, *Patr. Lat.*, vol. 172.
² Henryson, in his Sixth Fable, associates him with the Minotaur, the *Bellerophont* and the Werwolf. Barclay couples him with the Chimaera—monsters to be vanquished—in his Fourth Eclogue. The allusion is not to be found in his sources.
³ *De Genealogia*, x. 27, *Pegasus*. The theme is repeated in xii. 25, *Perseus*.
⁴ Ibid. xiii. 58, *Bellerophon*. Fulgentius, *Mythologiarum libri tres*, in the 1535 edition of Hyginus: Book iii, p. 148.
⁵ *The Lyfe of Seint Albon* . . . , St. Albans 1534, Prologue to Book i, ll. 15-17. See also the edition by C. Horstmann, Berlin 1882.

THE RIDER ON THE WINGED HORSE

> whiche hadde vnto name
> Pegase the swyfte / so fayre in excellence
> Whiche somtyme longed / with his premynence
> To kynge Percyus . . .[1]

Halle records the appearance, in a masque at Henry VIII's court, of 'a person called Reaport, appareled in Crymosyn satyn full of tõges, sitting on a flyẽg horse with wynges & fete of gold called, Pegasus'.[2]

As with poetry, so with fame: the figure engaging the imagination may be either horse or rider. The poet may mount the winged horse, or let his own wings grow; likewise, Pegasus may be, or bear, renown. Moreover, so pliant is the myth, so lively the mood in which it was originally applied, that the very shape of the rider is subject to vagaries of the imagination. Now the poet may set in the saddle that Muse whom he chooses to call his own. (Johnson, waked to particular attention by political antipathy, makes merry with Addison's clumsy performance of this feat.)[3] Now he may invoke Apollo himself in such a manner as to suggest that Pegasus carries a god:

> O, thou king of flames!
> That with thy music-footed horse dost strike
> The clear light out of crystal on dark earth,
> And hurl'st instructive fire about the world . . .[4]

For poetry enjoys one freedom denied to pictorial representation: we do not ask that its images shall remain constant when their significance can be conveyed by evoking other modes of sensation. What matters, here, is the sense of airy motion.

Comes, like Boccaccio, offers a threefold interpretation, in terms of natural, political, and moral philosophy; but, in this third kind of allegory, the difference between his age and Boccaccio's makes itself plain, for the moralization of the story now attaches itself not to

---

[1] Stephen Hawes, *The Pastime of Pleasure*, ed. W. E. Mead (E.E.T.S.), 1928, ll. 178–81.
[2] Edward Halle, *The Union of the Two Noble and Illustre Famelies of Lancastre & York* . . ., 1550, fol. lxvi^r.
[3] See his life of Addison (*Lives of the Poets*, ed. Hill, 1905, ii. 128), and Addison's culminating eulogy of King William in *A Letter from Italy*.
[4] Chapman, *Bussy d'Ambois*, v. 1.

Bellerophon's triumph but to his fall—he is no longer example, but warning:

> Alii vitę humanæ rationem propè omnem sub hac fabula contineri tradiderunt: nam neque aduersis rebus nimis tristari, neque prosperis & felicibus nimis gloriari aut extolli conuenit, quoniam horum omnium denique moderatorem Deum esse experimur. Is enim prosua singulari clementia & calamitatibus iniquè circumuctos adiuuat, quod accidit, dum calamitosus esset, Bellerophonti, & nimis elatos animos deprimit, quare præceps idem postea dicitur de cœlo detrusus.[1]

We may suppose that the triumphant fame-allegory, as Fulgentius and Boccaccio knew it and made it known, would have been to Comes mere childishness; and—but for that element of play in the poetic approach to myth—his contemporaries and successors should have rated it no higher. That the medieval interpretation of horse and rider persisted, however, we know, not only from the emblembooks,[2] but also from such compilations as the *Mundus symbolicus* of Picinellus, with its Biblical and Patristic analogies, and the *Hieroglyphica* of J. Pierius Valerianus, in which Pegasus is untouched by any recollection that his soaring flight could tempt the tragic hero to ὕβρις, or the Christian to self-will:

> Fama autem ubi primùm genita per hominum ora incipit uolitare, Musarum excitat fontem in Parnasso, quippe quòd illustrium uirorum præclara facinora uatibus scribendi suggerunt argumentum.[3]

This tradition may well explain an allusion in Marvell's *The Loyall Scot*. Promising to the young Douglas a duration of fame beyond that of the ancient heroes, the poet glances at their fame-bearer:

---

[1] Op. cit., p. 956.

[2] Alciati, for example, preserves the tradition attributing to Bellerophon the qualities that earn fame. I must plead want of space, as well as skill, for omitting references to pictorial art; to have included them would have doubled the length of this essay.

[3] Basle 1556, Book iv, fol. 32ᵛ. (In an alternative explanation, on the same page, Pegasus is a symbol of speed.) The passage, which is headed by a cut of a flying horse entitled *Fama*, allegorizes the birth of Pegasus. This is the tradition perpetuated by Bacon in the *De Sapientia Veterum* (also in *De Augmentis*), though his emphasis falls on political allegory—the importance of fame (that is, report of victories) in war. For George Sandys, some sixteen years later, the medieval moralization is still the accepted way of interpreting *Ovid's Metamorphoses Englished, Mythologiz'd, and Represented in Figures*, 1626.

> Skip Sadles: Pegasus thou needst not Bragg,
> Sometimes the Gall'way Proves the better Nagg—

the Scottish breed of horse will endure the longer journey.[1]

Such a passage, elegiac in purpose, reminds us that our reaction to the idea of fame cannot always be so simple and serene as it has appeared in the single strain of medieval allegory hitherto exemplified in this argument. Set aside, for the time being, any malign or ambiguous aspect of *Fama*—rumour, or good and bad repute capriciously allotted; dwell on what is simply benign in the conception and the myths embodying it; and this reflection persists: fame, as preserver of worthy names, claims to outlast life. The word indeed resounds splendidly; but let the imagination be disarmed and the heart laid open to impressions received through the unguarded ear, and grave overtones will become perceptible. Once aware of these, we are prompted to ask questions as to person and tense. Whose fame is the speaker asserting, and in what tense is the assertion delivered? Is the subject some hero of the mythical or historic past? Then it is fame's function to divert the shadow of death from his effigy, making it shine out amidst the obscurity of those whose names no poet has preserved:

> . . . omnes illacrimabiles
> urgentur ignotique longa
> nocte, carent quia vate sacro.[2]

But what if present merit and future renown compose the theme? To flatter a patron, or a mistress, with promises of deathless poetic memorials is indeed to acknowledge that this shadow must fall; but some element—whether of ceremony or of make-believe—in such flattery distances the event and makes the acknowledgement seem merely formal. Let tense and person be changed once again, however, even but a little, and fame be promised to one lately dead—one, moreover, who has died young, 'inheritor of unfulfilled renown'—and the ear will catch another tone; for the poet now

---

[1] *Poems and Letters*, ed. H. M. Margoliouth, 1952, ii. 173. These lines (63, 64) are part of a passage which Dr. Margoliouth regards as a postscript to the narrative of Douglas's death, designed to conciliate the Scots: a tribute to a valiant breed of men and horses.

[2] Horace, *Odes*, iv. 9.

charges himself with the affirmation of faith in a future that should have been.

Recognition of the extent of difference between the idea of fame in simple relation to the tale of Bellerophon's triumphant exploits, and in its complex associations with elegy, may help us to measure the distance between E. K.'s gloss on Spenser's April Eclogue and Spenser's own elaboration of the tradition this represents, in *The Ruines of Time*. *Helicon*, E. K. comments,

> is both the name of a fountaine at the foote of Parnassus, and also of a mounteine in Bœotia, out of which floweth the famous Spring Castalius, dedicate also to the Muses: of which spring it is sayd, that when Pegasus the winged horse of Perseus (whereby is meant fame and flying renowme) strooke the grownde with his hoofe, sodenly thereout sprange a wel of moste cleare and pleasaunte water, which fro thence forth was consecrate to the Muses and Ladies of learning.[1]

Spenser's development of the myth of the winged horse occupies two passages in *The Ruines of Time*: lines 421 to 427, and 645 to 658. How they came to be combined with other parts of this great, uneven poem and why they stand in this order need not be discussed here; the interwoven themes of fame, the preserver of heroic reputation, Pegasus, the bearer of fame, and Sidney, who was both hero and poet, are sufficient for consideration. Nevertheless, the particular contexts of these stanzas must be briefly indicated.

> But fame with golden wings aloft doth flie,
> Aboue the reach of ruinous decay,
> And with braue plumes doth beate the azure skie,
> Admir'd of base-borne men from farre away:
> Then who so will with vertuous deeds assay
> To mount to heauen, on *Pegasus* must ride,
> And with sweete Poets verse be glorifide.   (ll. 421–7)

This is the climax of some sixteen stanzas on the theme of the Muses and their servants the poets as guardians of worthy reputation; and these stanzas have followed directly on the first of those two passages of lament for Sidney which focus and define the elegiac purpose of the poem: lines 281 to 343.[2]

[1] All Spenserian passages are quoted from E. de Selincourt's edition, 1909–10.
[2] I accept the dedication and envoy as intimations of the central purpose of the poem as it now stands.

> Still as I gazed, I beheld where stood
> A Knight all arm'd, vpon a winged steed,
> The same that was bred of *Medusaes* blood,
> On which *Dan Perseus* borne of heauenly seed,
> The faire Andromeda from perill freed:
> Full mortally this Knight ywounded was,
> That streames of blood foorth flowed on the gras.
>
> Yet was he deckt (small ioy to him alas)
> With manie garlands for his victories,
> And with rich spoyles, which late he did purchas
> Through braue atcheiuements from his enemies:
> Fainting at last through long infirmities,
> He smote his steed, that straight to heauen him bore,
> And left me here his losse for to deplore. (ll. 645-58)

These two stanzas compose the eleventh of twelve 'tragic pageants'. The pageants, or visions, like the preceding lament of the Genius of *Verlame*, illustrate the transience of earthly glory and happiness, and fall into two groups, the second devoted to Sidney; each of these latter six being an emblem 'developed ... from these poetic symbols which are also constellations, to celebrate the entrance into immortality of the poet Philip Sidney, *Philisides, Astrophel*, the Star-lover'.[1]

Spenser's use of mythology—a poet's use—has been censured by some of his commentators.[2] I doubt whether it would have hindered the imaginative response of his first readers. The winged horse was already accustomed to bearing, now the fame of heroes, now the poets who cherished that fame; why not the heroic poet? Sidney's claim on that power which can stay the ruinous hand of time was twofold:

> So there thou liuest, singing euermore,
> And here thou liuest, being euer song
> Of vs, which liuing loued thee afore,
> And now thee worship, mongst that blessed throng
> Of heauenlie Poets and Heroes strong.

---

[1] W. L. Renwick's Commentary, in his edition of the *Complaints*, 1928, p. 201. The *star* symbol (as Professor Renwick observes) has not been traced in all six, but may surely be called the dominant figure throughout the group.

[2] e.g. those quoted in the Variorum edition, Johns Hopkins Press, *Minor Poems*, vol. ii, 1947—excepting W. L. Renwick.

> So thou both here and there immortal art,
> And euerie where through excellent desart. (ll. 337-43)

And the emblem of that power was traditionally wing-borne.[1] Pegasus had soared to heaven and shone there as a constellation: an apt figure, in a world familiar with the allegorization of myth, for the heavenly comfort which must conclude a Christian elegy. As to the choice of Perseus rather than Bellerophon as symbol for Sidney's soldiership, Spenser had not only Boccaccio's warrant for supposing himself free to choose, but also cogent poetic reasons for his preference. Whereas the story of Bellerophon runs contrary to any notion of courtly love,[2] Perseus' rescue of Andromeda is congruous with the romantic element in that tradition, and he therefore a not incongruous counterpart to Astrophel. Moreover, Perseus and Andromeda, with Pegasus hard by, are among the constellations. Not only is Bellerophon absent from this starry company; he fell in endeavouring to reach it; and that flight ended (as readers of Comes knew) with the arrival of Pegasus at the heavenly stable, riderless.

The idea of Sidney seems to run, like a twisted thread of black and gold, through the variously coloured web of *The Ruines of Time*. So intricate a pattern, so strange an alternation of themes one with another, each vanishing from sight only to recur, and all expressed obliquely, whether in terms of myth, allegory, or heraldry—this may indeed baffle or alienate the modern reader. But we need not suppose it to have been difficult or displeasing to Mary Sidney.

I suggested, in my opening juxtaposition of this poem with the proem to the seventh book of *Paradise Lost*, that medieval accretions might not be observable on the surface of this latter passage. Yet, having now approached it by way of earlier developments in the idea of the winged horse and his burden, we must surely be conscious of its complex and subtle texture of allusion. Milton gathers up, in twenty lines, Homeric, Pindaric, and quite other elements in the story of Bellerophon's fall; glances at widely dispersed interpretations of the myth of Hippocrene;[3] subdues both to his poetic

---

[1] Hence the winged figure, or figures, in ll. 421-7.

[2] The part of it which seems to have lingered in popular memory is of the same pattern as the story of Joseph and the wife of Potiphar.

[3] 'Sapientia enim bonae consultationis aeternus fons est . . . Sapientia enim dat musis fontem.' Fulgentius et al.

undertaking, and gives to the whole a personal application—not unsupported by tradition, but with a new poignancy.

Here the path of my argument grows suddenly much steeper. What hope can there ever be of translating into critical prose the purpose, even so much of it as is apparent at a single juncture, of such a poem? As for the personal application we divine here, the youngest reader of Milton can tell that he often refers to himself in his poetry; the oldest may well hesitate to define the scope of any particular reference. Indeed, I am dismayed at my temerity; and, but that so substantial a part of the material for this essay has been given me,[1] I should hesitate to proceed.

Among the elements of Milton's purpose in *Paradise Lost*, one surely is beyond dispute: he is to bring us to a point at which we must launch out from the imagined—what poets have feigned—to the almost unimaginable truth he has to relate. In this passage, for example, the Muses are recalled, only to be disclaimed—not flippantly, nor with the hesitation belonging to modesty—but as myth that must give way before revelation. Sometimes indeed fable foreshadows what he intends; but there are times when his intention is of such magnitude that human language has never been able to approach it more nearly than by saying what it was not. His truth may outgo fable or stand opposed to it. Thus, Bellerophon does not signify Milton even to the degree that Perseus signifies Sidney. Nevertheless, reference to him here has these two kinds of relevance: he would have invaded celestial regions; but that exploit (even if attained) would have been but a shadow of the poet's aspiration in writing of heavenly transactions; he climbed unbidden and was not saved from the consequences; but the poet, sure of vocation, may implore protection. Both comparison and contrast demand analogy. There seems no reason to suppose that Milton saw Bellerophon as symbol of the poet—though I believe this to have been in Meredith's mind, as it is certainly in that of Mr. Day Lewis.[2] For him, Pegasus alone afforded intimations of analogy sufficient for his purpose—that is, to suggest both comparison and contrast

---

[1] I am particularly indebted to Mrs. Henderson, Miss Labowsky, Miss Syfret, Mrs. Roaf, and Miss Hubbard. The responsibility for what I have made of the references they have given me, and their help in reading them, is of course entirely mine.

[2] Meredith's *Bellerophon*; C. Day Lewis, *Pegasus and Other Poems*, 1957.

with the famous ascent to heaven of the poets' horse, in a manner intelligible to the common reader, who might be trusted for some recollection of Comes, of Micyllus' edition of Boccaccio or his collection of mythographies, or at least the dictionaries compiled from these sources.

The personal application likewise shows *one* face turned towards Milton's audience, all of whom would recollect that a disclaimer of the Muses' aid was customary, not only in prologues but also in passages requiring the reaffirmation of poetic purpose. To those in sympathy with him, something more would be discernible: the proclaimed independence—no longer merely of patronage, but even of all human approbation; the new and tremendous meaning in the old assertion 'It is enough that I write to please Thee'. There is, however, another aspect of this personal application, which we may perhaps seek to descry—though interpretation must be tentative, and fall far short of the whole. A younger and happier Milton had written to his closest friend: 'Audi, Theodote, verum in aurem ut ne rubeam, & sinito paulisper apud te grandia loquar; quid cogitem quæris? ita me bonus Deus, immortalitatem. Quid agam vero? πτεροφυῶ & volare meditor. . . .' Let this confession be read in conjunction with certain passages, some of them earlier still, all forerunning *Paradise Lost*. Of the theme of fame in *Lycidas* little need be said: the poem has been closely investigated;[1] but one plain observation must nevertheless be offered here, as relevant to this argument. Of the man who is *called*, much is demanded; yet death may intervene, and against death his calling is no defence. ('What could the Muse herself that Orpheus bore . . .' '. . . nor could the Muse defend / Her son.') The answer given in *Lycidas* is that proper to an elegy on a man whom this has befallen: promise of continuity—not as to existence merely but also as to function, continuance in service. Death, however, is not the only, nor the most fearful threat. The Parable of the Talents haunted Milton's thought. That he had it in mind when he wrote

> How soon hath Time the suttle theef of youth,
> Stoln on his wing my three and twentith yeer!

[1] See Rosemond Tuve, *Images and Themes in Five Poems by Milton*, Harvard U.P. 1957.

THE RIDER ON THE WINGED HORSE

we know from the draft of a letter which accompanies this sonnet in the Trinity College Manuscript and contains a reference to 'the terrible seasure of him that hid his talent'.[1] It is implicit in the closing lines:

> All is, if I have grace to use it so,
> As ever in my great task-Masters eye.

In the sonnet on his blindness, it becomes explicit—

> ... that one Talent which is death to hide,
> Lodg'd with me useless—

for a fear like this, reassurance must be found elsewhere than in such thoughts as properly conclude an elegy. Its magnitude can be measured by the change that it works in the story of the unprofitable servant. Parable, like myth, stirs deep responses—so deep that not even veneration for scriptural text will prevent a man from reading his own thoughts into it. Milton having in mind his own poetic endowment, 'that one talent' grows from the single opportunity supposed too meagre to be worth cultivation into something known to be uniquely precious. He has, moreover, given a new and dreadful conclusion to the story, by making death, not deprivation, the penalty for failure. In this sonnet, another answer than that of *Lycidas* is vouchsafed. Yet the question, though it undergoes change, persists, and here, at the mid point of *Paradise Lost*, Milton discovers a reply to satisfy a poet in the very heart of a great undertaking.

> Up led by thee
> Into the Heav'n of Heav'ns I have presum'd,
> An Earthlie Guest, and drawn Empyreal Aire,
> Thy tempring; with like safetie guided down
> Return me to my Native Element:
> Least from this flying Steed unreind, (as once
> *Bellerophon,* though from a lower Clime)
> Dismounted, on th'*Aleian* Field I fall,
> Erroneous there to wander and forlorne.

The crucial phase of the story lies still ahead; but the equipoise of

---

[1] Facsimile, Cambridge 1899, p. 6. Milton evidently had St. Matthew's version in mind.

hope and fear has been tilted. Undaunted by all that appears unpropitious in the circumstances—in the very endeavour—Milton faces forwards. Celestial matters of more moment and greater delicacy than the war in heaven will presently confront him. This return to earth is not a simple event, nor escape from the field of error made once and for all; the petition for safety is not so to be understood:

The meaning, not the Name I call . . .

Yet the name *is used*; for the meaning could never be fully communicated without it. Moreover, since this name, or group of names, is charged with the associations of a myth, one often related, and usually with some accession of significance, the means by which we are made to understand all that is implied cannot be separated one from another without loss. Story cannot be translated into other terms. *Pegasean wing*, *Bellerophon*—these signify what no interpretation can hope to catch. And yet, as wrack upon the surface of the river shows which hay-fields have been plundered upstream and allows the eye to measure the force of the current, so these scattered fragments of myth and allegory to which I have here drawn attention may tell us something about the antecedents of a poem—even of one so well known as this—and enhance our sense of its volume and power.

SHAKESPEARE'S PASTORAL COMEDY

(1959)

CRITICISM bearing on the pastoral strain in Shakespearian comedy belongs to two widely separated groups: that of the distant past, broadly based, both as to what it asserts and what it takes for granted—which is why I mean to begin with it; and that, more pointed and particular, of the immediate present. It is this which poses a problem for me. When you have been teaching for more years than you care to reckon, a piece of fresh criticism will sometimes make its impact in successive waves. First: 'Why yes, but isn't this what I have been trying to say all this while?' Second (in the voice of conscience): 'Trying is the operative word—when have you succeeded in formulating this idea?' Nevertheless, the conclusion must always be: 'For me, it is never completely uttered until I have said it myself—or said what arises from this encounter of old and new ideas.' Thus, while it is the least I can do, to acknowledge indebtedness (bluntly, for brevity's sake) to a number of writers whose work has appeared of late—notably, in the eighth and eleventh volumes of the annual *Shakespeare Survey*[1]—it is also the most. For it still remains for me to find my own way forward, asking such questions as I can frame, and seeking answers for which I can find words.

Hazlitt prompts the first of these questions, by what he says about Shakespearian comedy. The immediate context is *Twelfth Night*, but I think that his comments on this play apply—and that he would have been willing that they should apply—more widely; at least to include all those of Shakespeare's comedies that are called romantic. 'This', he says, '... is perhaps too good-natured for comedy.... It makes us laugh at the follies of mankind, not despise them, and still less bear any ill-will towards them.' And, after contrasting it with the artificial and satirical comedy of the Restoration, he proceeds to

[1] Cambridge University Press. I must single out for special gratitude Professor Harold Jenkins (on *As You Like It*, in *Shakespeare Survey* 8).

generalize: 'Shakespeare's comedy is of a pastoral and poetical cast. Folly is indigenous to the soil, and shoots out with native, happy, unchecked luxuriance. Absurdity has every encouragement afforded it; and nonsense has room to flourish in.'[1]

I propose to consider what these conjunctions mean: comedy *but* good-natured; inviting laughter that is free from contempt, and of a pastoral, poetical cast. Why, in the first place, did Hazlitt plant that (implied) *but* between comedy and all these agreeable things—the laughter of sheer enjoyment, poetry, the world of the pastoral?

Perhaps I may be allowed a personal illustration. I happened once to be lecturing on *Henry IV*—to an audience that was, or chose to appear, decidedly non-committal. Therefore I was the more surprised when one member of it—a particularly grave-looking graduate from overseas—joined me as I walked back and told me that he had never really thought Falstaff funny until he listened to me. I replied with proper modesty that it was George Robey he should have heard. No, that was not what he meant. All the literary, all the learned people he had met hitherto had been insistent that comedy was meant to do something beneficial to you—to make you better, not to make you laugh. Now, if this seems far-fetched, le me point out that, according to some eminent scholars and critics, Falstaff *cannot* have been meant to amuse the judicious, since he is merely the traditional figure of Riot misleading Youth— an interpretation which, as Miss Gardner points out, has had an enervating effect on some recent productions of the play, 'in which Falstaff has seemed so oppressed by awareness that he is temptation incarnate that he has hardly had the spirit to present any serious temptation'.[2]

Were we meant to enjoy the rogues and fools of Shakespearian comedy? And does that enjoyment touch hands with liking? (Enjoyment and liking must, surely, go along together in actual life; but I think that they need not in art; we can enjoy the representation of what we by no means like—and that, in most other kinds of comedy, is what we are invited to do.)

[1] *Characters of Shakespeare's Plays*: 'Twelfth Night'.
[2] Helen Gardner, *The Limits of Literary Criticism*, O.U.P. 1956.

Coleridge's theory of comedy may help: he was hardly likely to devise one which would exclude Shakespeare. He calls it 'poetry in unlimited jest'. It entails, he says, 'the apparent abandonment of all definite aim or end, the removal of all bounds in the exercise of the mind'. It is (he continues) 'a display of intellectual wealth squandered in the wantonness of sport without an object'.[1]

Now I believe that such comedy as this description comprises asks certain conditions, a particular climate of the imagination. The world in which this pure comic spirit can operate must be at once like and unlike our own. Thus, there are in this world laws of cause and effect; but, against their very nature, they act intermittently. Here, as in our world, you may, if you touch fire, burn your fingers; for it is not a world in which fire never burns, but rather, one in which it sometimes forgets to burn—or even burns the wrong man, the one who has kept well out of its way. Retribution is not, as in satire, inexorable; the dispenser of justice may be entreated—or may prove absent-minded. The proper consequence of an act is sometimes suspended—now in favour of the fox, now on behalf of the goose. (Suspended only; where would be the sport if all law were annulled?)

Here, a doubt occurs. This is all very well so long as we are concerned with pure comedy; a game in which there is no finality—if the players desist, it is only because they wait for the impulse to renew itself; a country dance tune, whose last phrase is an irresistible invitation to a new beginning. It is natural and reasonable to contrast this 'intellectual wealth squandered in the wantonness of sport' with satire, which closes with a clang—the villain punished, the fools frightened into prudent behaviour. But what are we to make of romantic comedy? It also has its close, much like a resolution of discord in music. Theseus turns back to Athens with the words:

> ... in the temple, by and by, with us,
> These couples shall eternally be knit.[2]

Moreover, the knitting follows a pattern of poetic justice—or purports to do; we may have to exercise a little kindly forgetfulness in favour of Demetrius—and even of Helena. He was unfaithful

---

[1] *Lectures and Notes on Shakespeare*, ed. T. Ashe, 1884, p. 188.
[2] *A Midsummer Night's Dream*, IV. i. 177–8.

before ever the magic juice touched his eyelids; she has made us wonder whether faithfulness is really a virtue. After all, it is Shakespeare's way to overlook shortcomings; and the total impression stands: romantic comedy closes on true love rewarded. But will not its rewards be as alien to 'the abandonment of all definite aim or end', to 'sport without an object', as are the punishments of satire? So there *is* a problem involved in the conjunction of qualities which Hazlitt remarked—a conjunction peculiarly Shakespearian: comedy; good nature; pastoral—which, for the Elizabethan dramatist, signified first and foremost pastoral romance, a literary species brought from abroad, but naturalized with the good gardener's intuitive skill and boldness. It was (I believe) by way of this very Elizabethan approach to the pastoral way of writing—and thinking, and feeling —that Shakespeare attained what Milton calls 'heart-easing Mirth', and Johnson, 'the greatest end of comedy—making an audience merry'. For the qualities which set Shakespearian comedy apart from all other kinds are Elizabethan qualities, though raised to a higher power. The men who were born not far from the middle of the sixteenth century and grew up in the sixties, seventies, and eighties, rediscovered the lost land of pastoral on their own frontiers, recognizing that its language and customs were not strange. This discovery, like a fine early morning, was too good to last; it had to give way to the sultry brilliance of Jacobean romantic fashions; but Shakespeare never wholly relinquished his vision— even his last plays, which have provoked such a variety of explanations, ranging from boredom to theophany, are best understood in the light of this pastoral morning.

To support this proposition I should need the space of a sizeable book. For example, why 'lost'? Why 'rediscovered'? I can only say that what I assume to be the true significance of pastoral must have been overlaid by the use as a school textbook of Mantuan's *Eclogues* —satiric diatribes, attributed to shepherds, but resembling the original pastoral eclogues no more than a lecturer on drama resembles a dramatist—and seven worlds away from pastoral romance. What, then, was recovered, and where, and in what form? To answer this I shall have to ask your patience while I trace one tradition of pastoral writing a little way back towards its source.

Pastoral romance (as the Elizabethans practised it) derives—at some distance—from those many long, leisurely, extravagant prose tales written in the decline of the ancient world, among Greek-speaking peoples on either shore of the Mediterranean. One alone can truly be called pastoral—*Daphnis and Chloe*; yet all had something to contribute to the tradition of pastoral romance. Revived in the Renaissance, given currency in Latin and vernacular translations, they gained an influence out of all proportion to their merits, and took new life from better men than their original authors. (So it may happen that some vigorous future writer will derive inspiration from this or that group of minor novels which to our eyes shimmer only with the phosphorescence of decay—and a still more distant critic will wonder what he found in them.) Intricately patterned stories—the theme of love prevailing in Italy and France, of chivalry in Spain—captured the imagination of courtly audiences and were presently popularized. We, of course, expected to have it all ways: hence our mingling, on the stage and in print, of conventions proper to tales of both love and chivalry, to exotic and to homely narrative art. There was indeed some warrant for this boldness. I count it significant that three seminal pieces of Renaissance story-telling—Boiardo's *Orlando Innamorato*, Montemayor's *Diana*, and Sidney's *Arcadia*—were left each at the death of its author in a state to invite completion. For such romance, with its hint of improvisation to please a particular audience, seems to engage our imagination in such a way that, if the narrator cannot finish, it becomes an office of friendship to dream out his dream for him. (Imagine Walter Scott dying in his early thirties, with *The Lay of the Last Minstrel* incomplete—who but would wish to carry it further?) The *Arcadia*, which Sidney had relinquished in the midst of revision, owed its ending, as the Elizabethans knew it, partly to his sister. It has the air of an unfinished building which loving care and some regard for the original design have made habitable, and indeed elegant, but which still guards the secret of that full purpose which was growing in the builder's mind even as he worked. For this reason, and also because it has lately been studied in particular relation to Shakespeare, I prefer to use for my principal illustration that other romance which may have been

Sidney's initial inspiration, and was surely one of Shakespeare's: the *Diana* of Montemayor. About a year after its first appearance in print, its author was killed, leaving his slight but intricate tale with some threads still to be tied up—and therefore (like Boiardo's) at the mercy of continuators. What they added tended to stick, and, by the time that an English translation appeared,[1] Montemayor's pretty little book had become a bulky folio.

How am I to describe in a few words the total impression left in my own mind by the *Diana*—let alone its intrinsic character? If I assert—where I should rather suggest, substantiate, and so persuade —it is because I am forced to take the nearest way to a place which, when I reach it, will be no more than my point of departure. First, then: never believe those travel-weary historians of literature who tell you that this romance is unreadable—nor that its English dress is an ungainly makeshift. The translator, Bartholomew Young, has been hardly used.[2] His original, like most of its kind, was a medley of prose and verse, and the ill luck of inclusion in an Elizabethan miscellany has made some of his songs familiar; for them I will not enter the smallest plea. But his prose, which is often tart and fresh, and never insipid, has come to us only in those well-meaning, insidious, unavoidable extracts called Shakespearian sources—there must be few notable romances of his age which Shakespeare did not know and lay under contribution. But here, as so often, virtue resides in the whole, not in the part he can be shown to have used.

The pattern of the stories which (folded one within another) compose this whole can be intimated thus: A loves B, but B loves C —who loves nobody until, mistaking D for E, and being mistaken by G for H, he endeavours to extricate himself by feigning love for A, supposing her to be—well, you see how it goes, and with no more reason than that, as Puck says, 'Cupid is a knavish lad.' All this is set in a world where we may reckon with some three or four *constants*. The pastoral region is a place of refuge, and the dominant symbol of relief from danger, weariness, want, every ill, is water. By stream or spring forlorn lovers may linger, recounting their

---

[1] In 1598—it had, however, been completed in 1583.
[2] He is, however, no longer neglected. See Judith M. Kennedy, *A Critical Edition of Yong's Translation of George of Montemayor's 'Diana' and Gil Polo's 'Enamoured Diana'*, Oxford 1968.

former vicissitudes, until the completion of a prescribed cycle, the fulfilment of some oracular prediction, brings lost opportunity round again, and they—wiser than before—reach out and take it. Thus, time has a strange circular movement; it accords with the rhythm of the revolving seasons. True, the pastoral poet has often lamented that, while nature renews itself, man goes his way once for all. (This is, of course, mere human make-believe—the pretence that it is last year's rose or nightingale come back to us.) In pastoral romance, however, man may sometimes share in this self-renewal. It is as though, tilting the hour-glass (a much more vivid symbol than our clock), he could give himself, not the next hour, but the past hour over again. And so, surprisingly, the oracle, which in Greek myths of the prime had signified the inescapability of a man's destiny, and had usually been charged with tragic implications, has now, in the silver age and in tales deriving from it, assumed an almost contrary character and become a symbol of the second chance. In such a world, the shepherd boy may well pipe as though he should never be old, and the parents of a lost child make light of the years of waiting.

Here is another constant in such romance: loss and recovery—identity itself is very easily lost or mislaid, to be reassumed when the time is ripe. (The deserted girl who seeks redress in boy's disguise is much older than the need to provide fitting parts for boy actors.) Where none is known until he chooses to disclose himself, the odds are strongly in favour of an unknown champion proving a woman—or, if a man, one alienated from his rights, or his very name. And, where many do not know themselves for what they are, a shepherdess may well find herself a queen, or an outlaw prove the heir to a kingdom.

So far, you might truly say, the characteristics I have described could belong equally to romance or pastoral—and indeed these are not very easily distinguished in their Elizabethan forms. But there is this difference. Whereas, in romance, the final pattern is composed of rewards and punishments, ideally distributed, pastoral has a variant of its own. Here innocence is a protection, and contentment, set high among the virtues, is in a special sense its own reward, since the contented mind receives no injury from the blows of adverse fortune. An ideal world—yes; but not the world of enervating daydream.

I have now in my hands the main threads of my argument, and can gather illustrations (particularly from the *Diana*), and weave in Shakespearian analogies. Montemayor's story is, as you will have inferred, too cobweb-like to bear retelling, but one strand may be followed to its conclusion. Felismena, whose birth was attended by dark sayings, is deserted by her lover, follows him in boy's dress (as Julia follows Proteus) and serves him in his courtship of Celia (as Viola serves Orsino). Parted from him once more, she takes to arms and, championing the oppressed, finds herself in the midst of a shepherd community. After many exchanges of tale and song among these pastoral people gathered round a spring, all of them resolve on visiting the wise lady Felicia and the temple of Diana. For some lovers of small consequence, Felicia has magical remedies, not unlike Oberon's. To another, the man she mourns is restored; his death, which she believed herself to have witnessed, was an eye-cheating trick—one very common in the Greek romances. For Felismena, however, according to the oracular Felicia, further trials and greater happiness are reserved. Setting out on her quest again, she comes among other shepherds—gentle, dark-skinned, and speaking Portuguese, her native tongue, and Montemayor's likewise, though he wrote in Castilian. On an island in the river by whose banks they live, she rescues a hard-pressed knight. He is, of course, her lost love, and Felicia has only to give him the water of remembrance to bring about a perfect reconciliation. How much of all this (my general propositions and particular instances) may we, without ever labouring a point, relate to Shakespeare? I suggest that refuge among unworldly people and resort to a benevolent oracular power recur significantly in his pastoral comedy.

When Le Beau, in *As You Like It*, warns Orlando of the enmity of the usurping Duke, he is to all appearance acting out of character. Shakespeare can be very peremptory with one of his minor *dramatis personae* if he wants something done and there is nobody else at hand to do it. But the words in which this apparently shallow and time-serving courtier takes leave of the man whose life he has saved at some risk to his own are even more surprising than his action:

> Hereafter, in a better world than this,
> I shall desire more love and knowledge of you.[1]

And what else can this 'better world' be than Arden? And what is Arden but a pastoral region where lost children are found, parted lovers reunited, dispossessed men come to their own again, and repentance and reconciliation grow like the leaves on the trees? To support this I must ask your patience while I reach back and draw in yet another strand of argument.

I believe, first, that exotic myths will most readily take possession of minds familiar from childhood with story-patterns that in some way resemble them; and, secondly, that the English counterpart of that pastoral world in which

> earthly things made even
> Atone together[2]

was a legendary forest: Sherwood Forest, ruled by the gentle outlaw. It is evident that Shakespeare was familiar with the Robin Hood ballads and pageants and popular plays—these may have been the 'Whitsun pastorals' Perdita recalled—and the recollections he cherished of them seem to have been pleasant. The references to them are, it is true, given to disreputable characters or spoken in jest; but so are those to all figures of popular, native story in his plays, and this I take to be no more than a concession to the clever young men in the audience. It is certain at least that an undercurrent of allusion to the dispossessed man and the gentle outlaw runs through no fewer than three plays: *The Two Gentlemen of Verona*, *As You Like It*, and *Cymbeline*.

The first is a mere sketch: bold, even careless. Valentine, 'in disgrace with fortune and men's eyes',[3] is welcomed by the outlaws; he is the very man they have been waiting for, and he undertakes to lead them on condition that none shall offer violence to women or mere travellers. (So Robin Hood in the ballad claims:

> I never hurt woman in all my life,
> Nor man in woman's company.)

He muses on life in the forest, as Duke Senior will teach his followers to do in Arden. And, again as in Arden, when the end comes it will

---

[1] I. ii. 263–4.   [2] V. iv. 103–4.   [3] Sonnet 29.

compass the three conditions necessary to a happy ending in Shakespearian comedy: truth will be revealed; those on whom this revelation casts an ugly light will repent; the oppressed and the oppressor will be reconciled. Indeed, Valentine has but to find his enemy at his mercy to forgive him freely. Even the outlaws turn out to be 'men endu'd with worthy qualities'—or so Valentine tells the Duke.[1] Had he forgotten their original confessions, or did he claim that his brief rule had reformed them? Perhaps the forest had worked its magic.

Now in *As You Like It* we find such a strange mixture of the old Robin Hood legends and the newly rediscovered pastoral romance that I must remind you briefly of its origins. The oldest to survive is the *Tale of Gamelyn*: a lay (longer and more circumstantial than a ballad; more downright and homely than a romance) belonging to the second quarter of the fourteenth century, but, from the fifteenth onwards, attributed to Chaucer; shining, therefore, with a borrowed lustre. Rough it certainly is, probably representing an early phase in the development of that legend whose outcome is the cycle of Robin Hood ballads. It is a tale of rights lost and recovered; taken by cunning, regained by strength. The youngest of three brothers (hardy, bold, but something of a simpleton) is cheated of his due by the eldest, and calls into the balance against him other simple, wronged men. Their fortunes swing to and fro; but right finally gets the upper hand in that forest world where the outlaws have established a rule of their own. They have been driven from their homes by oppression; and, even if they are not quite so gentle as the foresters of later tradition, they know how to maintain order: that is, they are ruled by a king, not by force, fraud, or fortune. Before him Gamelyn is summoned to give an account of himself—together with Adam, his brother's steward, who has helped him to escape, and shared his wanderings and hardships.

> Than seide the maister · king of outlawes,
> 'What seeke ye, yonge men · under woode-schawes?'
> Gamelyn answerde · the king with his croune,
> 'He moste needes walke in woode · that may not walke in towne.[2]

[1] V. iv. 153.
[2] *The Tale of Gamelyn*, in Chaucer's *Works*, ed. Skeat, 1900, iv. 669–72, Appendix to *Canterbury Tales*.

At the end, it is by summoning his friends the outlaws that he redresses the balance of justice—in an episode suggesting the outlines of a popular cartoon: the poacher on the bench, the squire and parson in the dock. And, with a flourish of legality, the King of England himself makes Gamelyn and Adam justices of the peace, and hangs all their enemies.

Presently, the Robin Hood ballads bear this story some way down towards the rich lowland pastures of romance. There, the knight who has fallen into the clutches of the Church (by bankruptcy, not heresy) wanders gently and disconsolately about the forest, until the outlaws (rather by show of strength than outright violence) regain his lands for him. (It is strange to consider that, when we reach the broad plains of Elizabethan romantic comedy, the Church —once the most powerful landowner in all England—will be reduced to a few friars and hermits who offer sensible advice, perform convenient but slightly irregular marriage ceremonies, and convert usurping dukes in forest glades.) The ballads vary, of course, in tone; but their general tendency is towards a softening of the Gamelyn story, and this continues into Elizabethan drama, and probably the Robin Hood pageants also—which, with a touch of sentimental archaism, glorified the old English long-bow while it was falling out of use as a weapon of war. (Contrariwise, that mercenary soldier, Falstaff, carries a pistol—long before it was invented.)

Lodge's *Rosalynde*, the immediate precursor and substantial source of *As You Like It*, is a gay and graceful mixture of the old stories of Sherwood justice with the new, fashionable, pastoral romances. Lodge, an adventurous reader, was familiar with *Gamelyn*, Sidney's *Arcadia* (probably in manuscript), and, we may be sure, popular versions of the Robin Hood legend. And he had his share of the authentic Elizabethan magic, 'gilding pale streams with heavenly alchemy'. He has caught the happy timelessness of pastoral; any of his characters might say with Orlando: 'There's no clock in the forest.'[1] It has become the realm of 'love in idleness'. Replacing the 'wife good and fair' whom Gamelyn married in the last line but four—and a line is all she is allowed—princesses and shepherdesses (the princesses disguised as shepherdesses, the

[1] III. ii. 284.

shepherdesses as courtly in their bearing as the princesses) await the approach of their suitors, sonnet in hand. And these are better love-poems than Orlando's. Was it Shakespeare's whim, or was it his wisdom, to give us the very poetry of love—and not allow so much as one of his lovers to write a respectable piece of verse? Perhaps his motive was akin to Chaucer's, when he took for himself the Tale of Sir Thopas.

These unreckoned riches of pastoral leisure belong rather to narrative than to drama, and I think there are signs that Shakespeare recognized this as a problem confronting him. Orlando, though he is driven from his brother's house within the narrow compass of the play, is indeed the lost child of traditional romance: he has been reared as though a foundling; nevertheless 'he's gentle, never schooled and yet learned, full of noble device'.[1] Then, time-inconsistencies have been apparent to the critics, and by some set down to revision:[2] the rightful Duke's banishment seems to be news when Charles tells it to Oliver—yet, by Celia's account, it happened when she was too young to plead for her cousin; and the Duke himself speaks of his forest life as though it had endured the seasons' change. Presently, the usurping Duke gives Oliver a year in which to find his brother, though our impression of the play's duration is a few fleeting days. (The change from winter to summer, in a recent production, was—to my thinking—an innovation enjoyable while fresh, but not fit to establish a new theatrical tradition.) Is it fanciful to suggest that Shakespeare, when he began to write, had hardly counted the cost of the alterations he must make and, if he later noticed discrepancies, did not care to efface them, preferring a *past-indefinite* tense? The passage of the seasons, especially as it is reflected in the talk of the older men (Duke Senior and Adam), signifies an acceptance of the terms of mortal life:

> my age is as a lusty winter,
> Frosty, but kindly.[3]

The condition of this acceptance of change is the contented mind. In Arden, love fosters its own peculiar impatience, but those who are free 'fleet the time carelessly, as they did in the golden world'.[4]

---

[1] I. i. 149. [2] Notably by the New Cambridge editors.
[3] II. iii. 52–3. [4] I. i. 107.

Their contentment extends even to little things: Jaques's failure to disturb the equanimity of any but the lovers—and *they* give as good as they get. I suspect that a small illustration of this has been swept away in the process of tidying the text, and I would plead for its restoration. Who *should* sing the third stanza of 'Under the greenwood tree'? Jaques offers it to Amiens who, according to the First Folio, agrees to sing and launches into it with the words, 'Thus it goes.' But the subsequent Folios and modern editions and (so far as I can tell) stage tradition have transferred those three words, together with the stanza, to Jaques—only the New Cambridge editors offering a hesitant defence of the Folio text in a note. Now, the actor who plays Jaques is rarely a singer, and the stanza is usually declaimed to a little audience (Amiens and anyone else who can be mustered) with such acrimony that Amiens's subsequent question loses its point. But, let Jaques put a paper into Amiens's hand, and let *him* sing innocently this parody of his own two stanzas, asking with unruffled good humour, at the close, 'What is Ducdame?'—and there is some reason for Jaques's exasperated retort: ' 'Tis a Greek invocation to call fools into a circle.'[1] The satirist is baffled by the world of comedy.

Unexpectedness ranks high among the distinctive qualities of *As You Like It*. The play tingles with questions. I deny altogether the claim that it is a satire on pastoral convention. True, it returns an echo to the pastoral idea; but the tone of this echo has not the heart-searching melancholy of Raleigh's:

> If all the world and love were young,
> And truth in every Sheepheards tongue,
> These pretty pleasures might me move,
> To live with thee, and be thy love——

nor the scorching irony of Donne's:

> Come live with mee, and bee my love,
> And wee will some new pleasures prove...

It is the tone rather of a brisk challenge—one to which the sequel may yet be: 'Pass friend, and all's well'; and, if the pastoral idea is challenged, that is because it *is* an idea, a pattern for living laid up in the

---

[1] II. v. 45–55.

mind, and such ideas are in full flight, and the people of the play in full cry after them, all up and down the glades of Arden. Everything is set off by contrasts; and the alternations are so swift that we might as well try to tell the colour of a field of ripening barley combed by the wind as capture any of the successive moods by definition. If the idealism of the Duke is called in question by Jaques, why, so is the cynicism of Jaques by the Duke. Rosalind, herself 'many fathom deep in love' and pursued by Celia's keen raillery, undertakes to turn every convention of love-making inside-out; and against her romantic friendship with Celia is set her astringent treatment of Phoebe. None of the disputants has the last word; but, with the possible exception of Jaques, none of them wants it. The pursuer lets the quarry escape, sure that he will not go far, for fear of ending the pursuit. This is indeed Coleridge's 'intellectual wealth squandered in the wantonness of sport without an object'. How is it to be reconciled with the need inherent in romance, to resolve all discords in a full close?

In the first place, it is necessary that all the characters should go back where they belong. Do not quarrel with this; it is required by the pattern of loss and recovery. Dekker confuses this issue when—turning the story of patient Griselda into a play—he makes her father's home, to which she returns bringing her children, a place of pastoral felicity, where the loveliest of all his songs is sung. Only her brother, a spoiled scholar and a character of Dekker's own invention, is ignorant of what Griselda knows:

> ... adversity
> Dwells still with them that dwell with misery,
> But mild content hath eas'd me of that yoke;
> Patience hath borne the bruise, and I the stroke.[1]

Thus, when the story is pulled back into its course, we are haunted by remembrance of his pastoral world and would be glad to return to it. But the ring which is the proper symbol of pastoral romance is not rounded into completion until each of the characters has fulfilled the destiny to which he, or she, was born; and, to this end, the Duke must reassume his office—in a court where (as Professor

---

[1] *Patient Grissill* (attributed to Dekker, Chettle, and Haughton), V. ii.

Jenkins points out)[1] goodness has been restored and Jaques's occupation's gone, Rosalind must reign after him with Orlando, the dispossessed man come to his own again, and benignant powers must operate.

Now, I freely admit that Hymen is not a very impressive counterpart even of the *romantic* oracle. Nevertheless, I find it significant that Shakespeare should have employed, for the ending of *As You Like It*, these three agents: a symbolical figure, speaking such archaic verse as he gives to Jupiter and the ghosts in *Cymbeline*, Juno and Ceres in *The Tempest*; a mood of half-belief in Rosalind's tale of her uncle the magician ('most profound in his art and yet not damnable'); and a pattern of riddling stipulations, propounded by Rosalind in her character as *magician's boy*, to which the lovers must subscribe—and which, being fulfilled, resolve all discords.

The oracle in *Cymbeline* has proved a stumbling-block; and—not to pursue this question further than our purpose requires—it performs its function awkwardly: it bears no intelligible relation in time to those confessions by which the skein of the plot will presently be unravelled, nor any in place to that ideal country which Imogen has found and lost again, where outlaws offer refuge to the oppressed, and recognize an impostor, even in a true man's clothes. And yet I believe the use of this device to be in keeping with those pastoral intimations—with Imogen's wish, before ever she set out on the journey which led to the outlaw's cave, that she and Posthumus had been herdsmen's children; with the mountain-bred boy's victory over the court-bred ruffler and braggart. Suppose that Shakespeare was finding his way back to a source of imaginative fulfilment which had charmed him some years earlier, but was cumbered with too weighty and intricate a story, and had to rest content with something short of his full purpose.

Within a year or so, he recognized what he sought, hidden away in that old-fashioned and unprepossessing little tale, Greene's *Pandosto*. It had something he needed: an oracle which, as a source of infallible truth, could be credited with authority, even sanctity; which would inevitably punish the unbeliever and yet—so far had tragedy given ground to romance—let punishment teach repentance,

---

[1] *Shakespeare Survey* 8, p. 45.

and repentance cherish hope; and shepherds, the traditional guardians of that place of refuge in which hope might be realized.

To show why I believe that *The Winter's Tale* transcends the models on which it is framed by obtaining their ultimate purpose, I shall have to ask a question which must sound very simple and matter-of-fact: in those ancient tragic stories which turn upon oracular prediction, what would have happened if the people whom it threatens had taken no notice of it? If King Acrisius, warned that he would be killed by his grandson, had not imprisoned his daughter, nor, when her child was born, put them both to sea in an open boat, Perseus would not have caused the death of an unknown man, and found himself the slayer of his grandfather. For the point of these stories seems to be that it is a man's efforts to avert his fate which fasten it upon him. We are therefore (I take it) to understand that a man so visited can no more desist from struggling than could an animal caught in a trap. Does Shakespearian pastoral comedy shirk this knowledge, or see beyond it?

All I can now attempt is to point out some ways in which oracular truth—absolute truth regarding past, present, even future events—operates in *The Winter's Tale*. Notice, first, that Leontes no sooner acknowledges his suspicions than he sends to the oracle, supposing that he will obtain confirmation of them—a departure from *Pandosto*, in which the Queen asks that Apollo be consulted. Next, the crucial scene representing the messengers on their way back from 'the Isle of Delphos' is set as prelude to Hermione's trial: in some twenty lines it conveys an extraordinary impression of serenity and sanctity. Cleomenes and Dion are unshakably convinced of the truth of the sealed statement they carry; convinced, also, that it will clear the Queen.[1] It is evidently established that, while we remain in Sicily—that is, until the end of Act III, Scene ii—things are what they seem, to us and to everyone in the play, *except* Leontes.

Now, if I may revert to my simple question: what would have happened if Leontes had accepted the truth thus delivered? The prediction that 'the king shall live without an heir' would have been inexplicable; indeed, at the time when it was entrusted to the messengers, Leontes would still have a wife and two children with him.

[1] III. i.

But, possessed by the insane conviction that he and oracular truth are ranged together against false seeming, he does not wait for the revelation: he condemns the child he supposes Polixenes' to death. It is Shakespeare's way to accept character as the ultimate source of event. Therefore, when truth is revealed and he finds himself standing alone, Leontes is already committed to the utterance of his final, fatal blasphemy: 'There is no truth at all i' the oracle.'[1] Immediately and inexorably, the wheels begin to turn: word comes of Mamilius' death, and he interprets it as divine retribution:

> Apollo's angry; and the heavens themselves
> Do strike at my injustice.

Paulina's 'this news is mortal to the Queen' threatens complete fulfilment of the prediction, and Leontes' public confession and vow of amendment are answered by her passionate cry that repentance prolonged beyond the span of mortal life would not atone. Nothing further is said of reparation, nor is the oracle's stipulation, 'if that which is lost be not found', remembered again until the very eve of finding. It is mere critical officiousness to demand an oracular injunction against second marriage; Leontes has accepted the full implications of his misdeed.

Presently, a speaker only less august than the oracle intervenes. Time, in appropriately archaic verse, explains his own function as composed of contrarieties:

> ... it is in my power
> To o'erthrow law, and in one self-born hour
> To plant and o'erwhelm custom.[2]

He is alike founder, destroyer, renewer. He cannot (in the agonized words of Lucrece) 'return and make amends'; but, given time and kindly shelter, the seed will yield next year's harvest, and we have but now seen the lost child received into the pastoral refuge.

> I turn my glass ...
> ... but let Time's news
> Be known when 'tis brought forth.

From now on, growth proceeds underground: things will not be what they seem; honest characters (Paulina and Camillo) will be

[1] III. ii. 157.   [2] Prologue to Act. IV.

involved in a tissue of subterfuge; the truth, if it is told, will be uttered uncomprehendingly—as when Polixenes tests Perdita with gardeners' talk of crossing strains, and she maintains that like must mate with like. One certainty alone holds: in the pastoral world, the promise of the oracle will be fulfilled as surely as were its threats, and the lost will be found.

What, then, does this pastoral world signify? Not 'wish-fulfilment' —a new name for an old misuse of the imagination. *That* requires obliteration of the boundary which separates the imagined from the actual. But the world of true pastoral is always known for a country of the mind, to be attained only by force of the imagination. This, doubtless, holds good for all great imaginative story-telling (whether cast in narrative or in dramatic form). Pastoral fiction, however, has a distinction of its own to observe, and this may best be indicated in terms of time and space. Tragedy shakes us with its tremendous *here* and *now* (no matter how remote its subject). History (Shakespearian history, at least) makes a sharp impact of *there* and *then*— the sun rising on St. Crispin's day over the field of Agincourt. But pastoral romance is, and must always remain, *elsewhere* and *some other time*. Thus, though it is simply and immediately enjoyable, in a kind and degree beyond that of other story-telling, it no more invites us to identify ourselves with its happy people than the rainbow invites us to climb. In its realm, Shakespearian comedy is free to flourish. Its happy endings are not flattering fantasies, but tokens of a fulfilment to be imagined only, not hoped for. In this fulfilment, the partial and piecemeal returns and renewals which life grants us are capable of completion; not only does the future stretch before us, with its assured rhythm of the seasons and the generations—the past itself is no longer irretrievably lost. Not Perdita alone comes back, but Hermione also.

SHAKESPEARE'S COMIC INSIGHT

Read 25 April 1962

WHEN you did me the honour of inviting me to deliver this year's Shakespeare Lecture, I turned an anxious gaze on the names of my august predecessors and wondered, with deepening dismay, at my temerity in daring to accept the invitation; but in the titles of their lectures I found this morsel of reassurance: there was little mention of comedy; and to clarify and present some few ideas on Shakespearian comedy has long been a cherished project. That this subject has suffered general neglect I will not maintain. Nevertheless I am troubled by two signs in the weather of Shakespearian criticism as it relates to comedy: first, the assumption that Shakespeare's plays, with the exception of the great tragedies, are compounded of ingredients—like any nostrum, or pudding—amongst which one may be separated from the rest and designated comedy; secondly (does it follow from the first?), an ambition to explain this component, by reference to something other than itself—and the upshot of that is all too often success in explaining it away. How otherwise should it come about that, while Alfred Doolittle's defence of the undeserving poor[1] is hailed as comedy, Davy's plea to Shallow—'God forbid, sir, but a knave should have some countenance at his friend's request. An honest man, sir, is able to speak for himself, when a knave is not'[2]—that this is subjected to dispiriting sociological comment? (A reversal which might have annoyed Shaw, and perhaps have amused Shakespeare.)

A little before his death, James Thurber recounted a visit to a friend: ' "I have come to talk with you about the future of humour and comedy", I told him, at which he started slightly, and then made us each a stiff drink, with a trembling hand.' The conclusion of the little tale hints at the courage of despair: ' "I . . . remember

---

[1] Shaw's *Pygmalion*, Act II.
[2] *2 Henry IV*, V. i. 41.

when we used to write about . . . the human comedy. If there is no human comedy it will be necessary to create one." [1]

With Thurber, we have come to ascribe this alteration in the climate of comedy to our present discontents; but, reading the signs attentively, we should perhaps wonder when it really began. Those of Shakespeare's plays which we used to call romantic comedies have been (with honourable exceptions) least well served in recent criticism, and (again with due exceptions) very capriciously on the stage. I believe this to be significant and disquieting. If I attempt to account for it in terms of fable, it will not be in any flippant spirit, but because fable takes the shortest road.

As the Victorian age was drawing to its close, Satan (reviving a slander which had formerly failed of its purpose in heaven) went about the earth, whispering in one ear after another: 'Doth Job fear God for naught?' And the generation that was then coming to intellectual maturity looked back over a century and more of English novel-writing in which the imagination of their parents and grandparents had found satisfaction, and saw happiness treated as the proper reward of virtue. (And if, here or there, the tragic bent of one novelist's heart gave to the words in which the transaction was concluded a wry ambiguity, that only served to confirm them in their mistrust of all the rest.) Retreat is not easily halted. To the generations that followed, and supposed themselves wiser because they knew themselves sadder, it was not enough to ask: 'Has this happiness been rightly allotted?' They challenged an author's competence to bestow it, whether as reward or bounty—not considering that, in the world of the imagination, it is a gift at the disposal of anyone who can obtain credence for it. Now, the tradition of the English romantic novel, deriving as it does from Shakespearian comedy, could not thus falter without casting doubt on its progenitor. And so it has come about that Shakespeare's happy endings are either warily examined for hidden meanings, or else summarily dismissed as concessions to popular demand. But should we not sometimes be prepared to consider the possibility that they are intrinsic to the purpose and congenial to the mood of the comedies they crown? We may have been intended to take the whole context

[1] *Times Literary Supplement*, 11 Aug. 1961.

SHAKESPEARE'S COMIC INSIGHT

of many a comic predicament into account—including the felicitous outcome. Beatrice's question—'Would it not grieve a woman to be over-master'd with a piece of valiant dust, to make an account of her life to a clod of wayward marl?'[1]—how would this sound in a different context—if it were spoken, for example, by Lesbia Grantham (in Shaw's *Getting Married*)—or even by Lady Percy, whose piece of valiant dust will, at the close of the play, be that and nothing more? Whereas *hers* is Benedick; a man for whom twenty eyewitnesses in a tale together weigh light against her affirmation of her cousin's innocence; the man with whom she will eventually leave the stage in a dance which we recognize as the Shakespearian token of traditional happy ending. That question—'Would it not grieve a woman . . .?'—is at the heart of Beatrice's comic predicament. The answer—Yes; it would; and you will find fulfilment in accepting it—lies at the heart of the play. The integrity of particular comedies has been notably demonstrated—of *The Comedy of Errors*, for example, by Dr. Harold Brooks, of the first part of *Henry IV* by Professor A. R. Humphreys. But I think that a sense of the integrity of Shakespeare's comic vision is still to seek.

When Rosaline enjoins Berowne

> With all the fierce endeavour of your wit
> To enforce the pained impotent to smile—[2]

we may take her penance as signifying little more than one of those forfeits that compose the final pattern of the play. But when he expostulates, and she concedes

> A jest's prosperity lies in the ear
> Of him that hears it, never in the tongue
> Of him that makes it—[3]

we recognize a truth valid beyond the limits of this pattern. And when a great comic artist takes up this very challenge (to 'jest a twelvemonth in an hospital'), but with the whole world for his hospital—why then, it appears that happiness and comedy are to part company. But, should the precariousness of happiness cease altogether to be one of the common themes of tragedy and comedy,

---

[1] *Much Ado about Nothing*, II. i. 50.
[2] *Love's Labour's Lost*, V. ii. 841–2.   [3] Ibid., V. ii. 849–51.

what would remain? Only the comic fact of the precariousness of laughter, solitary and sterile.

You will surely not expect from me, however, any philosophical reflections on laughter. Indeed, I desisted (after a while) even from reading such exercises; not only because I found (like Rasselas) that I understood less as I listened longer, but also for fear lest I might never laugh again. Fortunately, the return to Shakespeare still lay open, with Johnson for company on the way.

Johnson arrived at his position by way of an exploratory defence of Shakespearian tragi-comedy (in *Rambler* 156), and fortified it in his Preface.[1] There he maintains that the mingling of grave and merry themes is consonant with life; that Shakespeare has admitted their interplay almost everywhere; that experience denies the force of the theoretical objection (attention will be dissipated); that no critical authority known to Shakespeare forbade this alternation of moods; and that in comedy he was following the natural bent of his genius. Thus, the central bastion of assertion—Shakespeare's comic vein is pervasive—is flanked by two pleas—no one can now object that it is ineffectual, no one could then tell Shakespeare that it ran counter to dramatic convention—and rests firmly on two justifications—it is level with life, it was congenial to Shakespeare. Questions of critical authority now seem remote; we do not wait to be persuaded that what *works* will do well enough. Into the mystery of Shakespeare's natural bias I will not follow Johnson. I therefore propose to examine the two remaining parts of his argument: the terms of his assertion that comedy is (very nearly) omnipresent in Shakespeare's plays; the validity of his appeal to our experience of life as a justification of Shakespearian practice.

Shakespeare [Johnson asserts] has united the powers of exciting laughter and sorrow not only in one mind but in one composition. Almost all his plays are divided between serious and ludicrous characters, and, in the successive evolutions of the design, sometimes produce seriousness and sorrow, and sometimes levity and laughter.

This statement takes for granted a pattern of alternating and contrasting episodes, tragic and comic in succession. Such analysis may

---

[1] (1765), pp. xiii–xv.

be called traditional, an expression of the customary response to Shakespearian diversity. William Seward records of Lord Chatham that he excelled as a reader of tragedy, delighting in both parts of *Henry IV* and in *Henry V*. Seward's informant, however, 'observed that when he came to the comic or buffoon parts of those plays, he always gave the book to one of his relations, and when they were gone through, he took the book again'.[1] (Unfortunately he does not tell us which of them read Mrs. Quickly's tale of the death of Falstaff.) At either level, whether of criticism or taste, this assumption of tragi-comic alternation plausibly corresponds with Shakespearian dramatic structure; but it is liable to hinder critical insight and harden into an unverified theory of comic relief. Alternation can afford relief from many different sorts of pressure. Is it tragic tension alone that Hamlet relieves when he assumes the antic disposition of the fool in his dealings with Polonius? Change of tone is sovereign against inertia: it can dispel unreceptive moods, avert impatience. It can give resilience to the narrative structure of comedy itself—Lyly and Greene had shown that. Raillery does not serve for amusement only—which is just as well, since some of it is not very amusing. The fool, or any character who borrows his untimely garrulity, is free to utter what we might have said if he had not forestalled us. Lucio's interruptions in the trial scene at the end of *Measure for Measure* are (in their tiresome way) useful: the Duke has to make his audience within the play understand what has happened, as well as what it signifies; for us, who are in possession of the facts, unbroken demonstration threatens tedium. There are, moreover, juxtapositions which elude any formula of contrast, or relief. In two successive scenes of *Henry V*, the King pronounces sentence of death on Cambridge, Scroop, and Grey, concluding:

> The taste whereof God of his mercy give
> You patience to endure—[2]

and Mrs. Quickly tells how she watched by Falstaff's death-bed:

Now I, to comfort him, bid him 'a should not think of God; I hop'd there was no need to trouble himself with any such thoughts yet.[3]

---

[1] *Anecdotes* (1795a), ii. 340.   [2] II. ii. 178–9.   [3] II. iii. 18.

This resembles not so much the effect of two colours placed side by side as an alteration in the light falling on a single colour.

Nevertheless, alternation, juxtaposition—however variously and subtly they may operate—these are not the whole matter: Johnson's statement does not reach far enough. But, since he is a poet, he will often tell us more in a single figure of speech than in a whole passage of argument. When he levels Shakespeare's practice with the condition of human life, he uses this figure:

> Shakespeare's plays are not in the rigorous or critical sense either tragedies or comedies, but compositions of a distinct kind; exhibiting the real state of sublunary nature, which partakes of good and evil, joy and sorrow, mingled with endless variety of proportion and innumerable modes of combination; and expressing the course of the world, in which the loss of one is the gain of another; in which, at the same time, the reveller is hasting to his wine, and the mourner burying his friend; in which the malignity of one is sometimes defeated by the frolic of another; and many mischiefs and many benefits are done and hindered without design.[1]

This surely aims at the heart of the problem, for it compels us to ask: what have the mourner and reveller to say to one another when they meet? A. P. Rossiter spoke of 'that frightening inclusiveness of the Elizabethan mind which attains its full scope only in Shakespeare'.[2] But inclusiveness may threaten artistic integrity, provoking so vehement a reaction as Ben Jonson's passion for relevance. Have the mourner and the reveller anything of moment to say when they encounter? Not unless each, looking in the other's face, should recognize the lineaments of his own.

Shakespearian characters do not consist of two sorts, those on whom the comic spirit shines his lantern, and those who are shielded from its beam. Compared with later, sentimental, comedy, and seen in relation to late-seventeenth- and early-eighteenth-century adaptations of his plays for the stage, Shakespeare's comic vision may be called unsparing. It is not mitigated by the seriousness of the occasion. With the kingdom falling in ruins about them, Hubert tells King John how the rumours of Arthur's

---

[1] Op. cit., p. xiii.
[2] *Woodstock: a Moral History*, ed. A. P. Rossiter (1946), Introduction, p. 37.

death and a French invasion are received, and mimics the amazed blacksmith

> With open mouth swallowing a tailor's news;
> Who, with his shears and measure in his hand,
> Standing on slippers, which his nimble haste
> Had falsely thrust upon contrary feet—[1]

tells his tale of disaster. (And, if this is ascribed to Shakespeare's alleged contempt for the common people, I reply that the Grecian princes who listen to Nestor in *Lucrece* are shown in equally grotesque postures.) But it is not only nameless persons in that notoriously undignified aggregate, a human crowd, that this comic vision exposes. According to the code of sentimentality, a character whom we are meant to regard as sympathetic must be spared the full rigour of acquaintance with comedy. (If the case *appears* otherwise, then we may guess that this character is being subjected to an ordeal or test, carefully, even clinically, controlled.) Shakespeare allows no exemptions on this score. Indeed, his favourite device of disguise or mistaken identity is most often employed to bring one of these 'sympathetic' characters face to face with his own image as it appears in the mirror of other men's minds—a proverbially disconcerting experience. The Duke, in *Measure for Measure*, must hear the common interpretation of his conduct; Hamlet, the popular account of his insanity; King Henry, before Agincourt, learns that Pistol alone regards him as a combatant—and to be Pistol's chosen champion would not raise a man in his own esteem. The discovery of Vienna's Duke, or England's King, helpless in such a comic predicament has driven some critics to the desperate explanation that Shakespeare must have intended such characters to alienate, repel, even disgust the intelligent observer—who would thus share a sour joke with him at the expense of simpletons ready to take this fellow for a hero. Under such a dispensation, who is to be saved? Not Posthumus in the gaoler's keeping; not Coriolanus among servingmen in the house of Aufidius; not Pericles suppliant to the fishermen —no, not Marina herself at odds with Boult. Of tragic and comic characters alike it may be said that, if dignity survives what they are called on to endure, it has not been preserved by aloofness.

[1] *King John*, IV. ii. 195–8.

Furthermore, they can all speak that middle language which was, for Johnson, the signal achievement of Shakespearian comedy;[1] all use imagery which carries what Wordsworth called 'the ballast of familiar life'.[2] When lesser Elizabethans use a homely idiom for tragic themes, we may fear they are 'for Alisander . . . a little o'erparted'.[3] No such anxiety attends Cordelia's declaration:

> Mine enemy's dog,
> Though he had bit me, should have stood that night
> Against my fire.[4]

Shakespeare's mourner and reveller meet (not merely intercept) one another, because they are akin; kinship is possible because diverse and even contrary moods interpenetrate (they do not merely alternate) throughout nearly all his plays. In the very heart of his pastoral romance, Jaques calls up a vision of human life which includes its first and last indignity—utter helplessness at the gates of birth and death. It is a far more daunting picture than Pope's:

> Behold the child, by Nature's kindly law,
> Pleas'd with a rattle, tickled with a straw . . .
> Scarfs, garters, gold, amuse his riper stage;
> And beads and pray'r-books are the toys of age:
> Pleas'd with this bauble still, as that before;
> 'Till tir'd he sleeps, and Life's poor play is o'er![5]

Strange, at first sight, that the satirist's should be the softer impression! But Pope is speaking in his own person, whereas Jaques is merely the voice of satire in the orchestration of *As You Like It*, and falls silent at the close.

Contrariwise, in a play whose plot retains some of the hard brilliance of its original (though Dr. Brooks has shown us in how romantic a light the Elizabethans could regard Plautus),[6] we are haunted by the 'piteous plainings of the pretty babes' which have rung in Aegeon's ears until they brought him

> to the melancholy vale,
> The place of death and sorry execution.[7]

---

[1] Op. cit., p. xviii.　　[2] *Prelude* (1805), vii. 603.
[3] *Love's Labour's Lost*, V. ii. 578.　　[4] *King Lear*, IV. vii. 36–8.
[5] *Essay on Man*, Epistle II, ll. 275. . .
[6] Harold Brooks, 'Themes and Structure in *The Comedy of Errors*', in *Stratford-upon-Avon Studies*, 3 (1961).　　[7] *Comedy of Errors*, I. i. 73 and V. i. 120–1.

The very theme of a play may submit to diversity of treatment. While the mimic warfare between men and women in *Love's Labour's Lost* treads the razor's edge that divides angry and merry laughter, Berowne turns the image of love this way and that until it reflects all the colours of a tempestuous April. He tells himself

> Go to; it is a plague
> That Cupid will impose for my neglect
> Of his almighty dreadful little might.

To his fellow subjects, he delivers a splendidly formal oration on their sovereign:

> And when Love speaks, the voice of all the gods
> Make heaven drowsy with the harmony.

To Rosaline, he extenuates their behaviour with the plea that

> love is full of unbefitting strains,
> All wanton as a child, skipping and vain.

And, at the last, the Princess's reply to Navarre's importunity resolves these rainbow colours to a white radiance:

> *King.* Now, at the latest minute of the hour,
> Grant us your loves.
> *Princess.*   A time, methinks, too short
> To make a world-without-end bargain in.[1]

In Shakespearian comedy we may again and again discern that 'inclusiveness' which Ben Jonson (as playwright though not as poet) discarded in the interests of comic relevance. It belongs to a region of thought and feeling which Professor Willard Farnham has characterized as 'the mediaeval comic spirit in the renaissance'.[2] Within the narrow compass of a lecture I cannot hope to do more than indicate where this region lies, and comparison with Ben Jonson may serve as finger-post. It is impossible to imagine Jonson treating any of his characters as Barnardine is treated—a reprobate who must be brought to realize that he is compounded of an immortal soul and a body desperately mortal, before authority will trouble to find

---

[1] III. i. 191–3; IV. iii. 340–1; V. ii. 748–9; V. ii. 775–7.
[2] *Joseph Quincy Adams Memorial Studies*, Washington 1948, pp. 429–37.

out what he has been doing, and stop him doing it. What Ben Jonson's artistic conscience exacted must have become always easier with changing assumptions as to man's nature and situation. Pope admits both to be paradoxical, but proceeds as though the problem were merely to reconcile 'self-love and social'. Our failure to reach this supposedly attainable good provokes the angry disappointment of the satirist. The age which brought the novel to maturity gave its whole attention to these often intractable partners, seeing the well principled social being yoked in every individual with the intransigent egoist: in those who are amiable, regard for others is able to subjugate self-love; in the unamiable, the knowledge that this is expected of them merely serves to regulate the appearance of selfishness. Response to the human comedy comes to depend for its diversity on variation of experience and temperament: those to whom both suggest despair, and those to whom they bring a sober hopefulness, will alike call their inference rational. But the yoke-fellows within man, as the Elizabethans conceived him, were not to be reconciled on reasonable terms. The mortal part would still cry out 'It is *I* who am undeniably sensible of life'. This claim (none the less insistent for being inadmissible) rings with a shivering hilarity through Doll Tearsheet's question to Falstaff: 'When wilt thou leave fighting a days and foining a nights, and begin to patch up thine old body for heaven?'[1]

In a region of thought and feeling comprehending such extremes, even kinship and common language will hardly avail to compose all differences. Moreover, when we have looked across the generations to Shakespeare's world, and seen it standing nearer to Chaucer's than to our own, we have still not measured the full magnitude of that capacity for reconciliation demanded of his comedy. We ask of it (surely it was he who taught us to ask) that it shall reconcile apparently incompatible states: ideal happiness, with all that this implies of grace and harmony; and those abject indignities to which error or misadventure may subject body and spirit—with all that they threaten of discord and disgrace.

Professor Coghill has taught us to look for two distinct strains in Renaissance comedy, and acknowledge that the one chosen by

[1] *2 Henry IV*, II. iv. 222-3.

Shakespeare has its own traditions of theory and practice.¹ But I would plead for recognition of a third, which, together with that narrative and romantic strain which he distinguishes, goes to the making of Shakespearian comic art. Coleridge has defined one property of comedy. It is, he says, 'poetry in unlimited jest'. It is 'the apparent abandonment of all definite aim or end... the removal of all bounds in the exercise of the mind'. Again, it is 'intellectual wealth squandered in the wantonness of sport without an object'.² These, however, are intellectual terms. Can they capture and hold up to view something that is not always and altogether intellectual? The term I would use for this property of comedy as it works at all levels, down to the humblest, is simply play. (It is a pity that we have not a distinct word for what I mean: gambol, game, sport for its own sake.) Although Christopher Sly is corrected for supposing that comedy has something to do with Christmas gambols, he may not be altogether at fault. Comedy is indeed, as his pretended lady tells him, 'a kind of history'³; but it is also a kind of revelry—he is himself playing a part in one of this sort without knowing it. That, surely, was what Berowne meant by 'a Christmas comedy'.⁴

Play is a faculty we share with the other creatures—as anyone knows who has watched hares at sunrise, or badgers after sunset, or young lambs engrossed in the game which children call 'king of the castle'. Now, those who play together contend with one another —or make believe to contend. Elizabethan taste fostered the contention in words, one player fending the other off by answering at cross purposes, as the servants answer their masters in Shakespeare's earlier comedies. (Who would have guessed that the dialogue of *Henry IV* could ever have developed out of this?) Or they play tricks —cheat one another's eyesight by disguise, dumb-show, or carefully planted misinformation. They are not always the first instigators of these illusions, but may be initially beholden to mischance: it is the trick played by fortune on Viola that compels her to cheat Illyrian eyes; and, since this subterfuge can be only partially

---

[1] Nevill Coghill, 'The Basis of Shakespearian Comedy', in *Essays and Studies*, 1950, collected for the English Association.
[2] T. M. Raysor, *Coleridge's Shakespearian Criticism*, i. 169.
[3] *Taming of the Shrew*, Induction, ii. 138.
[4] *Love's Labour's Lost*, V. ii. 462.

successful (someone in the play must see through the disguised girl, or she will seem to us a virago), there are those who divine that Cesario lacks a man's heart, and on this half-truth build their comic conspiracy.

Comic contention, in so far as it is really play, has certain characteristics which set it apart from heroic or tragic conflict and even from that of satire or corrective comedy. Finality is alien to it; if the players desist, they are waiting for the impulse to renew itself. The odds are a matter of indifference, and may well fluctuate from episode to episode, now one player up, now the other. What they are contending for is not so much the advantage as the initiative—which, in the nature of things, cannot be perpetuated, though it may be renewed. (In romance, on the other hand, the hero must be outmatched, must vanquish, and remain for ever the victor. But then he is, to borrow Saintsbury's happy misquotation of Tennyson, 'Grand, epic, homicidal, six-feet-high'.)

To illustrate Shakespearian comedy as play, I choose two episodes, one from either part of *Henry IV*. They happen to be numbered Act II, Scene iv, in both, and each is a scene of unusual length resourcefully diversified. In the first, the theme of the *play extempore* begins to declare itself when the Prince, having played his practical joke on Francis—as though he were indeed of little more account than Hotspur's 'sword and buckler Prince of Wales'—is asked by Poins what it signifies. (Poins is never inside the game—any more than a dog is, prancing at the heels of a boy intent on some ploy of his own; but he has this advantage, for us, over the dog: when he does not understand, he asks questions, and we benefit by the answers.) The Prince's answer, here as often elsewhere, is directed rather to us than to his inquisitive companion:

> I am now of all humours that have showed themselves humours since the old days of goodman Adam to the pupil-age of this present twelve o'clock at midnight.[1]

The sentence, as Johnson interprets it (and I concur), leads direct to that passage in which the Prince sketches, lightly but acutely, the humours of two men, each confined to his own orbit: poor

---

[1] *1 Henry IV*, II. iv. 89.

Francis, driven out of his few wits by being asked to think of two things at once, and that inflexible engine of war, Hotspur: 'I am not yet of Percy's mind', he says, and launches into a piece of mimicry of the man who begins his day by killing 'some six or seven dozen of Scots at a breakfast', and observing to his wife: 'Fie upon this quiet life! I want work'. There, he seems to say, goes such another one-idea'd man as simple Francis; and, delighted with his own insight and the freedom it confers, he resolves on calling in Falstaff to exploit its possibilities by playing Lady Percy to his own Hotspur.

Falstaff comes; but there is that not inconsiderable matter of what happened at Gadshill to be settled first between them; and when Falstaff has clambered to a pinnacle of effrontery he does not wait to be pulled down but proposes 'a play extempore'— on which the Prince of course suggests that the subject shall be Gadshill. The King's emissary, however, affords a diversion and respite, for Falstaff offers to treat with him on the Prince's behalf, and, when he returns from speaking with Sir John Bracy, he makes use of the information he has obtained to regain the initiative. The Prince, he reports, is summoned to give an account of himself at Westminster, for the Percies are joined in rebellion with Douglas and Glendower. 'Art thou not horribly afraid? Doth not thy blood thrill at it?' The Prince's rejoinder—'Not a whit, i' faith; I lack some of thy instinct'[1] —warns him that his brief absence has allowed his enemies to combine against him, and the way lies open, wider than ever, towards Gadshill. With a keen relish of his own predicament, leaving defence to lesser men, he attacks from another quarter: let the Prince join with him in rehearsing the answer he will be called on to make to his father. And so the play within a play, long promised, is after all presented, and on a subject of Falstaff's choosing; but it is prevented from reaching the culmination he has designed by yet another diversion, the Sheriff's entry. So robust is Shakespeare's comic invention that we may all too easily overlook its economy: he forbears to surfeit us; where suggestion is sufficient for his purpose, he rests content with the half-spoken.

In Act II, Scene iv, of the second part, the Prince and Poins, disguised as drawers, have been present while Falstaff has assured Doll

[1] Ibid., II. iv. 361.

(whom I would not play as an accomplice of authority) that they are both shallow young fellows—with even less complimentary additions. They discover themselves, and Poins, that too assiduous terrier, warns the Prince that Falstaff will get away—'drive you out of your revenge and turn all to a merriment'—unless he is prompt with his accusation. In seeming compliance, the Prince challenges Falstaff—'And you knew me, as you did when you ran away by Gadshill. You knew I was at your back, and spoke it on purpose to try my patience.'[1] The question is a trap: Falstaff is invited to use his former plea of instinct. The only answer to this invitation is a wary movement: Brer Rabbit seems to stir within the briar patch. 'No, no, no; not so; I did not think thou wast within hearing.' The Prince, with a mimic gesture of triumph, posts himself at the obvious bolt-hole: 'I shall drive you to confess the wilful abuse, and then I know how to handle you.' Still only a shuffling movement, as of a player who has lost the initiative: 'No abuse, Hal, o' mine honour; no abuse.' The Prince relentlessly reminds him of his very words of dispraise. Still Falstaff feigns helplessness, and Poins takes up his feeble 'No abuse' with a sharp yelp of triumph, thus giving Falstaff the opportunity he has been waiting for—the occasion to negotiate and break the enemy's ranks: 'No abuse, Ned, i' th' world; honest Ned, none. I dispris'd him before the wicked—that the wicked'—he swings round to face his other adversary—'might not fall in love with thee; in which doing, I have done the part of a careful friend, and a true subject; and thy father is to give me thanks for it.'

To admit the weather of actuality, to take into account the dependence of Falstaff and his companions on the Prince's whim of forbearance—this is to deny to this mimic warfare the spirit of play, of comedy as revel. Even the fire-eating Hotspur lays claim to a sort of prudence: 'Out of this nettle, danger, we pluck this flower, safety.'[2] Falstaff reaches out for the nettle, but, if he were to find the flower in his hand, would he not toss it away, for the sake of one more round in the game? And, despite his disclosure of a disquieting preoccupation with the future, I believe the Prince to be of the same mind while he is playing, to take the same delight as Falstaff in the

[1] *2 Henry IV*, II. iv. 295.   [2] *1 Henry IV*, II. iii. 9–10.

successive turns and reverses which bring now one, now the other, uppermost—that is, to a commanding position from which his very momentum must topple him down. Would he drive Falstaff into a thicket of prevarication if it were not for the sake of hearing that deceptively mild voice from within—'Born and bred in a briar-patch, Brer Fox'?

Translate game into earnest; turn Falstaff into the ingratiating parasite that a favourite dependent may be in actual life—and what are we to make of his tactics with his own shabby retinue ('devoted Falstaffians', Professor Humphreys happily calls them),[1] whose favour he is certainly not seeking? Like Bottom, he can create an element in which he is buoyant; but, while Bottom floats serenely in the smooth waters of his ascendancy over his fellows, Falstaff prefers the surge and swell of opposition. Unchallenged in Eastcheap, as Bottom was in Athens, he cannot desist from provoking his subjects to rebellion, in order that he may have the pleasure of sallying out to quell it. He enjoys giving a finished performance, if only for his own approbation: in default of better sport, he will rout Pistol.

I have still to meet the most forcible objection to any simply comic reading of Falstaff: that it fails to reckon with those two sombre episodes, rejection and death. That he must fall from favour is beyond question; the wild Prince cannot change into the trustworthy King on any easier terms; and where a character has to make a harsh choice, it is not Shakespeare's way to soften it: in his plays, whoever says 'no', man or woman, says it with the rude vehemence of a force of Nature. That he must die is less evident. It would be pleasant to accept Johnson's surmise, that Shakespeare 'made haste to dispatch him, perhaps for the same reason for which Addison killed Sir Roger, that no other hand might attempt to exhibit him'.[2] But the sense of old age and death has hung heavy in the air throughout the second part of *Henry IV*. So powerful is this impression that I could more easily believe his fellow players to have been forcing Shakespeare's hand when that incoherent epilogue was written than that he intended to carry Falstaff to the French wars

---

[1] New Arden Shakespeare, *1 Henry IV*, II. iv. 475, note on S.D.
[2] Shakespeare (1765), iv. 397; note on *Henry V*, II. iii.

and changed his mind. When the hour strikes—and it cannot be very far off—he must depart, like the Lord of Misrule, or the Christmas Prince. For them and their like, it is no grave matter; they will come again another year. (Miss Welsford has remarked the close relation of these figures, in England, with seasonal, recurrent revelry.)[1] Common sense forbid that I should ask you to regard Falstaff in terms of myth, as symbol of the winter solstice—as anything but himself. But there are certain characteristics that he shares with the figures of traditional revel, and fable. The Lord of Misrule cannot change, in respect of what he signifies—any more than the characters of beast fable can change, the fox turn vegetarian, or the sheep grow quarrelsome and vainglorious; but like them he can recur. If all these withdraw, it is to wait the proper occasion for return—and that is the recurrence of a mood in which we spontaneously demand another episode in a tale which properly has no end. In them, both changelessness and renewal result from simplicity of structure: only complex characters can change without loss of identity; only simple stories can be prolonged by successive episodes. Falstaff is not structurally simple; yet he cannot change, as Henry of Monmouth changes. And it is evident that he prompted the demand for recall—to Windsor, if not to France. If we object that we would rather take leave of him in Arthur's bosom than at Mistress Page's fire-side, we may fairly be accused of fastidiousness, and can but plead that this is what happens when genius works upon the stuff of popular imagination.

Supposing I am right—what becomes of the integrity of Shakespear's comic vision; what, of Falstaff's kinship with other Shakespearian characters—those, for example, who are simple and traditional in a different sense: braggarts, whose pretensions to valour are exposed, but for whom the exposure is not an invitation to begin the game afresh? I believe that the answer is to be sought in the tenor and function of the soliloquies allowed them on these very occasions. We know, of course, that the clown was furnished with opportunity for direct intercourse with the audience—if he had not been given it, he would have taken it. We are, moreover, aware that the world of the comic character is never private. Whereas in

---

[1] Enid Welsford, *The Fool: his Social and Literary History*, 1935, p. 211.

all drama the fourth wall is down, comedy has this peculiarity: from whatever quarter we cross the ruins of that wall, we may be sure the other three will cut off the quarry's line of escape. Life itself cannot (fortunately for us) equal the completeness of comic exposure. In Shakespearian comedy, however, this is seldom the conclusion; for the victim, if he does not turn to bay like Falstaff, may take refuge with us from his tormentors; and, in that case, soliloquy is his passport. As a fugitive from his own comic predicament, he throws himself upon our mercy. It is to us that Parolles turns, with his declaration:

> Simply the thing I am
> Shall make me live.[1]

It is to us that Pistol confides his plans for a campaign after the campaign[2]—like any black-marketeer, on the stage, at the end of the last war. Upon which Johnson (surely no lax moralist) is impelled to comment: 'The comick scenes of the history of *Henry* the fourth and fifth are now at an end, and all the comick personages are now dismissed.'[3] He enumerates them, with an observant eye for their several histories, and concludes: 'I believe every reader regrets their departure.' Who could say as much for Jonson's Bobadil? But *he* must continue to excuse his behaviour, under the merciless gaze of those who can testify against him[4]—the poor wretch is never alone with us.

Surely it is significant that Shakespeare should allow the fourth wall to be crossed, as it were, in both directions—and by such diverse fugitives, all of whom this device of soliloquy compels us to admit, even while we laugh, to sanctuary. This traffic indeed creates a sort of fellowship between those who are found out, and those who are witty enough to find themselves out: Berowne and Benedick outdo themselves in their soliloquies of self-discovery. Could we, and would we, claim exemption from this fellowship? Shall we not submit, because it is inclusive, and consent, because the vision that framed it is merciful?

---

[1] *All's Well that Ends Well*, IV. iii. 310–11.
[2] *Henry V*, V. i. 81–3.
[3] Shakespeare (1765), v. 474 (note on Pistol's exit).
[4] *Every Man in his Humour*, ed. Herford and Simpson, IV. ix.

I fear that I have done little but ask questions, and, when I could not arrive at an answer, send others chasing after them. It will therefore be appropriate to end by quoting (though I cannot interpret) a passage which by haunting my imagination has prompted many of them. In the close of the *Banquet* of Plato (as Shelley translates it), Aristodemus tells how he fell asleep, and woke to find that some of the company still slept, some had gone home, and Aristophanes, Agathon, and Socrates were still disputing:

The beginning of their discussion Aristodemus said that he did not recollect, because he was asleep; but it was terminated by Socrates forcing them to confess, that the same person is able to compose both tragedy and comedy, and that the foundations of the comic and tragic arts were essentially the same.

REVIEW

(1967)

King Lear. Edited by G. I. DUTHIE and J. DOVER WILSON. (The New Shakespeare.) Cambridge: University Press, 1960.

THE history of the textual study of *King Lear* is of such intricacy that every editor is obliged to recapitulate some part of it. The New Cambridge plan, of separating the account of the *copy* for each play from the general Introduction, to form a (sometimes substantial) chapter, invites an extensive survey. Moreover, Professor Duthie, with his 1949 edition of the play, is himself an important part of this history—which even the reviewer must attempt to recall.

Although P. A. Daniel opened the way in 1885 to the elimination (at least for some eighty years) of Q2 (1619), leaving only two contestants in the field—Q1 (1608, the Pied Bull Quarto) and F—yet there remained, and remain, difficult questions concerning the source of the earlier, its relation to the later, and the credit of both. These questions are further complicated by the circumstance that the dozen surviving copies of Q1 consist of sheets some of which have been corrected in the printing-house, and that traces of this partial correction are discernible in parts of F. (W. W. Greg, 1939/40). And, apart from other short-comings, both quarto and Folio versions have suffered curtailment—the omission of some 300 lines from F, and a (different) 100 from Q1 and its derivative Q2. Moreover, neither text can rank as satisfactory; and (to take the heart out of an editor) they are most suspect where they agree. Thus, for a play which intrinsically presents enormous difficulties of thought and language, the editor is obliged to compose an eclectic text; and, while much may be said against the quarto as witness, every editor is troubled by those idiosyncrasies of the Folio which are characterized as 'sophistication'—a term covering a variety of methods apparently employed by more than one person, to make it presentable.

In attempting to trace some of the main fluctuations in the discussion of these problems, I give dates, because the major authorities (Greg and Duthie, for example) have scrupulously reconsidered and sometimes modified their theories as those of other investigators demanded attention, and as the complexity of the whole situation became always more evident.

The source of the first quarto has been diversely conjectured: a manuscript in Shakespeare's hand, made illegible by his own revision (Madeleine Doran, 1931—since modified); a reported text (E. K. Chambers, 1930, and Greg, 1933). But acceptance of the term *reported* will no longer cover the possibilities envisaged. The persons and circumstances involved in obtaining copy, otherwise than by transcribing the author's manuscript or the prompt-book, are under dispute: a shorthand reporting (Greg, 1933), the Company assembling to reconstitute a missing prompt-book (Duthie, 1949); purloined foul papers from which an actor or actors dictated to a scribe, relying on memory rather than script for familiar passages—those in which Goneril and Regan appear—(Alice Walker, 1953; a conjecture by which Greg was impressed but not convinced, 1955).

One factor remains almost constant: distrust of the quarto texts. Q1 sinks from 'doubtful' (Greg, 1942) to 'bad' (A. S. Cairncross, 1955). Dr. Walker, though she argues that it must be *used* (as 'complementary' to the Folio), and believes the area of 'memorial contamination' to be limited, is outspoken on the proportion of sheer nonsense it contains, and would not advocate 'taking it as copy-text'. And though Q2 has been disinterred (Cairncross, 1955) it was not for the sake of rehabilitation. Yet since a relationship between one or both and F appears indisputable, the question persists: in what way—to what degree and with what authority—was the particular copy of Q1 which must have been used at some stage in the construction of the Folio text corrected, or 'edited'? The answer to this question will determine the lines on which the modern editor constructs his own eclectic text. Professor Muir, in the New Arden (1952), would admit Q readings only where F is 'manifestly corrupt', or Q 'palpably superior'—though in his notes he is careful to show what sort of case can sometimes be made for the alternative reading.

NEW CAMBRIDGE SHAKESPEARE

Mr. Duthie, with his partner's general assent and occasional comment, takes a course which may be briefly indicated thus. Reconsidering in certain respects the standpoint of his 1949 edition, he relinquishes the hypothesis of Q1 as a reconstruction by the Company of a lost prompt-book. He argues for a modification of Dr. Walker's theory: suspicion of memorial corruption cannot be confined to the Goneril–Regan passages; not all the nonsense is attributable to negligence. Retaining his faith in a reputable transaction behind this text, he posits a scribe dependent on mutilated foul papers, and driven to the expedient of patching from memory: 'Transcription from foul papers by dictation, the persons involved having had some memorial knowledge of the play, seems the most convincing solution.' Reporting he rules out, on the score that Q1 (which he will not allow to be simply 'bad') attains a degree of fullness and accuracy beyond the reach of shorthand. Prompt-copy he rejects as basis not only because discrepancies (notably as to length) will not allow both F and Q texts to derive from a prompt-book, but also on account of those many defects which would make the manuscript from which Q was set up quite unfit for such use in the theatre.

Of the making of the Folio text, Mr. Duthie offers this provisional account—provisional, because (even when the suggestions of A. S. Cairncross and P. Williams (1953) have been related to one another and modified by further consideration) there remain unresolved problems. The Company were unwilling to part with their prompt-book to the printing-house. One or perhaps two scribes therefore used it in the process of editing leaves taken, some from Q1 (already partially edited, when it was set up), some from Q2. The influence of the prompt-book is reflected in theatrical cutting—its omission of 300 lines being all, or nearly all, due to exigencies of performance, whereas the absence of 100 from the quarto text is ascribed to negligence. There is no trace of Shakespearian revision, unless (perhaps) in this curtailment. Yet, 'it is uncertain whether what was sent to the F printing-house was these edited pages themselves, or a transcript of them. And it is uncertain whether there are any passages in F which can be held not to depend on edited quarto at all, but to depend on manuscript pages of prompt-copy or on a transcript of manuscript pages of prompt-copy.'

Thus, even for expert and rigorous bibliographers, much still turns on divination of character: and not only on Shakespeare's character (this was where Greg took issue with Madeleine Doran), but on that of unknown persons, whose part in the transmission of the text is hypothetical—actors and scribes. A choice of reading may even turn on the capacity of the corrector, or correctors, of Q1.

In sum, the final court of appeal must be the editor's own judgement. Mr. Duthie has clearly shown why, after considering every variant on its merits, he inclines towards the Folio more often than the quarto. If he has any discernible bias, it is for the harder reading.

Apart from the 'horrible obscurations' of the text, what are the principal difficulties to which an editor must devote his introduction and notes? The language; the movement, in time and space; the significance. The second of these occupies little of this edition—perhaps because it has been so fully and ably examined by Sir Walter Greg, Harley Granville Barker, and others. On the language Mr. Duthie does not expatiate; therefore it may be allowable to suggest that its salient characteristic can be conveyed only by paradox: it is most enigmatic where it is plainest. Again and again we are confronted by a short, apparently plain speech, composed of simple words in customary, idiomatic order, and must say: 'I recognize the meaning, but cannot apprehend the import.' What, for example, is the relevance and significance of the last line but two:

Speak what we feel, not what we ought to say (v. iii. 324)?

An actor, studying a part in the play, must often ask: 'With what are these words charged?' Mr. Duthie finds Kent's

I am come
To bid my king and master aye good night (v. iii. 235-6)

charged with foreknowledge of his own death, but insists (in agreement with other good authorities) that Kent must not die on the stage. How is the actor to convey this premonition?

The characters likewise, for all their apparently simple opposition of innocent and guilty, often prove inscrutable, and, together with the words they speak, are drawn into that terrible vortex: the question of the play's total significance. The editor is aware that his predecessors in criticism have swung between irreconcilable extremes, of pagan horror and pious hilarity. Few besides Johnson have been content to rest in doubt; they have desired to formulate a solution. Mr. Duthie is outstanding in a notable body of critics who have found what they were seeking—concept and formula—in a phrase which the present reviewer has come to dread: the presence of a Christ-like figure. The objection to it, briefly stated, is twofold. It carries inescapable reflections on another Person of the Trinity. If Cordelia's

> O dear father,
> It is thy business that I go about ... (IV. iv. 23–4)

is intended to evoke more explicit scriptural overtones than a reference to filial duty, then God the Father is likened to an angry old man, who can learn only through the sufferings he brings on his child and on himself the scope of his own authority. Unintended implications are indeed found in the cruder sort of medieval allegory, stuff of the *Gesta Romanorum*; but, in attempting to recover this older simplicity, the critic is surely overshooting the mark, if he attributes to Shakespeare such unbelievable moral insensibility. And there is no telling how many other characters may be drawn into this net of hypothetical symbolism. It is with a feeling stronger than dismay that I find Lear's garland (mentioned in a stage-direction with which the New Cambridge has taken its usual dangerous liberties) likened to the crown of thorns. Mr. Duthie regards Lear's education as the play's central theme; but it surely costs too much—to too many people. From time to time, explanations have been offered of that condition which Granville Barker calls (in relation to *Lear*) the 'capricious cruelty' of life. An overruling purpose is descried, or alleged. 'But surely, the quiver of Omnipotence is stored with arrows, against which the shield of human virtue, however adamantine it has been boasted, is held up in vain: we do not always suffer by our crimes; we are not always protected by our innocence.' It was against a particular sort of optimistic certitude that Johnson was protesting; but in challenging the assertion that temporal affairs display a legible text of the divine will he may yet speak for Christians of other times besides his own.

My second objection to this unitary explanation of *Lear* is that, precluding all others, it empties the play of much of its human content. It forbids us to interpret any part of it in terms of that tension which can develop between the generations—most dangerous where a great inheritance is in question, most apparent to an age for which all history was dynastic history. And not between the generations only: the whole pattern of allegiance and dependence, mutual obligation and mutual indebtedness—manifest in the very denial—operates as a centripetal force, holding the huge, rough fabric of the play together. The particular instances of strife between brothers, between sisters, are shown to be representative by means of juxtaposed likenesses and differences: the diverse provisions of English law as it relates to inheritance by sons, or by daughters; by the legitimate, or the illegitimate. (Sidney gave Shakespeare the unkind bastard, but in a quite different context.) Nor is this pattern confined to blood relationships: it is present in Cordelia's ironical reference to her sisters' implied unconcern with the obligations of marriage—true dramatic irony in that, though seriously spoken, the words carry a meaning which extends beyond the speaker's intention. Its political significance has been illustrated by Professor L. C. Knights (1957).

Shakespeare has taken a threadbare tale and even balder play, an episode from a courtly romance, and fears drawn from common life, and out of these has woven an intricate expression of his own tragic vision, conveyed to us through the insights which one and another of his characters experience. Lear discovers that, in the dissolution of every tie sanctioned by law and custom which has followed from his own wilful act, *age is unnecessary* (a result Shakespeare's More had foreseen); Kent, that his crowning service to a master who has learned this, is to let him die. Severally, these may indeed be simple; it is by their manifold interplay, within a complex human situation, that they baffle understanding, leaving

> the fierce dispute
> Betwixt damnation and impassion'd clay

to be *burned through* again. *King Lear* asks more questions than it answers.

To oppose an interpretation which Mr. Duthie upholds with the authority of many years' study of the play—years which have yielded the closest and fullest account of its text that we have got or are likely to get—must seem indefensible. Conviction drives me to it.

This is not an edition for the common reader, who—if unable to follow up its clues to Jacobean demonology and vagabondage—may turn back to the Arden. It does not offer a complete account of sources, though the relations between *Leir* and *Lear* are elucidated —a strong case has been made, and a still stronger could be made, for the influence of Sidney's *Arcadia*. The reader may sometimes think wistfully of Johnson's sturdy paraphrases—but when Johnson wrote an editor was free to choose the easier reading for this purpose. What the New Cambridge *Lear* does give is given in ample measure.

IMPLICATIONS OF *KING LEAR*
A POSTSCRIPT

(1971)

THE passage from one of Johnson's essays, which I quoted in the foregoing review, would appear—on a superficial glance—to be at variance with the tenor of his criticism of the play, particularly with his plea for a happier ending. But look at both steadily and squarely and in their proper context, and a true relationship, one with another, may be clearly discerned. The subject of the essay (*Adventurer* 120) is the conduct of life; that of the commentary on *Lear*, the practice of art. And, in the context of man's ideas on divine dispensation, these may well conflict.

The argument of the essay runs thus: mortal life cannot be the whole. This is inferred from two positions: a just God would not create beings capable of enjoying such happiness as they can never hope to experience; the distribution of unhappiness bears no relation to desert—it is not to be spelled out in terms of punishment. To substantiate this analysis, I must quote with some fullness.

After counting up the diverse calamities, public and private, to which mankind is liable, Johnson rounds upon the exponents of philosophical optimism:

> Affliction is inseparable from our present state; it adheres to all the inhabitants of this world in different proportions indeed, but with an allotment which seems very little regulated by our own conduct. It has been the boast of some swelling moralists, that every man's fortune was in his own power, that prudence supplied the place of all other divinities, and that happiness is the unfailing consequence of virtue. But surely, the quiver of Omnipotence is stored with arrows, against which the shield of human virtue, however adamantine it has been boasted, is held up in vain: we do not always suffer by our crimes; we are not always protected by our innocence.

A POSTSCRIPT

From this inexplicable distribution, 'the moralists have always[1] derived one of their strongest moral arguments for a future state'. On such a supposition rests their confidence in divine justice; but it is likewise necessary if we are to believe in divine mercy:

> It is scarcely to be imagined, that Infinite Benevolence would create a being capable of enjoying so much more than is here to be enjoyed, and qualified by nature to prolong pain by remembrance and anticipate it by terror, if he was not designed for something nobler and better than a state, in which many of his faculties can serve only for his torment.... There will surely come a time, when every capacity of happiness shall be filled, and none shall be wretched but by his own fault.

The essay, which contains several Biblical references, concludes with one more explicitly Christian than Johnson often permits himself:[2] 'The Redeemer of mankind himself was "a man of sorrows and acquainted with grief".'

The position is clear: we apprehend, not what is, but so much of it only as is vouchsafed; and we acquiesce in this partial knowledge because we recognize it to be incomplete and look forward to acquaintance with the whole. How, then, did Johnson come to plead for such a mitigation of the distress he felt at Cordelia's death—and supposed us all to feel—as the practice of the contemporary stage afforded? The answer which (I believe) he would give rests on two arguments. One, the lesser but more explicit, is to be found in his concluding note: Shakespeare has allowed Cordelia to perish 'contrary to ... the faith of the chronicles'. (Johnson has been censured for failing to read the story in 'the chronicles' through to its bitter ending; but I have yet to find the critic who takes into consideration the latter part of Sidney's tale of the 'unkind bastard'.)

This appeal to received tradition, however, merely sets the edge on Johnson's larger argument, implicit not only in that final note, but also throughout his commentary on the play.

---

[1] 'The moralists have always'—Johnson clearly intends a distinction between moral thinking which has proved durable, and temporary aberrations, notably of his own day.
[2] I distinguish between general references to religion and passages such as this and the end of *Rambler* 185.

> A play in which the wicked prosper,[1] and the virtuous miscarry, may doubtless be good, because it is a just representation of the common events of human life; but since all reasonable beings naturally love justice, I cannot easily be persuaded, that the observation of justice makes a play worse.

And he proceeds from a general proposition about the response of any audience, to the particular assertion that the audience of his own day has demonstrated incontrovertibly this preference for 'poetical justice'.

Here, then, is the crux of the difference between Johnson's view of the conduct of life, and that idea of the operation of poetic justice in art which impels him to protest against the death of Cordelia. On his reckoning, we demand something of art which a Christian would not ask of life. He evidently takes this for granted, never guessing that as a double criterion it might one day be challenged. It therefore becomes necessary to trace those changes in the climate of opinion which have made Johnson's assumptions appear questionable, and have substituted for them others which he would probably have called in question.

To go no further back than yesterday, art was and had long been regarded as serving to impose order and clarity on life: to make it, not more comfortable or propitious, but more intelligible.[2] To this end, story—whether presented in narrative or dramatic form—must convey an impression of completeness: must seem to give us motive or prompting as well as act, and the consequences of all significant actions; to intimate that the reverberations which followed have died away, the dust has settled, and what happened may be grasped in its entirety. But what apprehension of the whole is possible to those who know, and reckon to know, only the part? Comedy and tragicomedy have their allowed conventions, but tragedy is impatient of make-believe—notably in the conclusion. What if it tells a traditional story in which (as everyone knows) poetic justice is not seen to be done? It cannot, like comedy, end

---

[1] As Johnson has admitted in the preceding paragraph, they do not ultimately prosper. They have, however, inflicted on Lear and Cordelia sufferings far greater than any they must endure themselves.

[2] For a philosophical development of the implications of this idea in relation to *King Lear* see D. G. James, *The Dream of Learning,*, 1951, Lectures III and IV.

with a flourish while the prospect is still fair; nor, like tragicomedy, recall and reverse happenings which have appeared no less irreversible than death itself. Richardson was prepared to offer a solution which was in accord with the theme of *Adventurer* 120. His promise of redress for Clarissa Harlowe in a future state may be exceptionally explicit; but it was not at variance with the sentiment of his age. What separates us from his original readers can be regarded in more than one way. It may seem a small matter that taste has veered towards the open-ended, inconclusive story—unless this should signify surrender of the demand that art make life intelligible; but such a surrender would itself need to be explained, and other consequences than this considered. Why and how has the ballast shifted?

As social and intellectual change in the nineteenth century gathered momentum, as the novel took over from the drama and novel-readers became more numerous and more vociferous, prudential morality gained ground in literary criticism—and, I dare say, elsewhere. The intelligibility of a story was too often measured merely in terms of the author's disposal of rewards and punishments at the close. Shakespeare was submitted to these 'swelling moralists', and even Cordelia was judged to have got her deserts. Such a way of reading imaginative literature was bound to lose credit among thinking men. It had reflected a demand for reassurance in a world slow to admit how secular its deepest thoughts had become. With secularity openly declared, however, critical theory could frame its own assumptions about human life, and was ready to impose them on authors who had lived under another dispensation. Drawn into the void which had been formed by the ebb of religious faith and practice, emboldened by the withdrawal of the theologians, the critics advanced. They looked to find in Shakespeare's more disturbing plays religious thought expressed in the idiom prevailing among their own poetic contemporaries—an allusive idiom. So they came to furnish Shakespeare with fragmented theology. Symbolism was their password. Their method was eclectic. They were like children playing with their elder brothers' discarded tools, unaware of the injuries these were capable of inflicting. Hypnotized by associations, they are now in danger of overlooking the further implications of the religious allusions which they claim to have discovered.

In order to illustrate this danger, I develop my objection to a particular claim—one which does not originate with the New Cambridge *King Lear*, but to which this edition lends its authority. On a passage from Cordelia's speech before the battle—

> O dear father!
> It is thy business that I go about—   (IV. iv. 23-4)

Mr. S. L. Bethell comments: 'We find Cordelia ... using a language which directly echoes a saying of Our Lord from St. Luke's Gospel.' After quoting this saying (Luke 2: 49), he continues: 'Does this bold comparison suggest a poetic reason for her innocent yet ignominious death?'[1] The Arden edition reports the suggested comparison, emending the Biblical quotation to give a version which Shakespeare is more likely to have used.[2] The corresponding note in the New Cambridge edition implies acceptance of Mr. Bethell's suggestion; and this implication is borne out by a passage in the Introduction.[3]

For an allusion to serve any purpose whatever, it must make its impact on the mind in one at least of two ways: the words[4] it is meant to recall must be memorable, even unforgettable; the meaning must be apposite—that is, the analogy must be not only recognizable but also acceptable to the reader for whom it is intended. Now, the import of the speech in which these words occur is unambiguous, and their content quite inapposite. Cordelia is protesting that she would not lead an armed force against her own countrymen, were it not for her father's necessity; and the course of the play has shown Lear as the prime agent of his own distresses. What analogy can this afford with the passage in St. Luke?[5] Nothing beyond the reference to filial duty. On the score of verbal analogy likewise I

---

[1] *Shakespeare and the Popular Dramatic Tradition*, 1944, p. 60.
[2] 'Knew yee not that I must goe about my father's businesse?' For the translations of the Bible known to Shakespeare see Richmond Noble, *Shakespeare's Biblical Knowledge*, 1935, Ch. iv.
[3] p. xxi.
[4] Verbal allusion alone has hitherto been under consideration.
[5] The New Cambridge note suggests a duality—if not duplicity—of implication: 'patriotic spectators' could take Cordelia's protest at its face value.

raise an objection. The critics are surely betrayed to a subjective reading by the force of an experience which cannot have been that of Shakespeare or of his first audience: I mean, familiarity with a version of scripture current among all those who read the Bible in English. The long reign of the Authorized Version could not fail to condition the mind's ear, alike of those for whom it had authority and those whose response was merely aesthetic: as time added strangeness to majesty, the cadences became more memorable. But, for the sixteenth-century reader and hearer, there was no one version of indisputable authority; none that had been known and quoted over many generations. I cannot believe that this is the direction in which the religious implications of *King Lear* are to be sought.

To say that they should not be looked for at all is quite another matter. I therefore in my turn put forward a train of suggestion. The play is bursting—charged to combustion point—with religion. In no other of Shakespeare's plays does it occupy so much room in the minds of the characters. A concordance can register how many times the gods are mentioned; a list of proper names can enumerate loans from the classical pantheon. But neither will disclose how often nor how vehemently the elements are challenged and interrogated as to their part in this divine hierarchy. For the religion of Lear's Britain is no decadent paganism; nor is there that listless agreement as to the formalities appropriate for calling upon the gods which betrays that no one really expects to find them at home. Their existence and function are passionately affirmed, and as strongly denied. The subject has been much debated—most succinctly in Mr. J. C. Maxwell's 'The Technique of Invocation in *King Lear*'.[1] But there is, I believe, another dimension still to be considered. Religion among these characters is something of Shakespeare's own imagining—almost to the same degree as that of Caliban, though it serves so much larger and more complex a purpose that I offer the comparison for emphasis only, not for illumination. Lear and his subjects give utterance to an extraordinary variety of beliefs, conjectures, hopes, and fears. What they say, however, even

---

[1] *Modern Language Review* (Apr. 1950), pp. 142–7. See also William R. Elton, *King Lear and the Gods* (Huntington Library, 1966).

in its contrariety, raises always that same question about divine dispensation: whether it is the part that we see, or the whole. Some think they know, others demand to be given the answer.

Edmund—the atheist, as Johnson flatly calls him—can conceive nothing in the universe to match himself. He therefore asks no questions—but at the last he gets an answer. Lear calls upon the gods to justify *him* and register his imprecations in a celestial court; and there is a terrible suavity and a terrifying plausibility in the assurance of Goneril and Regan that his appeals for divine intervention signify nothing but the unreason of age. Albany, as his mind opens to the situation, calls upon them to justify *themselves* by bringing retribution on wrongdoers. Kent, that bewildering compound of irascibility and patience, commits Cordelia to their care, but does not afterwards arraign them. To this impiety Gloucester is reduced in his misery. What the women believe may be inferred from their conduct. (Cordelia's appeal to the virtues—that is, benign properties—of the earth arises so simply from the doctor's reassurance that I cannot discover in it a religious affirmation.[1])

It could be argued that the play is merely about *man's distressed estate*. It presents mankind in Johnson's sombre terms, as a being capable of happiness (without this capacity there would be, not tragedy but desolation)—yet forever in a state which precludes it; 'qualified by nature to prolong pain by remembrance and anticipate it by terror'. Lear and Gloucester, after initial error and great suffering, learn much about mutual obligation between man and man,[2] and, even more ineluctably, about mutual love.[3] But does their experience, or that of any other character who commands attention, teach them anything about the gods?

It should be remembered that the paganism of *Lear* originated in dramatic necessity. A family quarrel about property, even if that property is part of a kingdom—could anything be more ignoble? An old man turned out of doors on a stormy night—here indeed is pity; but its proper complement of terror, the immensity and elevation of tragedy is due to the setting of the action: in a great darkness, where

[1] IV. iv. 15–18.
[2] e.g. III. iv. 28–36 (Lear); IV. i. 67–72 (Gloucester).
[3] e.g. IV. vii, from Lear's waking until his exit, and V. iii. 8–25. Gloucester is allowed no such reconciliation, but see, e.g. III. vii. 90–1 and IV. i. 22–4.

visible and invisible forces, the elements and other powers, may or may not be charged with our affairs, and may or may not be just. Though we may still believe, as Shakespeare's generation believed,[1] that all is not *dark and comfortless*, it nevertheless remains right to ask what is revealed to the significant characters in the play.

Since there is no priest, no interpreter of mysteries (unless that office can be ascribed to Edgar), each one must learn—must, in the words of Keats, *burn through*, and *humbly assay*—the experience for himself.

I discount the sole reference to a future life—Lear's

> Thou art a soul in bliss; but I am bound
> Upon a wheel of fire. (IV. vii. 46–7)

Regarded as a verbal allusion, it cannot be called scriptural, being traceable only to the New Testament Apocrypha—an investigation summed up in Professor Muir's Arden note. I accept his interpretation of Lear's speech as an expression of the pain of reawakening to life and sanity (Introduction, p. lv); but I would suggest that the image—of a soul in torment looking up to a soul in bliss—may be derived from recollection of some pictorial representation, of wall-painting, glass, or illustrated book.[2]

Those characters who have not, by word or conduct, proclaimed themselves atheists, share a speculative concern about the government of the universe, and an inclination to propose their own as a test case. Albany and Edgar are satisfied with the evidence they find for a just dispensation. But it is to 'the eldest' who have 'borne most' that I turn for a deeper insight.

Gloucester accepts his own punishment as deserved. (It has been accepted on his behalf by the critics, with indecent alacrity: the symbolism of spiritual and physical blindness, with his own words and Edgar's to warrant it, has proved irresistible.) Beyond this, he accepts the omnipotence of the gods, their 'great opposeless wills';[3] contending deities, with whom conflicting vows may be registered,

---

[1] D. G. James would except Shakespeare himself—'the most powerful secular imagination the world has yet known' (op. cit., p. 80). But Shakespeare compels each reader to fashion his own image of that inscrutable mind.
[2] I hope to develop this argument presently, elsewhere.
[3] IV. vi. 38.

will not again be invoked. Moreover, he acknowledges their mercy: *gentle* is no mere propitiatory epithet—he commits to their care the son he loves.

Lear, recovered from his madness, has less to say about the gods; perhaps, because he is wholly absorbed in cherishing Cordelia. But into his only distinct reference to them there enters a sense of mystery and awe not hitherto expressed:

> Upon these sacrifices, my Cordelia,
> The gods themselves throw incense.[1]

Mystery and awe are not incompatible with the surmise that there is more to be known than we can know.

Beyond that? Nothing. What should there be? Those to whom Shakespeare spoke could contemplate a pagan Britain as a historical phenomenon. It is we who, living in a world no longer Christian, are assailed by the desire for a theophany within the play.

[1] v. iii. 20–1. Some of the most frequent, and most graceful figures in medieval church sculpture and wall-painting are the censing angels.

SIR DAGONET IN ARTHUR'S SHOW

(1960)

WHETHER by chance or bias, my argument radiates from a position in the mid eighteenth century, and I shall begin by quoting passages from an exchange between Samuel Johnson and Thomas Warton in 1754. In the first edition of his *Observations on the Fairy Queen*, published that year, Warton had advanced a claim which many of us would willingly defend:

And here it may be observ'd, that in criticising upon Milton, Johnson, Spenser, and some other of our older poets, not only a competent knowledge of all classical learning is requisite, but also an acquaintance with those books, which, though now forgotten and lost, were yet in repute about the time in which each author respectively wrote, and which it is most likely he had read.[1]

Writing to thank him for the book, on 16 July 1754, Johnson characterizes it with his usual discernment, and perhaps with this very passage in mind:

I . . . pay you a very honest acknowledgement for the advancement of the literature of our native Country. You have shown to all who shall hereafter attempt the study of our ancient authours the way to success, by directing them to the perusal of the books which those authours had read.

He instances some who had failed in the performance of this duty, and concludes:

The Reason why the authours which are yet read of the sixteenth Century are so little understood is that they are read alone, and no help is borrowed from those who lived with them or before them. Some part of this ignorance I hope to remove by my book. . . .[2]

---

[1] p. 243.
[2] *Letters*, ed. R. W. Chapman, Oxford 1952, 53. The last sentence, as Dr. Chapman tells us, refers to the 'Preface, Grammar, and History' of the Dictionary.

Let me endeavour, first and foremost, to make it clear that I am nowise concerned with the allocation of this or that share of credit to any scholar for any particular discovery. While I need hardly say that I accept the full implications of Professor Nichol Smith's claim —'It is in Warton's *Observations on the Faerie Queene* that Malory makes his entrance into literary criticism'[1]—, I am none the less impressed by the sociability of eighteenth-century studies in this field, anxious to show by what small accretions men thus engaged advanced knowledge (or, in their eagerness, obscured the issue), and aware how little we can hope to know of the particulars of these informal and friendly transactions. As Johnson wrote to Warton four years later: 'A commentary must arise from the fortuitous discoveries of many men, in devious walks of literature.'[2]

For Warton, Malory was an important Spenserian source. It was natural, therefore, that he should cite in his *Observations* the more strikingly romantic strains in Malory's work. Of the fidelity of his impression his contemporaries were to judge; he had shown them where to look in a work which he presented thus:

> It is entitled Morte Arthur, *The Lyf of Kyng Arthur, of his noble Knyghtes of the round table, and in thende the dolorous deth of them all.* This was translated into English from the French, by one Sir Thomas Maleory, Knight, and printed by W. Caxton, 1484.

A footnote adds this information: 'This Book has been reprinted twice or thrice. The last Edition is dated 1634.'[3] Some six years later, Johnson was engaged on that edition of Ascham's English works for which he allowed Bennet to take the credit.[4] It is at least probable that he was responsible for the transcription of a note from Upton's second edition of *The Scholemaster*,[5] relating to 'La Mort d'Arthure':

---

[1] *Warton's 'History of English Poetry'* (Warton Lecture: British Academy 1929), p. 6.
[2] *Letters*, 114 (Apr. 1758).
[3] p. 15. It is clear that Warton used the 1634 edition. Particulars which he could not have got from it were available in Ames's *Typographical Antiquities*.
[4] Roger Ascham, *English Works*, 1761—'with notes and observations on the Author's Life by James Bennet'. The Life has long been known for Johnson's, and his supervision of the whole work seems not to be in doubt.
[5] *The Scholemaster* 'by Roger Ascham, Esq; now revised a second time, and much improved, by James Upton', 1743.

so the book is intitled, tho' it treats of the birth, life and acts of the said King *Arthure*, and of his noble knights of the Round Table, and their marvailous conquests and adventures. I find it was reprinted at London 1634.[1]

In the same year (1761) Percy and Warton were corresponding about 'that Old Romance intitled Mort. Arthur'.[2] In the following year Warton brought out the second edition of his *Observations*. Here, the Arthurian material is amplified, notably by a reference to Shallow's remark in *2 Henry IV*, III. ii. 272—'I was then Sir Dagonet in Arthur's Show'—and a commentary on the passage, including Theobald's note (with its illustration from *The Knight of the Burning Pestle*), the statement that 'Sir Dagonet is an important character in Morte Arthur', and the appropriate quotation from Ascham's *Scholemaster*.[3] Thus, the connection between Sir Dagonet and Malory's romance is established, but two other items of information accompany this, each liable to prove misleading: Theobald's citation of a play some ten years later than *2 Henry IV*, and Warton's own designation of Sir Dagonet as 'an important character'.

When Johnson came to annotate the passage, he took over the note from Theobald's Shakespeare and quoted from Ascham, but added a characteristic comment of his own:

In this romance Sir *Dagonet* is King *Arthur's* fool. *Shakespeare* would not have shown his *justice* capable of representing any higher character.[4]

For his Appendix, however, he accepted and acknowledged information from Warton. In a substantial note, designed to lead up to an amplification of Theobald's illustration with another from Heywood's *Four Prentices of London*, Shallow's reminiscence is thus explained:

Arthur's Shew seems to have been a theatrical representation made out of the old romance of MORTE ARTHUR, the most popular one of our author's age. Sir *Dagonet* is King Arthur's 'squire.[5]

---

[1] Upton, pp. 86–7; Bennet, p. 254. The note in the 1761 edition is taken verbatim from that of 1743, with slight differences of spelling and punctuation. It includes matter of more direct relevance to Upton's edition than to Bennet's.

[2] *The Percy Letters: Correspondence of Thomas Percy and Thomas Warton*, ed. M. G. Robinson and Leah Dennis, Louisiana 1951, p. 2. There are other references to the work in this correspondence.

[3] pp. 58, 59, and 61.   [4] Johnson's Shakespeare, 1765, iv. 300, 301.

[5] Ibid. viii, keyed to this passage.

Whether Johnson was indeed 'induced to glance through the *Morte d'Arthur*' by Warton,[1] or by Percy (who had his own notions as to the composition of the work), or had long known it as one of the vernacular writings among which he moved with easy familiarity, he was evidently in no doubt about the part Sir Dagonet played in it. Critical curiosity, however, was taking another road—away from Arthur and towards Arthur's Show.

The tale of this investigation must be briefly recounted. Warton, drawing upon Shallow's reminiscences to illustrate his passage on 'interludes in the inns of Court' in the *History of English Poetry*, allowed himself to be entangled in speculation as to what it really was that the old gentleman had to remember; but he solved this little problem by separating Shallow's residence in Clement's Inn from his military exercises on Mile-end Green, and concluding that he was equally ridiculous for the tangled skein of his memory, and his unconsciousness of

> the satire implied in making [him] act Sir Dagonet, who was King Arthur's Fool. Arthur's Show, here supposed to have been presented at Clement's—inn, was probably an interlude, or masque, which actually existed, and was very popular, in Shakespeare's age: and seems to have been compiled from Mallory's Morte Arthur, or the history of king Arthur, then recently published, and the favourite and most fashionable romance.[2]

The solution did not wholly satisfy Malone, and the hint of *actuality* prompted him to further exploration: after quoting from both Johnson and Warton, he brought forward a work to which his attention had been drawn by a friend—Richard Mulcaster's *Positions*. This happily reconciled Arthurian legend and Elizabethan archery: Mulcaster, in his chapter 'Of Shooting', pays tribute to those

> who profess it throughly, & maintaine it nobly, the friendly and franke fellowship of prince Arthurs knightes in and about

---

[1] W. B. C. Watkins, *Johnson and English Poetry before 1660*, Princeton 1936, p. 49. See also Arthur Sherbo, *Samuel Johnson, Editor of Shakespeare*, Illinois 1956, p. 26. Both works are valuable, but Johnson's wide knowledge of early English prose—a knowledge independent of the anthologies which were bringing early verse to the notice of his contemporaries—is not within the scope of either. He possessed Ames's *Typographical Antiquities* (Sale Catalogue, item 323).

[2] 1774, ii. 404, 405.

the citie of London, which of late years have so revived the exercise. . . .¹

It now needed only the citation of Richard Robinson's *Auncient Order, Societie, and Unitie Laudable, of Prince Arthure, and his Knightly Armory of the Round Table* (1583) by Douce,² and R. P. Cowl's indication of allusions to Sir Dagonet in *Every Man out of his Humour* and *Cynthia's Revels*,³ to establish the supposition of an archers' pageant in which a buffoon appeared and was called Sir Dagonet.

Useful and amusing as are these illustrations, I question whether they may not have obscured something which the common sense of Johnson's original note makes plain: that the Shakespearian passage which has occasioned them derives ultimately from a particular source: the vein of pleasantry in the book of Sir Tristram de Lyones, in Malory's *Morte d'Arthur*. 'Ultimately?' I will ask a bolder question: what reason have we to suppose that there was ever a Dagonet in Arthur's Show, until Shallow played the part? If we set out the surviving fragments of evidence in chronological order, this is the impression we shall receive. In 1581, Mulcaster salutes those worthy citizens who, banding themselves together to revive the exercise of archery, have called themselves an Arthurian fellowship and taken the names, one of Arthur, one of Lancelot, others of 'the whole table, of those wel known knights. . .'. In 1583, Richard Robinson, amidst popular heraldry and popular history in doggerel verse, lists the names of fifty-eight Arthurian knights, similarly appropriated. Sir Dagonet is not among them; and this is not surprising if, as I infer, those who played a part in these pageants took themselves very seriously indeed. About 1596 or 1597, we are told, Jonson wrote his *Tale of a Tub* in its original form;⁴ and in those

¹ 1581, p. 102. Malone, perhaps inadvertently, alters the tone of the reference a little by reverting to Warton's earlier description of Sir Dagonet as King Arthur's squire. See his edition of Shakespeare (1790), v. 365, 366.
² *Illustrations of Shakespeare* (1807), i. 464. Warton was familiar with Robinson's work, of which he gives an account in the third volume of his *History of English Poetry* (1781), p. 391, note g.
³ Arden edition of *2 Henry IV* (1923); revised and amplified by A. R. Humphreys in 1966.
⁴ *Works*, ed. Herford and Simpson, Oxford 1925–52, ix (1950), p. 268. The editors conclude that Jonson 'reshaped it in 1633, rewriting old work and adding new scenes'. There seems reason to believe that this simple, good-humoured, topical satire belongs to the early version.

years the satire of his simpleton's Arthurian pretensions would still be freshly topical. Their heads in a whirl of fable and legend, Turfe, Medlay, and Clench choose for themselves the most aristocratic names they can recollect—and again Dagonet is not among them.[1] Thus, *2 Henry IV* forms, in 1597–8, a kind of watershed; and Jonson, in *Every Man out of his Humour*, records the change by making merry with folly in a new way. Carlo Buffone points out the country fellow, Sogliardo, and his follower Shift, to Macilente, in these words: 'Looke here, man; Sir Dagonet, and his squire!' And, when Saviolina has been fooled into taking Sogliardo for a fine gentleman, Fastidious Briske comments: 'This is a kinsman to justice *Silence*.'[2] It is clear that Shallow has already become a household word, and his performance in the archers' pageant a standing joke: oblique allusion will serve to recall either. Presently, the context of the jest loses its original distinctness: in *Cynthia's Revels*, Sir Dagonet is already a nickname for any fool or fop;[3] *The Knight of the Burning Pestle* recalls the serious simplicity of civic pageant or play, but loses the thread of Arthurian allusion.

Is it too much to suggest that at the core of this Shakespearian passage lies a familiarity with part at least of Malory's story; and that the force of the pleasantry consists partly in this very familiarity, shared between dramatist and audience? It may be claimed, first, that editions of the *Morte d'Arthur* within the preceding century were sufficiently plentiful to permit this supposition; secondly, that the misadventures of Sir Dagonet are no mere incident: they run, a thread of homespun humour, throughout Books IX and X. Let me instance some representative passages—furnishing for the cursory reader a reference to Professor Vinaver's plain text of 1954 (from which I quote), and for the more curious inquirer references both to the 1634 edition which Warton, Percy, and probably Johnson knew, and the 1557 edition in which Shakespeare may perhaps have read the tale.

Sir Kay sends Sir Dagonet, 'kynge Arthurs foole', after La Cote Male Tayle, the youth who has still to prove himself, and Sir Dagonet

---

[1] III. vi. Herford and Simpson, iii. 51. See the editors' note, ix. 293.

[2] IV. iv. 119; and V. ii. 22. Herford and Simpson, iii. 543 and 567. See the editors' note, ix. 466.

[3] V. iv. 549. Herford and Simpson, iv. 155. The name signifies no more in Davenant's *Wits*.

SIR DAGONET IN ARTHUR'S SHOW

gets a fall.[1] Sir Dagonet, again called King Arthur's fool, lingers unwarily beside a well haunted by Tristram in his wild mood; Sir Tristram 'sowsed sir Dagonet in that welle, and after that his squyars, and thereat lowghe the shypperdis'.[2] Sir Dynadan plans to expose Mark's cowardice, and Sir Gryfflet joins him, saying, 'Here have I brought sir Dagonet, kynge Arthurs foole, that is the beste felow and the meryeste in the worlde.' Mark is persuaded that he has to do with Lancelot, and takes flight:

> Whan sir Uwayne and sir Brandules saw sir Dagonet so chace kynge Marke, they lawghed all as they were wylde, and than they toke their horsys and rode aftir to se how sir Dagonet spedde, for Arthure loved hym passynge well and made hym knyght hys owne hondys. And at every turnemente he bega[n] to make kynge Arthure to lawghe.[3]

Dagonet's pursuit of Mark lives long afterwards as a jest of the Round Table.[4]

It would surely be a nice stroke of humour to insinuate such a figure into the mummery of an archers' pageant—where he had every right to be, but was unlikely to be found. It would be intelligible, and laughable, to any reader of Malory; and, among those who relished an occasional reminder that Falstaff's name had once been Oldcastle, this laughter would hardly be quenched by traditional denunciation of the religious and moral temper of *Morte d'Arthur*.[5]

Having ventured so far, I mean to go further. That Shakespeare had some acquaintance with Arthurian story has long been recognized; but it seems to have been assumed that his knowledge was confined to those popular versions current in humble verse forms. Let this assumption be reconsidered, however, and the possibility of some reading in Malory's *Morte d'Arthur* admitted, and it becomes pertinent to ask whether traces of this reading are to be

---

[1] 1557, Book IX, Chapter iii; 1634, Part II, Chapter xliv: *The Works of Sir Thomas Malory*, ed. Eugène Vinaver, Oxford 1954, p. 344.
[2] 1557, IX. xix; 1634, II. lx; 1954, pp. 369, 370.
[3] 1557, X, xii; 1634, II. xcvii; 1954, pp. 437 and 438.
[4] 1557, X. xx; 1634, II. cv; 1954, p. 451.
[5] The old censure had been revived by Nashe, among others. See his *Anatomie of Absurditie*, 1589, in *Works*, ed. McKerrow and Wilson, Oxford 1958, i. 11.

found, beyond the single allusion on which I have poised my argument. I believe there are such traces, one of them at least within that group of plays which may be called the Henry of Monmouth cycle—the two parts of *Henry IV*, and *Henry V*.

Falstaff is a character of many aspects—so many, that all attempts to reckon the sum must be distrusted; but one of them is happily caught in Maurice Morgann's phrase: 'a kind of Military freethinker'.[1] There is a character in Malory's story of Tristram to whom this same phrase might fitly be applied: Sir Dynadan. We know from Professor Vinaver that Malory has toned down his cynicism, finding the flavour of his French original too dry. And yet, with what equanimity and critical detachment does he hold his ground amongst the fire-eaters of the Round Table! Whether with King Mark, to whom he defends his own refusal of a challenge with the words 'Hit is ever worshyp to a knyght to refuse that thynge that he may nat attayne',[2] or with the disguised Tristram, who bids him avenge Sir Gareth's overthrow—' "That sall I nat," seyde sir Dynadan, "for he hath stryken downe a much bygger knyght than I am" '—, he remains constant to himself. This is his retort to an unknown challenger:

'Sir, whether aske you justys of love othir of hate?'
The knyghte answerde and seyde,
'Wyte you well I aske it for loove and nat of hate.'
'Hit may well be,' seyde sir Dynadan, 'but ye proffyr me harde love, whan ye wolde juste with me wyth an harde speare!'[3]

He even has the hardihood to dispute with La Beall Isode, denying the sovereignty of love and telling her that, though she is as fair a lady as ever he saw, he does not mean to joust with three knights for her sake.[4] He accepts the fortunes of combat imperturbably: Lancelot, having taken him captive,

brought hym to the quene, and tho the Haute Prynce lowghe at sir Dynadan, that they may nat stonde.

---

[1] *Essay on the Dramatic Character of Sir John Falstaff*, 1777, p. 99.
[2] 1557, X. viii; 1634, II. lxxxiii; 1954, p. 432.
[3] 1557, X. xx; 1634, II. cv; 1954, p. 452.
[4] 1557, X. lvi; 1634, II. cxlii; 1954, p. 516.

'Well,' seyde sir Dynadan, 'yet have I no shame, for the olde shrew sir Launcelot smote me downe.'
So they wente to dyner, all the courte, and had grete disporte at sir Dynadan.[1]

These, it may well be urged, are but trifling particulars of resemblance, insignificant in comparison with all that separates the characters of Falstaff and Sir Dynadan. True; but my inference is likewise a small matter. I do not argue that Shakespeare *owed* anything to Malory. This talk of indebtedness, idle even where scholarship is in question, must always dissolve to absurdity where the subject under discussion is great imaginative art. This only I would suggest: that, as the relationship between Falstaff and the other persons of these three plays develops, a pattern becomes apparent, the pattern of a situation which Shakespeare may perhaps have observed in that happy strain in the *Morte d'Arthur*. The Haute Prince and his Round Table laugh at Dynadan, not because he is a fool and plaything (like Dagonet), but because he is at once loyal and disengaged, because he stands apart and yet is one of them. For, although he may appear as the antithesis of their chivalric code, without that code he could not have come into being. Where there is a Hotspur, we may fairly expect a Falstaff also. Thus, the resemblance between Sir John and Sir Dynadan, though slight, is not superficial. Whether it touched surface in Shakespeare's mind we cannot know. If it pleased him, then the pleasure it gave was one which did not require to be communicated. But whether he was aware of it or no, it seems to have left a ripple near by. Mrs. Quickly's valediction[2] teases the imagination. Those who see Falstaff merely as a figure of Riot misleading Youth are clear why he must die; the rest of us acknowledge that he cannot continue to live (*Our revels now are ended*). Yet the terms in which his death is related transcend any clear-cut explanation; and they contain an expression which hints at subconscious recollection: 'Nay, sure, he's not in hell: he's in Arthur's bosom, if ever man went to Arthur's bosom.' Such commentators as have deigned to notice this line have remarked that the speaker meant Abraham. No doubt—if *meaning* is to be attributed to Mrs. Quickly. To

---

[1] 1557, X. xlvii; 1634, II. cxxxii; 1954, p. 495.
[2] *Henry V*, II. iii. 9–26.

determine what she means is as much to the purpose as deciding what Shallow remembered. It seems more pertinent to ask, why Shakespeare gave her these words. If there is an answer, it is to be formulated in terms rather of impulse than of intention: of the rhythm of the *Morte d'Arthur* prevailing upon his inner ear. Such a rhythm, haunting the imagination with the sense of something at once comparable and incongruous, might be accountable for the mingled tones of humour and pathos in this valedictory passage.

'A PHYSICIAN IN A GREAT CITY'

Presidential Address to the Johnson Society of Lichfield,
September 1951

AN invitation to preside on this occasion is indeed an honour, and a pleasure also; but it is none the less daunting. I am reminded of a proverb which was current in more than one European language about the time of the revival of learning. It ran: *Do not speak Latin in the presence of scholars.* (I cannot find it in the recent *Oxford Book of Proverbs*; doubtless the risk has diminished, one way and another.) But speaking Latin in the presence of scholars is a minor indiscretion beside that of speaking about Johnson in the presence of the Johnson Society of Lichfield, and in a company including some of its former presidents—those particularly who have done the work of giants in the world of scholarship, who have laboured to give us the text by which we may learn to know Johnson. Coming from a University whose Press has been responsible for the great editions of Johnson and of Boswell, I am bound to claim that Johnson has been faithfully served there. This piety would surely have pleased him. The unhappiness of his early years at Oxford was healed by his honorary degree, and there seems to have been no tincture of bitterness in any of his recollections. Not every author, revisiting this world, would care to be confronted with his editors. I am inclined to surmise that Johnson would have liked it very well. But then, it is not every author who remains a hero to his editors, as Johnson has done. From them (and I include among them those who may be said to have edited his unpublished works, the editors, for example, of Boswell and Mrs. Thrale)—from these, we have the finest criticism, the truest recognition of his greatness. It would be bold in anyone to suppose that he could add anything to the knowledge of Johnson that they have given us; in me it would be foolhardy. But Johnson, who gave courage to so many, encourages me here. 'It is', he says, '... not necessary that a man should forbear to write, till he has discovered some truth unknown before; he may be sufficiently useful, by only diversifying the surface of knowledge, and luring the mind by a new appearance to a second view of those beauties which it had passed over inattentively before.'[1] In the hubbub of mere gossip which has lately come to us from those who have *not* been Johnson's editors, and even in the criticism of some who *have* been Boswell's, Johnson's own works have not always received their proper share of attention. It was in a pleasant little book, by an approachable and friendly man of letters, that I found this extraordinary judgement: 'Johnson had himself almost every quality that makes for survival except genius; and that, by the happiest of fates for himself and for us, he found in his biographer.'[2] Do not imagine that I grudge one farthing of the universal tribute paid to Boswell's work. What he did was incomparably well done. But, for the generation that had known them both, it was Johnson's writings that counted.

A little while after Boswell's admission into Johnson's circle, Sir David Dalrymple wrote to congratulate him:

> It gives me pleasure to think that you have obtained the friendship of Dr. Samuel Johnson. He is one of the best moral writers which England has produced. At the same time, I envy you the free and undisguised converse with such a man. May I beg you to present my very best respects to him, and to assure him of the veneration which I entertain for the author of the Rambler and of Rasselas? Let me recommend this last work to you; with the Rambler you certainly are acquainted.[3]

(And, if we are not so certainly acquainted with it, the more is our loss.)

Those who knew Johnson best were quick to recognize that his writings and his talk were one: that a peculiar integrity united his opinions, however and whenever expressed. Too much has been made of the difference between his early formality and the easy manner of his later comments on men and books.

> To be able . . . to furnish pleasure that is harmless, pleasure pure and unalloyed, is as great a power as man can possess.[4]

---

[1] *Adventurer* 137.
[2] John Bailey, *Dr. Johnson and his Circle*, revised edition, 1947, p. 22.
[3] *Life*, i. 432–3.   [4] Ibid. iii. 388.

'A PHYSICIAN IN A GREAT CITY'

That kind of life is most happy which affords us most opportunities of gaining our own esteem.[1]

Sorrow is a kind of rust to the soul, which every new idea contributes in its passage to scour away.[2]

They who complain, in peace, of the insolence of the populace, must remember, that their insolence in peace is bravery in war.[3]

Where should we place these, on happening to hear them for the first time? Only one of them comes from Johnson's talk as reported by Boswell, and it is not (I think) the one we should look for there.

It is well known that, from the time he received his pension, Johnson wrote less. Boswell was bold enough to call him to account for this, within a little of their first meeting—and lucky enough to get a mild answer. When this *bad habit*, as Johnson acknowledged it, had continued some while, Boswell and Goldsmith together took him to task, urging their claim upon him. Johnson would not allow it. (He never liked to be told of obligations.)

'No, Sir, I am not obliged to do any more. No man is obliged to do as much as he can do. A man is to have part of his life to himself.... A physician, who has practised long in a great city, may be excused if he retires to a small town, and takes less practice. Now, Sir, the good I can do by my conversation bears the same proportion to the good I can do by my writings, that the practice of a physician, retired to a small town, does to his practice in a great city.'[4]

The analogy is exact; closer, perhaps, than Johnson himself recognized. As we go to consult a physician, so people of many different kinds went to consult Johnson. What they divined of him, through their reading of his essays and prefaces, his poems and *Rasselas*, made them think he could help them with their lives. Has any other English author occupied just such a position? Mrs. Thrale, glancing on and off the mark as usual, records that

with all his odd severity, he could not keep even indifferent people from teizing him with unaccountable confessions of silly conduct which one would think they would scarcely have had inclination to reveal even to their tenderest and most intimate companions; and it

---

[1] *Adventurer* 111.   [2] *Rambler* 47.
[3] *On the Bravery of the English Common Soldiers, Works*, 1825, vi. 152.
[4] *Life*, ii. 15.

was from these unaccountable volunteers in sincerity that he learned to warn the world against follies little known, and seldom thought on by other moralists.[1]

The fact is well attested: Johnson's more presentable friends were time and again surprised at his association with queer, uncomfortable, and undeniably faulty companions; but I distrust Mrs. Thrale's inference. It can be no more than a shrewd guess, based on the tales of odd characters he told to amuse *her*, for the social satire in his essays was some way behind him when their friendship began; and, as a guess, it does not ring quite true. Johnson's tolerance was not of that kind which a writer's acquaintance sometimes learn to distrust. He did not use them for *copy*. I do not suppose he ever turned to account either a friendship, or a draft upon his bounty. He relished the company of Bet Flint for its own sake—not, as grist for his mill when he wanted bread. It might indeed be serviceable to him, but in quite another way. Beyond the help they gave in keeping his melancholy at bay, those who came to him for any good office were as tug-boats to an ocean-going vessel, when they take her out of harbour. Johnson was seldom able to liberate his huge energies himself. 'Tom Tyers', he told Boswell, 'described me best: "Sir (said he), you are like a ghost: you never speak till you are spoken to."' Malone is circumstantial as to this peculiarity: 'I have always found him very communicative; ready to give his opinion on any subject that was mentioned. He seldom however starts a subject himself; but it is very easy to lead him into one.'[2] Once out of harbour, he was able to move strongly and freely. 'To receive and to communicate assistance', he had written, 'constitutes the happiness of human life.'[3] But the opportunity must, so to speak, present itself in person—must, as man or woman, walk in at the door.

Even supposing this to be the main reason for Johnson's readiness to welcome his oddly assorted visitors, we may still wonder what brought them. Not, surely, curiosity: the King could hardly conduct his life more openly; there was besides nothing mysterious about his opinions, nor enigmatic in his utterance of them. Moreover, contemporaries familiar with the tenor of his published works

---

[1] Hesther Lynch Piozzi, *Anecdotes of the Late Samuel Johnson, LL.D.*, 1786, pp. 223–4.
[2] *Life*, iii. 307 and note 2.   [3] *Adventurer* 67.

could not hope that he would tell them what they liked to hear—of progress, human perfectability, and the infallible reward of merit. Some of them had been shocked by the conclusion of *Rasselas*: Mrs. Chapone was sure that it would 'extinguish hope, and consequently industry'.[1] It certainly offered no easy comfort. Those whom his writings brought to Johnson must have reckoned on getting counsel framed in, and for, the rough weather of common experience.

When Rasselas and his sister Nekayah were travelling in search of happiness, they resolved to visit a celebrated hermit, and 'enquire . . . whether a man, whose age and virtue made him venerable, could teach any peculiar art of shunning evils, or enduring them'.[2] They found him sitting outside his cell. 'As they approached him unregarded, the princess observed that he had not the countenance of a man that had found, or could teach, the way to happiness.'[3] (She was, as usual, right.) No one who came to Johnson can have read in his countenance the witness of success in this quest. And yet it seems plain that they found what they sought.

Such counsel, if it is to avail, must be inexhaustibly applicable. No private nostrum will serve. (How well we know, and how rightly we distrust, those who offer to tell us, in common with a crowd of others, the *secret* of their success, in this or that enterprise!) At the same time, no judgement on the art of living is of any force without personal credentials. To the author of the *Rambler* and *Rasselas* those in need looked for ideas to scour away rust from the soul: general ideas, which yet carried the particular stamp of his own life, and what it had cost to live it.

It may seem odd that Johnson was able to furnish, out of his own experience, provision against 'the multiplicity of human passions, and the variety of human wants'. For that experience had not been every man's—still less, every woman's. Ever since his failure to take by storm the protected citadel of scholarship, it had been the experience of the professional writer, at its most rigorous. What should such a man know of any life beyond the desk to which he was bound? Hawkins, with his deep but narrow attachment to his strange friend, judged the question unanswerable.[4]

[1] *Posthumous Works*, 1807, p. 410.
[2] *Rasselas*, p. 52.
[3] Ibid. p. 55.
[4] *Life of Johnson*, 1787, p. 243.

It is true that Johnson's compassionate imagination showed him much that lay beyond the range of his vision: what it was like to be a private soldier in an ill-conducted campaign, an unprovided girl in a shiftless family—to be in any way at a disadvantage, in the robust society of that age. But, as he himself says, 'It is impossible for any man to rid his mind of his profession.'[1] And the remarkable thing is, that he does not even try. Time after time, in his essays, he puts some human problem to this test: how would it shape for the writer, in his peculiar predicament? Sometimes the proposition is playful: love he calls 'the state which fills the heart with a degree of solicitude next that of an author'.[2] But it is more often advanced seriously: 'Perhaps no class of the human species requires more to be cautioned against this anticipation of happiness, than those that aspire to the name of authors.'[3] I believe that in this very paradox may be found the clue we are looking for. It is because Johnson proposes that the author shall be the *average man* of surmise or speculation that the outcome stands up to everyone's weather.

It was, so far as I know, Johnson who originated a phrase now generally current—the *common reader*;[4] and I believe it might almost be said that out of that same capacious mind came a corresponding idea: an image of the *common writer*. Earlier literary criticism, when it undertook to praise the writer, pitched its claim so high as to invite the rebuff Rasselas gave Imlac, when he was proceeding to aggrandize his own profession: 'Enough! Thou hast convinced me, that no human being can ever be a poet.'[5] The poet, it was claimed, must be regarded as the counsellor of kings—high priest of mysteries; or else, as the shepherd-boy piping as though he should never grow old. Johnson is prepared to call him friend and benefactor on easier terms: by his reckoning, all may rank as authors who bring to the world's market a piece of that commodity —at once strange and familiar: the written word. And, among authors, every one who ministers to our needs—not excluding our

---

[1] Note on *The Winter's Tale*, IV. iv (IV. iv. 21–2).
[2] *Rambler* 1.   [3] *Rambler* 2.
[4] Johnson had first used the phrase in *Rambler* 4, and again in a note to *Othello*, I. iv (I. ii. 2); but it was the famous declaration ('I rejoice to concur with the common reader') in his Life of Gray which made it proverbial (*Lives*, iii. 441).
[5] *Rasselas*, p. 29.

need to be beguiled—may prefer a claim to his interest and fellow-feeling. I do not mean that he is easily satisfied with the stuff. Indeed, some of his verdicts have come to seem harsh, as those of a fellow craftsman may sound in the ears of a mere buyer. But, in the singular mixture of candour and astringency with which he treated the members of his own profession, there is no infusion of professional snobbery. He recognizes no hierarchy, no inner ring of initiates, in his commonwealth of letters: all alike are candidates for the suffrage of the common reader, all alike must submit to the same test—'continuance of esteem'.[1] For none will he claim special dispensation; and he makes relentless fun of those who claim any for themselves, who sit down to coddle their genius, or suppose themselves exempt from ordinary human obligations. He will not even allow them to magnify the significance of their success or failure; his estimate of the writer's influence on human thought and action is measured out with sparing hand: 'The most general and prevalent reason of study', he reminds him, 'is the impossibility of finding another amusement equally cheap or constant, equally independent on the hour or the weather.' What remains from such casual intercourse with books, he describes as though it were a sort of natural deposit: 'Perhaps, it seldom happens, that study terminates in mere pastime. Books have always a secret influence on the reader's understanding; we cannot, at pleasure, obliterate ideas.'[2] But he encourages no writer to suppose that his readers await improvement. 'Whatever professes to benefit by pleasing', he warns the self-appointed teacher, 'must please at once.'[3]

To please, then, is the writer's inescapable task. 'That book is good in vain which the reader throws away.'[4] But this acknowledgement of obligation—this admission that it lies with the reader to decide whether the obligation has been fulfilled—must never be mistaken for servile complaisance. Johnson was regarded by his friends as a proud man; taxed with it, he confessed to a defensive pride. If, as spokesman for his own profession, he carries himself humbly, it is with the humility of the incorruptible servant—and, beside this, all other pride is seen as mere ostentation. The literary

---

[1] *Preface to Shakespeare* (second paragraph). [2] *Adventurer* 137.
[3] Life of Cowley, *Lives*, i. 59. [4] Life of Dryden, *Lives*, i. 454.

sins he cannot find it in his heart to pardon are the sins of servility. 'There is often to be found', he says, 'in men devoted to literature a kind of intellectual cowardice.'[1] It is his gravest indictment. Towards the pretensions of a glossy scholarship he turns a withering aspect: 'I have inserted this note', he observes of one of Warburton's, 'rather because it seems to have been the writer's favourite, than because it is of much value. It explains what no reader has found difficult, and, I think, explains it wrong.'[2] On false pretensions in the realm of general ideas he is severe according as he judges them dangerous: there can be few more formidable verdicts than that which he delivers on the substance of Pope's *Essay on Man*: 'Having exalted himself into the chair of wisdom he tells us much that every man knows, and much that he does not know himself.'[3] And yet, to how many an unpretending literary enterprise will he give safe-conduct, forestalling others' challenge! 'Nay, it is an honest picture of human nature.'[4]

Johnson does not aim at aggrandizing his own profession, because he recognizes that the common reader and common writer are made out of the same stuff; that the writer is an eager reader of the works of his fellow-commoners in the realm of literature; that the reader may sometimes like to put pen to paper. He was accustomed to inquiries alike from friends and strangers, requiring his opinion as lexicographer on the right use of word or phrase, and he would expatiate in any company on the associations of words, their power to engage, or antagonize, or distract attention—knowing them for what they are: every man's tool, and the toys of a mind at play. This it is, surely, that draws us in—when we consult the *Dictionary* or the *Shakespeare*—as to a shared enterprise. Thus it is that we look to Johnson for authority, and find companionship. His critical manner has been called magisterial; and certainly there are critics in whom it is easier to recognize a companion. But there is surely none on whom we may more securely rely to come his fair share of the way to meet us, to carry his full share of the responsibility for communication—nor ever bear us down with reminders of the trouble to which this has put him. (Perhaps he had forgotten it himself; most

---

[1] *Rambler* 25.   [2] Note on *Henry VIII*, I. iv. (I. ii. 35).
[3] Life of Pope, *Lives*, iii. 243.   [4] *Life* iii. 228.

of it had been taken long beforehand; he had so schooled himself to think, and write, upon demand, that he seemed to any friend who watched him to be writing without effort.) The indolent writer knows more ways of shirking this responsibility—this obligation to take the reader with him—than his victim guesses: the assertion that commits him to nothing; the allusion which convicts the other of ignorance; the delicate hesitation which glances at our stupidity; the air of sustained effort which reminds us what it costs him to condescend within our reach. Johnson never magnifies the distance between himself and his readers. 'It is', he says, 'as possible to become pedantick, by fear of pedantry, as to be troublesome by ill-timed civility.' And, in a few lines—lightly drawn but not easily effaced—he sets before us the likeness of this variety of pedant: one who 'apologizes for every word which his own narrowness of converse inclines him to think unusual; keeps the exuberance of his faculties under visible restraint; is solicitous to anticipate enquiries by needless explanations; and endeavours to shade his own abilities, lest weak eyes should be dazzled by their lustre.'[1] The rule which he framed for himself was simpler: ' "Some people" (Boswell heard him say) "tell you that they let themselves down to the capacity of their hearers. I never do that. I speak uniformly in as intelligible a manner as I can." '[2]

Thus, whatever Johnson's visitors may have hoped to obtain by talk with him, this at least is certain: when they came away, they knew what they had got. Some, no doubt, were disappointed: of such was the young man who pestered him with trivial scruples of conscience until (according to Mrs. Thrale) he exclaimed: ' "I would advise you Sir, to study algebra... your head would get less *muddy* and you will leave off tormenting your neighbours about paper and packthread, while we all live together in a world that is bursting with sin and sorrow." '[3] Not all could take what he had to give.

What this amounted to, I will not now undertake to say. It is too big for me, and too grave for the occasion. It is, besides, known in some measure to all who care to know Johnson. But perhaps I may be allowed to separate one strand from the fabric of his argument,

[1] *Rambler* 173. [2] *Life*, ii. 323. [3] *Anecdotes*, p. 227.

if only because that strand is of the same colour and texture as some which I have already drawn out. I mean, his unfaltering sense of human solidarity. This it is which lends force to Imlac's counsel: 'Keep this thought always prevalent, that you are only one atom of the mass of humanity, and have neither such virtue nor vice, as that you should be singled out for supernatural favours or afflictions.'[1]

When Imlac enjoins on the Princess and Pekuah good faith in all their dealings with 'the great republick of human nature,'[2] he is expressing an idea which runs through Johnson's thought. (How otherwise account for his benign use, here, of that word *republic*—in any other context, abhorrent to him?)

'The power' '[he elsewhere observes] ... of every individual is small, and the consequence of his endeavours imperceptible, in a general prospect of the world. Providence has given no man ability to do much, that something might be left for every man to do. The business of life is carried on by a general co-operation; in which the part of any single man can be no more distinguished, than the effect of a particular drop when the meadows are floated by a summer shower; yet every drop increases the inundation, and every hand adds to the happiness or misery of mankind.'[3]

It was not any superstitious regard for public opinion that led Johnson to conclude, with an equanimity tried alike by failure and success in his own transactions with the common reader: 'About things on which the public thinks long it commonly attains to think right.'[4] To every man (he believes) it is given to effect something; and since, for this efficacy, he has but the one scale of measurement—his own—every man is credited, in his reckoning, with his own power to *think long*. Of power with which we are credited, by a friend who commands our respect, we may come at length to find ourselves possessed—in some degree.

The counsel, then, which Johnson gave, and gives, in his writings and his talk, avails because it was framed to endure the adverse weather of every life, and tested by his own. (And we may marvel

---

[1] *Rasselas*, pp. 124–5. The advice is offered to a man in an exceptional state of mind; but its tenor is not exceptional.   [2] Ibid., p. 120.
[3] *Adventurer* 137.   [4] Life of Addison, *Lives*, ii. 132.

how *his* deeply laden vessel could live in those terrible seas through which he had to voyage.) It is therefore not hard to believe the report that, in a recent time of adversity, men were heard, in common talk one with another, quoting Johnson's lines:

> Yet hope not life from grief or danger free,
> Nor think the doom of man revers'd for thee:
> Deign on the passing world to turn thine eyes,
> And pause awhile from letters, to be wise.[1]

[1] *The Vanity of Human Wishes*, ll. 155-8.

RASSELAS RECONSIDERED[1]

(1951)

'To a lady, who signified [to Johnson] a great desire to increase her acquaintance with authors, conceiving that more might be learned from their conversation and manner of living, than from their works —"Madam," said he, "the best part of an author will always be found in his writings."' So Hawkins reports.[2] That succeeding generations have sided with the lady against Johnson is surely indisputable, so far as Johnson himself is concerned. And, even when we deliberately disengage ourselves from the incomparable record of his 'conversation and manner of living', are we not apt to confine our attention to a few established favourites among his works, leaving the rest in Limbo?

Rasselas has lain there for a long while. On its first appearance, Mrs. Chapone spoke her mind about it; and in the declaration of a plain-spoken eighteenth-century lady we may sometimes discern thoughts that other thinkers—less stupid, perhaps; certainly less candid—have scrupled to utter. 'Do for once give your judgement fair play against the man's name,' she writes to Mrs. Carter, 'and tell me whether you do not think he ought to be ashamed of publishing such an ill-contrived, unfinished, unnatural, and uninstructive tale?' Its moral implications particularly offend her: 'I think the only maxim one can deduce from the story is, that human life is a scene of unmixt wretchedness, and that all states and conditions of it are equally miserable; a maxim which, if adopted, would extinguish hope, and consequently industry, make prudence ridiculous, and, in short, dispose men to lie down in sloth and despondency.' And she is 'scandalized above measure' at the final return to the outworn pleasures of the happy valley—for so she interprets the concluding words.[3]

---

[1] References to the text of *Rasselas* in this and the following essay have been revised, and now relate to *Rasselas*, ed. Geoffrey Tillotson and Brian Jenkins, 1971.

[2] *Life*, 2nd edition (1787), p. 410.   [3] *Posthumous Works* (1807), i. 108–10.

Mrs. Chapone was not quite alone in her opinion. Indeed, her point of view, and that more edifying conclusion to *Rasselas* for which she vainly looked, are alike exemplified in the *Dinarbas* of Miss Knight, published some thirty years later.[1] Here is reward according to desert; here, 'conscious merit'; here, those maxims of prudence and piety in which the reader may find means of self-improvement: 'There is no profession in which a man may not be virtuous and respected: the fault lies not in the state of life, it depends on the manner of acting.'[2] In so far as these aspersions, the direct and the oblique, may be supposed to represent eighteenth-century opinion, *Rasselas* seems hardly to have obtained even the 'success of esteem' which was all that Raleigh claimed for it. They are, of course, not representative. Nevertheless, the encomium of Hawkins (for example) is oddly mixed: 'Considered as a specimen of our language, it is scarcely to be paralleled; it is written in a style refined to a degree of immaculate purity, and displays the whole force of turgid eloquence.' But the substance has little to commend it: 'I wish I were not warranted in saying, that this elegant work is rendered, by its most obvious moral, of little benefit to the reader.' Only the circumstances in which it was composed can excuse its general tenor.[3] Murphy's criticism, though more happily expressed, sustains this contrast between the manner, which can be admired, and the substance, which must be regretted:

It is remarkable that the vanity of human pursuits was, about the same time, the subject that employed both Johnson and Voltaire; but *Candide* is the work of a lively imagination; and *Rasselas*, with all its splendour of eloquence, exhibits a gloomy picture.[4]

Even Boswell qualifies his tribute with the doubt whether Johnson's constitutional melancholy may not here override his sagacity.[5] It was no wonder that, when the tide turned, the next generation was disposed to reject so 'debilitating [a] moral speculation'[6] outright. Scott's reaction is significant—far more telling than that of a willing

---

[1] Ellis Cornelia Knight, *Dinarbas; A Tale: being a Continuation of Rasselas, Prince of Abissinia* (1790). [2] p. 15. [3] pp. 368, 371.
[4] *Essay on the Life and Genius of Samuel Johnson* (1792), p. 165.
[5] *Life*, i. 343.
[6] Hazlitt, *Lectures on the English Comic Writers* (*Works*, ed. Howe, 1930–4, vi. 102).

detractor: committed to a critical account of *Rasselas*,[1] he veers, drags his anchor, and runs for the lee of a favourite passage in *The Vanity of Human Wishes*, a poem for which he cherished a life-long affection.[2] Where he could not praise, he would not scrutinize; and it is clear that he could not praise *Rasselas*.

Is the grave tenor of *Rasselas* the true and sole cause of this dismay? The occasion of composition was indeed melancholy: contemporary references agree in associating it with the death of Johnson's mother. The evidence is closely examined in the Introduction to Dr. Chapman's edition,[3] which establishes Boswell's well-known account of the circumstances as substantially true:

> The late Mr. Strahan the printer told me, that Johnson wrote it, that with the profits he might defray the expence of his mother's funeral,[4] and pay some little debts which she had left. He told Sir Joshuah Reynolds that he composed it in the evenings of one week,[5] sent it to the press in portions as it was written, and had never since read it over.[6]

Rasselas, then, was a task to be performed. It sometimes happens to an author, however, to find that he has *written himself into* a piece of task-work: has discovered, in what he has perforce undertaken, opportunities which were not at the outset present to his unwilling attention. I believe that the 'little story book' which Johnson promised Lucy Porter on 23 March 1759, and which issued from the press on Thursday 19 April, may witness to some such experience. Hawkins gives a bleak enough account of the considerations determining Johnson's choice of direction:

> The fact, respecting the writing and publishing the story of Rasselas is, that finding the Eastern Tales written by himself in the Rambler, and by Hawkesworth in the Adventurer, had been well received, he had been for some time meditating a fictitious history,

---

[1] *Miscellaneous Prose Works* (1834), iii. 264 ff.
[2] Lockhart, Chapter xx.   [3] *Rasselas*, ed. R. W. Chapman, 1927.
[4] Mrs. Piozzi, Hawkins, and Murphy agree that money was needed for some purpose connected with his mother's death, and disagree merely in detail.
[5] Mrs. Chapone had heard 'three mornings'.
[6] *Life*, i. 341. Dr. Chapman points out that we are to accept this with such minor reservations as, that not all of the work was necessarily sent to the printer piecemeal; and, that Johnson included in his recollection of the writing of *Rasselas* a revision of the text for the second edition, which appeared but two months after the first.

of a greater extent than any that had appeared in either of those papers, which might serve as a vehicle to convey to the world his sentiments of human life and the dispensations of Providence, and having digested his thoughts on the subject, he obeyed the spur of that necessity which now pressed him, and sat down to compose the tale abovementioned, laying the scene of it in a country that he had before occasion to contemplate, in his translation of Padre Lobo's voyage.[1]

Was this, indeed, all that the notion of an Abyssinian tale signified to Johnson's preoccupied mind, or have we here no more than a half-truth, casting as much shadow as light on the subject?

Geoffrey Tillotson pointed out the *Persian Tales* as a possible factor in the situation,[2] but I found myself unable to accept this suggestion even with such reservations as he himself proposed. The *Mille et un Jours* of Pétis de la Croix, which Ambrose Philips translated,[3] flicker and twinkle with a polite French irony alien to *Rasselas*, and to its author; Johnson's irony was never polite. The tale of Bedreddin Lolo cited by Professor Tillotson as bearing some relation to Rasselas's quest of happiness appears indeed to be held together by the king's quest for a man who will admit that he is happy; but it is composed of a succession of romantic reversals of fortune, following no other rule than that which the story-teller in the market-place must observe: variety. When the king comments slily, at the close of one of these tales of extraordinary vicissitudes—'Tout le monde n'a pas perdu comme vous une princesse'—we are surely nearer to *Candide* than to *Rasselas*. Grant that, for the eighteenth-century reader, 'Persian Tale' spells entertainment—Johnson himself epitomized Goldsmith's power to please in the remark that he would make his Natural History 'as entertaining as a Persian Tale'[4]—and you have, I believe, all that Pétis de la Croix stands for, in the development of *Rasselas*.

Pleasure was not the sole train of association carried by this literary convention. Since Addison's time, it had served a variety

[1] p. 367.
[2] *Essays in Criticism and Research* (1942), '*Rasselas* and *The Persian Tales*'.
[3] Johnson's reference to this translation, in his Life of Philips, betrays no particular interest.
[4] *Life*, ii. 237.

of didactic purposes, traversing the polite world easily with its light burden of ideas—very much as Joseph Emin ('as good and as oriental as ever') traversed the world familiar to Catharine Talbot, expatiating on 'the management of states and kingdoms', and recounting 'Eastern tales and poems, as he had heard them repeated by some Persians he travelled with, when they sat down to pass the heat of the day on the banks of a river.'[1] And a more deeply rooted tradition, regarding the character and intention of such tales, had lately been revived. When Gibbon drily remarks, of his former tutor's romance, *Automathes*,[2] that it 'aspires to the honours of a philosophical fiction',[3] he wakes the echoes in a wide valley. The story of Hayy Ibn Yaqzan, written by Abu Bakr Ibn al Tufail in Muhammadan Spain of the twelfth century, is beyond the scope of this essay (as of the writer's capacity); but the descendants of this work, in England of the seventeenth and eighteenth centuries, cannot be ignored. Briefly, the tale is an allegory of the attainment of a purer religious apprehension—more mystical and more philosophical than that attained in the common traffic of mankind—by a boy reared in solitude on an island, who, when he brings word of this apprehension to his fellow men, finds them incapable of receiving it. The Arabic original was translated into Latin by the younger Edward Pococke, son of the great Oxford orientalist, in 1671,[4] and thereby set in motion a train of versions and imitations. From Pococke's Latin, two English versions were made before the end of the seventeenth century;[5] and these in their turn provoked the Cambridge orientalist, Simon Ockley, to translate afresh from the Arabic,[6] and to accompany his translation with a warning against the interpretation of the allegory by the Quakers, 'who imagin'd that there was something in it that favoured their Enthusiastick Notions'.[7] From one of these versions, or an abridgement, John Kirkby drew much

[1] Elizabeth Carter, *A Series of Letters*, ed. M. Pennington (1808), i. 441.
[2] John Kirkby, *The Capacity and Extent of the Human Understanding exemplified in the Extraordinary Case of Automathes* (1745).
[3] *Memoirs*, ed. G. Birkbeck Hill, (1900), p. 33.
[4] *Philosophus Autodidactus*. The Arabic text, with an Introduction by the elder Edward Pococke and translation by the younger.
[5] By George Keith (1674), and George Ashwell (1686).
[6] *The Improvement of Human Reason* (1708, reprinted 1711).
[7] The second page of 'The Preface'.

of the substance of his romance. This purported to be a manuscript account (washed up on the Cumberland coast) of the experience of an English Benedictine priest, expelled from Japan and shipwrecked on the shore of an earthly paradise. Here he encounters one Automathes, who, as a boy, had been reared in the same manner as Hayy Ibn Yaqzan, remote from human beings but fostered by kindly creatures. Unlike his original, however, he has been recovered by his father, at the age of nineteen, speechless indeed, but (as to his state of mind) 'more like a polished Christian, than an ignorant Savage'.[1] Now, in Kirkby's romance the attraction which this allegory held for eighteenth-century readers can be clearly descried: it spoke directly to their curiosity regarding man's inherent powers, and it could be adapted to express some of their favourite trains of speculation as to the noble savage and the life according to nature.[2]

Whether Johnson was acquainted with this story in any form, I have not been able to ascertain; but his dispersed reading makes such acquaintance appear by no means impossible. Adaptations of it, deistical in tendency, would have pleased him no better than they had Simon Ockley:[3] it is surely significant that he should set *his* story in Abyssinia, where—as his recollection of Lobo's *Voyage* would assure him—he might refer indirectly to Christianity as already known, and disembarrass himself of surmise as to religion without revelation.[4] The original tale, however, in Pococke's plain translation, establishes its own world, and informs it with some of that 'sentiment' which Johnson found wanting in the 'oriental fictions and allegorical imagery' of his friend Collins.[5]

In effect, the 'eastern tale' had more to offer to the imagination and taste of the eighteenth century than we can easily grasp. It gave occasion for idealization in the grand manner—the manner recommended in Reynolds's *Discourses*—and this is now an almost forgotten language. Moreover, when it would abstract this ideal

[1] pp. 76, 77.
[2] In particular, as to the connection between thought and language.
[3] Appendix.
[4] Notice the references to Palestine and its significance (p. 31), and (less explicit) to the intention of the monastic rule (p. 126), and the expectation of a future life (pp. 72, 132).
[5] *Lives*, iii. 338. Johnson here quotes from a *character* he had written of Collins not long after his death in 1759.

grandeur, it could command a field of reference more widely and simply acceptable to that generation than to this. In Johnson's happy valley, there is surely a tacit allusion to the ideal beauty of Eden in the fourth book of *Paradise Lost*, the ideal energy and variety manifest in the whole creation, as related in the seventh book. Johnson could count on something like unanimity of response. To the writer, this convention of oriental fiction and allegory held out particular opportunities. It was well enough acclimatized to combine easily with social satire and admonition, for which it had sometimes afforded a transparent disguise.[1] Nevertheless, it was still sufficiently exotic to admit whatever departure from naturalism might best serve its purpose, moral or artistic; it enjoyed a freedom denied to the novel. Its characters could address one another without observing the set forms of civility prescribed by that ceremonious generation. (And how tedious these forms can become, in the too faithful reporting of Fanny Burney! They threaten the very life of the dialogue.) The writer was at liberty to invent a code of manners; the lofty courtesy between Rasselas and Nekayah, recalling the conversation of Adam and Eve before the Fall; the simplicity of access to those whom they would observe: 'The laws of eastern hospitality allowed them to enter'[2]—what easier formula could any story-teller desire? Thus, eastern fiction spoke to the imagination of the eighteenth century in a language not unlike that which pastoral fiction had used to the Elizabethans. Each, in its own way, was free to simplify human relationships; either, mismanaged, was liable to reduce them to insipid uniformity; but the later convention had this advantage, that it was associated with no very august names, and might therefore be developed, alone or in conjunction with other literary conventions, by a writer who had the art of moving freely within traditional forms. To Johnson, who never troubled to invent new literary modes—he would probably have found them as uncomfortable as new clothes—it was thoroughly congenial.

Popular eastern fiction was episodic. This suited Johnson's inclination and circumstances. He was an improviser: that is, his pre-

[1] Its happiest use, for disguise, lay in the near future, with Goldsmith's *Citizen of the World*.
[2] p. 54.

paration for any undertaking was general, and had been made long beforehand; when the time came to entertain some new project, he drew on accumulated resources, and drew deepest when he wrote under pressure—as in the *Rambler* and *Rasselas*. Behind *Rasselas* lay his practice in the periodical essay: practice in illustrating his view of life and manners facet by facet. The episodes of a tale in which the principal characters move—without the urgency which an intricate plot must dictate—from one group of illustrative figures to another, need differ little from a succession of such essays. Contrariwise, *Idler* 75 might well be a tale told to the Prince by a newcomer to the happy valley; and *Rambler* 204 and 205 have been cited as 'obviously an earlier draft of *Rasselas*',[1] because they tell how an Abyssinian prince sought happiness, in vain. Moreover, the periodical essay had maintained, ever since its Addisonian golden age, its own tradition of allegorical vision: an ample, leisurely, pictorial tradition, inviting the mind's eye to dwell on the symbolic landscape and the typical figures that occupy it, until the forms of both assume a dream-like certitude. And here also an acknowledged alliance with oriental fable was of some standing.

Johnson liked, and needed, more room to turn in than a single periodical number allowed him. To *begin* anything was always an effort to him; in these papers, this initial difficulty is surmounted tardily; and indeed, nice proportioning of space and content must always be difficult for a man who writes under pressure, and without opportunity for revision. He had found comfortable room in that extended Addisonian allegory, *The Vision of Theodore, the Hermit of Teneriffe*. Here, in *Rasselas*, he obtained a still wider freedom, together with variety, by composing his story of two sorts of episode, corresponding with two types of periodical essay: that which levels particular criticism at observed phases of social life, and that which conveys general warning and exhortation obliquely, through representation of imagined states of being. And, whereas the essays forming a series in a periodical must be all of a length, these episodes vary both in bulk and density. The *mechanist*, who projects a flying machine, and the astronomer, who supposes himself to control the

[1] M. P. Conant, *The Oriental Tale in England in the Eighteenth Century* (1908), p. 123.

weather, are alike illustrative figures—but how differently they are handled!

Now, whether Johnson had any recollection of the fable of the boy reared in solitude, or whether *his* tale reflects only the mood to which that other spoke, he chooses for his observers of social life two characters who belong to the imaginary world of allegory, in that they are able to turn on all the familiar appearances of our world an innocent and curious gaze. And this freshness of apprehension he preserves untarnished by keeping them untouched by time, like the heroes and heroines of romance: Rasselas, by computation, has reached thirty-two before he is equipped for his inquiries, but neither in him nor in Nekayah is the first sense of wonder ever extinguished, and to the end Imlac treats them both as children. When Nekayah says that 'youth reverences virtue',[1] she is speaking out of character: it should rather be Imlac's observation on his young companions.

In this peculiar conjunction of allegory and anecdote, Johnson found (I believe) the proper vehicle for what he wanted to convey. *Rasselas* expresses such a tension of contrarieties as no other medium could sustain. It urges, with equal cogency, the necessity, and the danger, of hope. For moderation in both, a *Rambler* paper could offer a sufficient plea.[2] But for a stronger and subtler tension; for the presentation of contrary states of mind alike valid; for the annihilation of distinction between successive and simultaneous phases of experience—only this will serve. In Johnson's view of the human predicament, man, forbidden to despair, is bound for disappointment: he is for ever dissatisfied because he must seek the satisfaction proper to his nature elsewhere, but what he is, here, for ever hinders this search. Thus he becomes an inveterate gambler with hope—and, in matters of small moment, does well to divert and beguile his own restlessness.[3] But, in respect of graver concerns, this would be a dangerous frivolity; and yet, he dare scarcely reflect on the

---

[1] p. 68. Cf. *Life*, i. 445: 'Young men have more virtue than old men; they have more generous sentiments in every respect.'

[2] e.g. numbers 2 and 29.

[3] 'It is necessary to hope, though hope should always be deluded; for hope itself is happiness, and its frustrations, however frequent, are yet less dreadful than its extinction' (*Idler* 58).

incapacity of his known self to receive the bounty on which he is dependent;[1] or listen to experience, when it insists that he cannot avail himself of what he most requires. It has been said that all the characters in *Rasselas* speak with Johnson's voice; and so they should; for it is not the diversity of several views that they were created to express, but the complexity inherent in one.

Narrative, however—especially such narrative as Johnson's age knew—customarily attains in the close at least a conventional resolution of discords. How are we to regard the conclusion of *Rasselas*, in which *nothing is concluded*? Does it reflect weariness and irresolution —the exhaustion of resources and inability to improvise further? Or does it express Johnson's considered opinion on the problem his story had posed?—And, if it does, by what name are we to call that opinion? Is it, after all, despair?

There can be no doubt as to the dejection in which *Rasselas* was written: disappointment was Johnson's prevailing mood in these years, and his mother's death did no more than deepen it. For the origin of this mood, circumstances, together with more questionable causes, have been alleged. It should not be forgotten, however, that disappointment must always be measured in terms of hope. Circumstances might still alter in his favour, but Johnson could never forget the older men—his father among them—who had expected a brilliant career for him, and were dead before his late, frost-bound spring came to answer their expectations. This theme —of success deferred until those to whom it was to be offered are out of reach of the offering—obstinately recurs in his writings, especially about this time. The best-known expression of it is the close of his *Preface* to the *Dictionary*: 'I have protracted my work till most of those whom I wished to please have sunk into the grave, and success and miscarriage are empty sounds...' But the parallel between *Rambler* 165 and Imlac's account of his home-coming is equally significant. In both, a young man returns, full of his achievements in the world of letters, to his native place, only to find all those whom he had expected to astonish dead, or unmindful of him. Imlac certainly would seem to have been unlucky: he sets out as a very young man and, returning twenty years later, finds none to

---

[1] On schemes of self-improvement, Johnson in *Idler* 27 looks askance.

recognize him: 'My father had been dead fourteen years... Of my companions the greater part was in the grave.'[1] But a similar foreshortening appears in Rasselas's dissertation on the drawbacks of late marriages: the parents must 'go out of the world before they see those whom they love best either wise or great'.[2] Johnson's conscience was tender towards his parents. Moreover, melancholy in him was accompanied by its familiar associate, pride; and a proud young man accepts help in the confidence that he will be able, in due time, to show an ample return. The death of his mother was for Johnson an occasion not only of sorrow, but also of self-reproach; and, like the deaths of his father and his wife, a token of faith betrayed.

Rasselas, however, is not merely a reflection of a personal experience; it is a deliberate challenge to false optimism. Here, the comparison with Voltaire's *Candide* is useful. Over more than one stretch of their journey, the two men are travelling the same road. Johnson's philosopher, who complacently recommended his pupils 'to concur with the great and unchangeable scheme of universal felicity [and] to co-operate with the general disposition and tendency of the present system of things', would have enjoyed the society of Dr. Pangloss; but, in *Rasselas*, he is a mere illustration; when the Prince discovers him to be 'one of the sages whom he should understand less as he heard him longer',[3] we turn the page and leave him behind. Likewise, Voltaire's episode of the sinking of the ship, which Candide takes for retribution on the man who has wronged him—'Oui, dit Martin; mais fallait-il que les passagers qui étaient sur son vaisseau périssent aussi?'—this is incidental; in *Rasselas* it would not have been so soon forgotten. For Voltaire's indignation against false systems[4] occupies the centre of *Candide*, and is a judgement passed by the intellect. Johnson's condemnation of optimism gives central place to commonplaces of morality coldly felt; and it comes from his heart.

Rasselas challenged the assumption (easily formed in a prosperous age) that success is always distributed according to merit, and

[1] p. 35.   [2] p. 78.   [3] p. 60.
[4] Johnson's closest counterpart to this assault on a system comes two years earlier than *Rasselas* in his demolition of Soame Jenyns's *Free Inquiry into the Nature and Origin of Evil*.

happiness is necessarily evidence of superior virtue. Johnson called this in question, not merely because his own experience did not tally with it, nor solely because it was unworthy of a thinking man. His compassionate heart was angered by what lay underneath: a tacit supposition that the unhappy must have brought their troubles on themselves; that they, beyond the rest of us, deserve to suffer. This had been his theme six years earlier, in *Adventurer* 120:

> It has been the boast of some swelling moralists, that every man's fortune was in his own power, that prudence supplied the place of all other divinities, and that happiness is the unfailing consequence of virtue. But, surely, the quiver of Omnipotence is stored with arrows, against which the shield of human virtue, however adamantine it has been boasted, is held up in vain: we do not always suffer by our crimes; we are not always protected by our innocence.

And this indignation still burns in his arraignment of the philosophy of Pope's *Essay on Man*, more than twenty years later:

> To these profound principles of natural knowledge are added some moral instructions equally new; that self-interest well understood will produce social concord; that men are mutual gainers by mutual benefits; that evil is sometimes balanced by good; that human advantages are unstable and fallacious, of uncertain duration and doubtful effect; that our true honour is not to have a great part, but to act it well; that virtue only is our own; and that happiness is always in our power.[1]

Prosperity had not changed Johnson.

Some of the optimistic notions which Johnson attacked appear to us now so simple that we may wonder why he expended such energy in demolishing them. I believe, however, that he measured the force required not so much by the degree of public assent they obtained, as by a motion that he felt within himself: an insidious propensity for day-dreaming. He was, in his own estimation, one who 'let year glide after year in preparations to live'.[2] To this Rasselas also was prone—together with an inclination 'to feel some complacence in his own perspicacity, and to receive some solace of the miseries of life, from consciousness of the delicacy with which he felt, and the eloquence with which he bewailed them'.[3] Imlac

---
[1] *Lives*, iii. 244.   [2] *Adventurer* 108.   [3] p. 7.

likewise had been a day-dreamer: had, at the outset of life, 'amused myself during the voyage, sometimes by learning from the sailors the art of navigation, which I have never practised, and sometimes by forming schemes for my conduct in different situations, in not one of which I have been ever placed'.[1] He supposed himself to have outlived such foolishness; but our youthful follies withdraw only to revisit us in another guise; and one of the most deeply humorous episodes in the story reflects Johnson's rueful self-knowledge:

Imlac now felt the enthusiastic fit, and was proceeding to aggrandize his own profession, when the prince cried out, 'Enough! Thou hast convinced me, that no human being can ever be a poet. Proceed with thy narration'.

'To be a poet', said Imlac, 'is indeed very difficult.' 'So difficult', returned the prince, 'that I will at present hear no more of his labours.'[2]

'Perhaps', as Johnson remarks elsewhere, 'no class of the human species requires more to be cautioned against this anticipation of happiness, than those that aspire to the name of authors.'[3] All through life, his own imagination was occupied with grandiose projects in the realm of letters.

Though Johnson may see this 'invisible riot of the mind, this prodigality of being',[4] as an inherent foible, both ineradicable and open to laughter, he does not regard it with an indulgent eye. The final confessions of the three young day-dreamers are called forth by Imlac's account of the rooted insanity of his friend the Astronomer, and the reflections with which it has filled his own mind:

'Of the uncertainties of our present state, the most dreadful and alarming is the uncertain continuance of reason. . . . Perhaps, if we speak with rigorous exactness, no human mind is in its right state. There is no man whose imagination does not sometimes predominate over his reason, who can regulate his attention wholly by his will, and whose ideas will come and go at his command.'

When we are alone, the imagination is hardly to be controlled:

'He who has nothing external that can divert him, must find pleasure in his own thoughts, and must conceive himself what he is not; for who is pleased with what he is?'[5]

[1] p. 24. [2] p. 29–30. [3] Rambler 2.
[4] Rambler 89. [5] pp. 113, 114.

This is the formidable context in which Pekuah confesses that she has played the princess in her dreams; Nekayah, the shepherdess of romance; and Rasselas, that he has indulged in a more perilous flight of fancy:

> 'I have frequently endeavoured to image the possibility of a perfect government, by which all wrong should be restrained, all vice reformed, and all the subjects preserved in tranquility and innocence. ... This has been the sport and sometimes the labour of my solitude; and I start, when I think with how little anguish I once supposed the death of my father and my brothers.'[1]

Thus, the end of *Rasselas*, in which Nekayah's grave words ('To me, said the princess, the choice of life is become less important; I hope hereafter to think only on the choice of eternity') are followed by more, and yet more projects[2]—this is but a candid recognition of that tension of contrariety which Johnson found in all men's lives, and of which he was poignantly aware in his own. Indeed, he possessed in special measure one characteristic which was bound to impose on his story a confined motion—like that of a ship riding at anchor, which can move, but never remove. He was tenacious; he did not relinquish easily, nor think it prudent to let go; he was dubious of one sort of religious conversion, because he thought it meant relinquishing too much.

It is not well enough remembered that in *The Fountains*[3] we have much of the wisdom of *Rasselas*, more simply and less sternly[4] expressed. This little story follows the course of one of the world's oldest fables: a mortal obliges an immortal being, and is rewarded with the magical means of obtaining his every desire, but uses that gift so ill that he must needs beg to be relieved of it. Here, the child

---

[1] pp. 115, 116. Cf. *Rambler* 8: 'He that fancies he should benefit the public more in a great station than the man that fills it, will in time imagine it an act of virtue to supplant him.'

[2] Are we to regard the projected return to Abyssinia as a final confession of defeat? Not unless Johnson remembered the circumstances which he had borrowed, for his opening, from his own recollection of Ethiopian rule: that every young man of royal blood must endure seclusion 'till the order of succession should call him to the throne' (p. 1).

[3] Contributed to Anna Williams's *Miscellanies in Prose and Verse* (1766).

[4] Lady Knight, however, found it 'a fine written but gloomy tale' (G. Birkbeck Hill, *Johnsonian Miscellanies*, ii. 173).

Floretta, having won the favour of the fairy Lilinet, is invited to drink at either of two enchanted fountains, and makes every mistake that we have learned to expect in such a tale. From the fountain of joy she obtains beauty—only to find herself less generally liked than when she was 'merely agreeable'; riches, and becomes the object of fortune-hunters—and so on. Each time, she has to acknowledge her error, and drink the water of sorrow to rid herself of the unwelcome gift. Every supernatural advantage but one she at length resigns, and thankfully accepts her share in the common lot of mortals. That one exception is discernment, the 'obstinate rationality'[1] which Johnson himself could not or would not surrender, even in exchange for serenity of mind. This tension he preferred to any relaxation of which he believed it capable.

Though we may—and surely should—set aside the charge that *Rasselas* is but a condensation of the vapour arising from despondency, yet there remain some hindrances to its enjoyment. The story creaks: vicissitudes are awkwardly brought about and stiffly related. The happenings are indeed not to be compared with the talk; some, such as the loss and recovery of Pekuah, should ring sharply, but return a leaden echo. Their episodic succession forbids formal symmetry; and there is reason to suspect that Johnson concerned himself little with their disposition. The fortuitous old man by the banks of the Nile rises like an exhalation in the midst of the Astronomer's story, and vanishes in like manner.[2]

To these objections one answer, together with its roots and branches, should be sufficient. When a man writes *out of himself*, we may expect that the writing will be *characteristical*—to use a favourite word alike of Johnson and Dryden: that it will express him in his entirety. And I believe that there is more of Johnson in *Rasselas* than is generally recognized.[3] There is the gift for comic narration which impressed and even startled his associates.[4] Rasselas's observations on the unreason of common life more than once recall the humour of the Rambler in his homelier moods: in the very fatigue of idleness, a 'youth and maiden, . . . having little to divert attention, or

[1] *Life*, iv. 289.   [2] pp. 116–19.
[3] True valuation of *Rasselas* is to be found just where it was to be expected: in Professor Nichol Smith's chapter in *C.H.E.L.*
[4] Hawkins, p. 258; Mrs. Piozzi, *Anecdotes*, p. 118.

diversify thought, ... find themselves uneasy when they are apart, and therefore conclude that they shall be happy together.'[1] We are not far from the social comedy of Jane Austen—who might well recognize a sister in the Princess, despite differences of idiom:

> 'But surely, interposed the prince [when Nekayah spoke of unprosperous marriages], you suppose the chief motive of choice forgotten or neglected. Whenever I shall seek a wife, it shall be my first question, whether she be willing to be led by reason?'
> 'Thus it is, said Nekayah, that philosophers are deceived. There are a thousand familiar disputes which reason can never decide. . . . Wretched would be the pair above all names of wretchedness, who should be doomed to adjust by reason every morning all the minute detail of a domestick day.'[2]

Within this husk of humour is folded the sagacious counsel for which his contemporaries sought Johnson's society: the sagacity of Imlac, when he confers with the Astronomer,[3] comforts the Princess,[4] or is echoed by his apter pupil: 'He does nothing,' (Nekayah warns her brother) 'who endeavours to do more than is allowed to humanity.'[5]

In any comparison with other eighteenth-century 'eastern tales' —Hawkesworth's, for example—the sanity of *Rasselas* is manifest. And, even in comparison with work of like quality, the peculiar character of this sanity must make itself felt. For the freshness of great classical, and great romantic, work is preserved in diverse ways. What renews itself with each re-reading of the romantic affirmation is a recovered sense of the initial force with which the particular experience assailed the particular poet. What renews itself with each re-reading of the classical affirmation is a sense of its unexpended applicability. This is the salt that seasons Johnson's writing: the recognition, not blunted by familiarity but sharpened with every return of attention, of the warrant that common experience affords it.

Sanity is a daylight colour; but it need not banish splendour. Cadences in *Rasselas* haunt the ear: '. . . that hunger of imagination

---

[1] pp. 75-6. [2] p. 77. [3] pp. 124-5.
[4] p. 89.   [5] p. 78.

which preys incessantly upon life;'[1] '... treason against the great republick of human nature';[2] '... from the wonders which time has spared we may conjecture, though uncertainly, what it has destroyed.'[3] These are Imlac's; but he has not been granted a monopoly.

In calling *Rasselas* a satire, Hawkins signally fails to take account of the difference between visitors and visited. All unreason—except that of hoping against hope for a rational solution of life's perplexity —is to be found among the visited; and, although the unhappiness attending human relationships is a dominant theme in this wide survey of human distresses, yet between the four visitors (three of whom travel for love) there survives a relationship never clouded. Rasselas and Nekayah are indeed open to the very objection that Johnson levelled against Milton's Adam and Eve: 'The man and woman who act and suffer are in a state which no other man or woman can ever know. The reader finds no transaction in which he can be engaged, beholds no condition in which he can by any effort of imagination place himself; he has, therefore, little natural curiosity or sympathy.'[4] And, unlike Adam and Eve, they keep their innocence even after they have left their original seclusion and mingled with humanity in its ordinary state. In the absence of self-reproach, the quest for happiness is surely altruistic; and these two can reproach themselves with nothing worse than expense of time —a commodity they have not to reckon at the common rate. It would, however, be dishonest to use against a man a charge which, when *he* used it, was judged invalid; and, if we reject Johnson's censure of the choice of ideal beings by Milton, we may, on like grounds, accept his own choice of such characters—provided only that the representation satisfies. Like the boy reared in a sort of solitude alien to experience, they are fashioned for the proper purposes of 'philosophical fiction'. And this particular fiction is the easier of acceptance because it follows that most durable of allegory's traditional patterns, the pattern of a journey. Thus it speaks to us in terms of our sense of continuity in our own experience: of identity persisting through and beyond change. And as we surrender to its rhythm, so

[1] p. 85. [2] p. 120. [3] p. 79.
[4] *Lives*, i. 181.

we accommodate our gait to the stately motion of those four travellers, all but one of whom accost us in Johnson's own voice.

> Would that they three could know
> How yet burns on in me
> Love—from one lost in Paradise—
> For their grave courtesy.[1]

[1] Walter de la Mare, *The Three Strangers*.

RASSELAS: A REJOINDER

(1970)

It is open to question whether anyone who has formerly expressed an opinion on a particular book has the right to re-enter the controversy about it. I claim no rights; but 1951[1] is now a long while ago: much has since then been written about *Rasselas*, and I should like to comment on some positions assumed in recently published work; former critical writings have fallen into perspective and need to be reconsidered; some of my own opinions I should like to reaffirm, whether with fresh evidence or merely with accumulated conviction; and to develop a few.

These appear to me the most important recent studies: Gwin J. Kolb, 'The Structure of *Rasselas*' (*P.M.L.A.* lxvi (1951), 698–717); Alvin Whitley, 'The Comedy of *Rasselas*' (*E.L.H.* xxiii (1956), 48–70); Frederick W. Hilles, '*Rasselas*, an "Uninstructive Tale" ' (*Johnson, Boswell and their Circle, Essays Presented to Lawrence Fitzroy Powell*, Oxford 1965); Emrys Jones, 'The Artistic Form of *Rasselas*' (*R.E.S.* N.S. xviii (1967), 387–401); and the Introduction to *The History of Rasselas Prince of Abissinia* by J. P. Hardy, Oxford 1968.

Behind us all appear the magisterial forms of Walter Raleigh, W. P. Ker, and David Nichol Smith. These spoke out of their own authority, which was great, and to a world which shared their scale of literary values and seldom asked for argumentative analysis. Yet within some of their judgements there seems to be an element of paradox and, when they are heard together, they do not always seem to be talking about the same book. Recent criticism is, not surprisingly, more various and more contentious. Indeed, I suspect the one unassailable judgement to be that of Mr. Emrys Jones: 'It is, after all, not altogether unknown for works of art of exceptional vitality to be interpreted in similarly diverse ways.'[2] I propose to increase, by a little, this diversity of interpretation, and, to that

[1] '*Rasselas* Reconsidered' in *Essays and Studies* 1951 (English Association).
[2] Op. cit., p. 389.

end, frame these complementary questions. What insight can we hope to obtain into the context of *Rasselas*, literary as well as biographical: not only of Johnson's circumstances and mood, but also the tradition in which he was writing? What kind of artefact is *Rasselas*—a performance, something deliberately planned and executed, or an improvisation? What is its mood, its author's intention, his design upon us?

I begin by reaffirming that Johnson undertook the work in deep dejection—a position seldom denied; and that he wrote himself into some sort of equanimity. As evidence for the first, we have his known circumstances, and his insistence, especially in the early chapters, on modes of unhappiness with which he was at that time all too familiar.[1] Of equanimity when the work was completed, at least in regard to the outcome, we may discern some intimation in his letters to Lucy Porter of 23 March and 10 May 1759: 'I am going to publish a little story book which I will send you when it is out'; and 'I beg you, my dear, to write often to me, and tell me how you like my little book'.[2] Surely Lucy Porter, that very unimaginative woman, would have been surprised to learn that the 'little story book' is now the subject of grave controversy—notably on the question whether it is a profound essay in moral philosophy or a satire on the moralist's search for a clue to the riddle of life. Johnson might have been surprised too. I suggest, and hope presently to show, that the *weather* of his mind had undergone some change in the course of the story.

Of the literary context of *Rasselas* I have likewise something to reaffirm. I see no reason for supposing that Johnson thought the 'oriental tale' other than a reputable literary form, worthy to associate even with *Paradise Lost*, or with that Moorish allegory which was accessible in Latin and in more than one English version.[3] Pope's allusion to this tale of a *Self-taught Philosopher* in *Guardian* 61 ('Against Barbarity to Animals') persuades me that the likelihood

---

[1] The recurrent theme of success delayed too long is pointed by Nekayah's reference to late marriages and their result: parents 'must . . . go out of the world before they see those whom they love best either wise or great' (p. 78). Johnson was himself the child of such a late marriage.
[2] *Letters*, nos. 130 and 131.
[3] See '*Rasselas* Reconsidered', above, p. 106.

of Johnson knowing it is stronger than I formerly surmised. The vein of irony running through *Rasselas*[1] need not imply contempt for the literary conventions it observes—any more than the satire in a 'mock heroic' poem implies contempt for the epic.

Raleigh claimed, in *The English Novel*, that 'the structure of the plot is masterly, the events are arranged in a skilful climax'.[2] But he did not particularize, beyond designating that climax 'darker than death itself'; nor did he develop this claim in his *Six Essays on Johnson*. Moreover, before it is tested, there is another question to be asked: with what sort of structure are we here concerned? You cannot judge an old house in the country by the same criteria as a modern house in a 'dormitory' suburb: assume a norm, and you will condemn the one for possessing, or the other for wanting, stable-yard and outbuildings. Thus, when W. P. Ker found in *Rasselas* little to admire and nothing to enjoy,[3] he was evidently taking for granted a unitary structure, all of a piece throughout: 'As a moral essay, *Rasselas* is monotonous and weak, through the repetition in different forms of the same situation.' It is, he continues, nothing but a series of experiments conducted by two characters, who relinquish one merely to turn to another, and are never themselves implicated in any. Most readers, however, recognize at least one sharp dividing line: that between the Happy Valley and the world outside. And among recent critics, Mr. Alvin Whitley is singular in seeing the movement of the tale under the guise of a journey which must inevitably bring the travellers back to their starting-point, because they have all along been tracing a circle—and the 'conclusion in which nothing is concluded' as grimly appropriate, because a circle has no end. Therefore the theme is, for him, futility. Professor Kolb is content with the division into two parts, inside and outside the valley. This corresponds with an initial, because instinctive, reaction we may all have experienced. But Professor Hilles shrewdly points out an objection to this simple analysis: within the valley the subject is, as often as not, the world outside. He therefore maintains

[1] This is most clearly shown by Professor Hilles, op. cit., pp. 115–16.
[2] *The English Novel*, 5th edn., London 1907, p. 206.
[3] 'Prose Writers from Locke to Gibbon' in *On Modern Literature*, ed. T. Spencer and J. Sutherland, Oxford 1955, p. 258. (The text from lecture notes not revised by the lecturer.)

that *Rasselas* is composed of 'three roughly equal parts, each related to the other two'.[1] Mr. Emrys Jones likewise finds three well-proportioned parts; for him, they are exactly equal, but he has to relegate the conclusion to 'a trailing coda' in pursuit of this symmetry.[2] (The problem of that enigmatic last chapter is inescapable.) I side with Professor Hilles and Mr. Jones in finding the work composed of several distinct and well articulated parts—or, as I should prefer to call them, phases, appropriate to the narrative design.

Mr. Whitley's essay, of 1956, stands (in my view) a little apart from those that precede and follow it. He, even more explicitly than W. P. Ker, treats *Rasselas* as though it were all of a piece, a single train of events; and, although he does not call it 'monotonous and weak', he makes it appear so. This 'futile journey in a circle' coheres, logically and organically, because all 'conditions and theories of human life are to be sought out' in its course; therefore nothing can be irrelevant. (To Miss Bates, nothing is irrelevant; but she is in her right place, inside a book.) Variety of tone is admitted, in so far as the sky is always darkening towards the final 'grim subject of religion'. After this, it comes as no surprise to be told that 'the subject of death and immortality' is 'the gloomiest subject in *Rasselas*'.[3]

Beneath some superficial differences, the rest are concerned to discover Johnson's central intention through observation of the story's successive phases and their interrelation; and, accepting the idea of progression, they look to the last phase for the answer to their questions. Professor Kolb, arguing that Johnson's purpose is to demonstrate the inescapable unhappiness of mortal life and recommend consoling thoughts of eternity, leans a little towards the severity of Mr. Whitley, and is forced to explain the humour which plays about this 'little story book' as satirical censure of the fashionable 'oriental tale'. For Professor Hilles, the travellers, when they enter the second phase and settle in Cairo, assess the threats to happiness and find them formidable. There is for man no such thing as a safe choice, and the visit to the Pyramids reminds them, and us, that there never has been. The final phase leads them from

[1] Op. cit., p. 111.
[2] Op. cit., Section iii. Particular references scarcely do justice to this closely-reasoned essay.
[3] Op. cit., pp. 52 and 68.

observation to experience: they 'learn what suffering is'. And 'the last sentence takes us back to the first one' (with its warning against fallacious hope), 'neatly rounding off a skilfully organised tale'. In its course Rasselas and his companions have 'acquired wisdom', and so the tone, however grave, is not dispiriting.[1] With Mr. Jones and Professor Hardy, we move still further from a vision of *Rasselas* as livid in colour and enervating in tone: they rightly point out that, whereas the delusions of the Astronomer form the climax of the third phase, this culminates in his recovery.[2]

Here I take up my tale. First, I suggest but do not insist upon a four-part division. Not that I would relegate the last chapter (any more than the closing lines of *The Vanity of Human Wishes*) to a mere coda; but I would open the third phase with Pekuah's abduction—the point at which life may be said to *hit back*, and a fourth with the first mention of the Astronomer. With this proposal I join another, though more tentatively: that the old man by the bank of the Nile be regarded as parenthetical—and, like a bracket in a sum, he must be considered first. He has a chapter to himself (XLV), and, relating neither to what precedes nor what follows, it is very awkwardly placed. We have had five chapters about the Astronomer, whose tale will be taken up immediately after this interruption. Thus, the complaint of old age and approaching death breaks into a narrative passage which had begun with the serene opening of Chapter XL: 'They returned to Cairo, and were so well pleased at finding themselves together, that none of them went much abroad.' (Imlac is the exception, but his *going abroad* is required to draw the Astronomer into their charmed circle.)

I suggest that Chapter XLV may be part of an earlier plan—perhaps the original ending: Johnson had meant the several accounts of those ills which we make, or make worse, for ourselves to lead up to those two which are inescapable. It would have been a dreadful conclusion. Not merely a general proposition, commanding easy assent, it is charged with the bitterness of a personal application: 'I have neither mother to be delighted with the reputation of her son, nor wife to partake the honours of her husband.' Is it not

[1] Op. cit., p. 119.
[2] 'The Artistic Form of *Rasselas*', p. 399; Introduction to *Rasselas*, p. xxi.

possible that Johnson, having drafted this episode—in his mind, if not actually in writing—decided that it should not end the book, and placed it where it is (I maintain) offset by the development of the Astronomer's story?

So everything turns on our reading of this final episode and its central character. How is the Astronomer to be taken? I deny altogether the position most explicitly stated by Raleigh: that his 'delusions supply the picture with a shade darker than death itself'. It is something, but not enough, to retort that the Astronomer's case, unlike that of the old man, admits of cure. We must penetrate deeper. Johnson's fear of madness is well known—perhaps too widely known and too narrowly understood. It seems to be forgotten that he was not afraid of madmen. The tenor of his friendship with Collins and Smart may show merely another aspect of his personal courage—or else that he had faced an issue commonly shunned. A man who has experienced no more than uneasy suspicions of his own equilibrium does not like to have it disturbed, and avoids disquieting company. It was Charles Lamb who, knowing (surely) the very worst, wrote on the sanity of true genius.

If, among our present discontents, we can yet find cause for satisfaction, it is in the changed attitude to mental disorders. (What the relationship between this and the increased recognition of their frequency—cause, effect, coincidence—I have no authority to determine.) In this respect, Johnson shows himself a modern thinker, notably in *Rasselas*. Contrast with Imlac's view—which, on this topic, is clearly his—that represented by Hogarth's Bedlam. The Astronomer's case, according to Imlac, is not the result of guilty indulgence:

> No disease of the imagination . . . is so difficult of cure, as that which is complicated with the dread of guilt: fancy and conscience then act interchangeably upon us, and so often shift their places, that the illusions of one are not distinguished from the dictates of the other. (p. 124)

The initial cause is a 'dangerous prevalence of imagination' (to which all the sympathetic characters sooner or later confess themselves prone) over reason.[1] And it is to the Astronomer's incorruptible

[1] Imlac generalizes this confession to include all mankind (pp. 113–15).

reason that Imlac appeals—not to that capacity for reason which stirred Swift's deepest despair, nor that misuse of reason which provoked Pope to call man 'the glory, jest, and riddle of the world'. Reason, for Johnson, signifies a source of strength which may remain accessible to those who will observe one rule—not to insulate themselves:

> When scruples importune you, which you in your lucid moments know to be vain, do not stand to parley, but fly to business or to Pekuah [that is, stretch your mind with men or relax it with women], and keep this thought always prevalent, that you are only one atom of the mass of humanity, and have neither such virtue nor vice, as that you should be singled out for supernatural favours or afflictions. (pp. 124-5)

The negative—do not withdraw yourself—is fortified by the positive injunction: acknowledge your kinship with your fellow beings. Johnson's thinking on the most disquieting problem his tale poses —no matter what the validity of his answer—is upheld by his faith in human solidarity: we are *all* akin because the difference between sanity and madness—much like that between genius and common powers—is one not of kind but of degree. The world he presents in *Rasselas* is indeed sombre, but it breeds no monsters.

Boswell records an occasion on which Johnson was provoked by Morgann's *Character of Falstaff* into remarking: 'Why, Sir, . . . as he has proved Falstaff to be no coward, he may prove Iago to be a very good character.'[1] I should be sorry to forfeit a hearing for an opinion in which I believe, merely because it wears at first sight an air of paradox. Its real seriousness may be discerned if it is seen in the whole context of Johnson's treatment of the Astronomer. This character is important, and understanding of him crucial to the interpretation of *Rasselas*, for three reasons. He is the first denizen of the outside world to whom the travellers open their hearts, and with whom they abandon their incognito. Thus he belongs rather with those who observe and experience than with those who are observed. He brings into sharp focus Johnson's ideas on the danger of the unguarded imagination. While I agree with Professor Hardy

---

[1] *Life*, iv. 192, n. 1.

that the Astronomer's studies have been, on Johnson's reckoning, ill directed,[1] I see the power of imagination working on a scrupulous temperament in solitude as even more dangerous. Nevertheless, being composed of quite another substance, as to density and complexity, than the Hermit, he does not merely signal 'Solitude is injurious' and quit the story. Joining the other characters, he combines with them to illustrate Johnson's achievement in transcending the limitations of contemporary allegory, and drawing on an older and greater tradition. Here I develop a suggestion tentatively advanced in my former essay.

The allegorical dream which occurs among the *numbers* of eighteenth-century periodicals—frequently enough to remind us that periodical *essay* is generally a misnomer—suffers from a fatal lethargy: each figure stands for something, and continues so standing until we ache with it; shapes cannot dissolve and re-form, colours undergo change, as in *Pilgrim's Progress*. It follows that, once you have grasped the writer's intention, there is nothing whatever to whet expectation; the way leads straight to a foregone conclusion and, your destination being obvious, you are impatient to reach it. Only a stubborn sincerity distinguishes Johnson's *Rambler* allegories from the rest of their kind. Much more than this distinguishes *Rasselas* from them all. It has recovered the allegorical way of thinking. In conventional eighteenth-century allegories, the end is predictable not only because the morality is trite, but also because the seeing eye and the thinking mind are one: that is, they are assigned to the same person. The writer has not availed himself of allegory's peculiar privilege, fragmentation of personality. The end of *Rasselas* may be predictable, but the way to it is not: we have to reckon with subtle changes not only in the characters but also in their functions, and therefore in the relations between them. This cannot all be due to the influence of the stripling novel. There, characters may change (or seem to change), in accord with the apparent variability of human nature; but their functions in the story, which are the reasons for their being there, should not.

In the great dream allegories we are concerned with a dreamer, or someone seen in his dream; and the difference between these two

[1] Op. cit., p. xix.

is negligible, for what the one knows about the other comes to him rather by intuition than observation. This visionary can, however, tell us a part only of the import of his vision; but, standing at a point where paths diverge—Bunyan's field with the City of Destruction behind and the wicket gate in front—he is presently joined by another figure. This other may serve as guide and interpreter, or he may contribute that missing piece of significance whose recovery will make sense of the whole. Even he may not fully understand the meaning of what he contributes. It must be diligently sought among the persons of the story, now from one, now from another. Thus we are not to expect in *Rasselas* any of those personified qualities or abstractions which make Johnson's own *Vision of Theodore* explicit and a little dull. And it is unprofitable to set one against another, as though we were opposing truth and falsehood. The Prince has been harshly censured.[1] Imlac is indeed a fallible guide: his resorting to the valley shows that life has defeated him; his claims on his own behalf, under the guise of professional zeal, are sheer comedy; and at the end he is content to 'be driven along the stream of life'—a choice which Johnson could not approve. Nevertheless, he is given—he does not merely claim—the title of poet, which furnishes him, in that age, with intellectual credentials. He has wisdom and courage to impart, not only to his companions but also to the Astronomer. He is to be likened, not to Bunyan's Evangelist or Interpreter, but to his Hopeful, who fell into snares with Christian, but upheld him in the river.

Thus, it is not really strange that the Astronomer should, for all his aberrations, be credited not only with abstruse knowledge but also with wisdom. True, we have to take the author's word for the manifestation of this. But he has come late into the story—can the development of this episode have been an afterthought?—and must carry his share of its meaning shrunk to a token. *Rasselas* is not bound by the rule of equivalence which governs eighteenth-century allegory: 'This figure on the right stands for truth; that on the left, for error.' Its meaning pervades the whole. The danger of imagina-

---

[1] 'A silly young man eagerly swallowing a fatuous theory and an earnest young man turning away in fear from the very truth he is seeking', Alvin Whitley, op. cit., p. 54.

tion's power is implicit in the opening invocation. It is sharply explicit in the Astronomer's tale. But, as that and the travellers' story draw towards the dismissive close, we come to realize that without imagination there can be no insight.

The theme of *Rasselas*, which it develops according to the laws of its own literary being, is the function, not in art but in life, of the imagination.

JOHNSON'S LAST ALLUSION TO MARY QUEEN OF SCOTS

(1957)

JOHNSON's last allusion to Mary Queen of Scots confronts us with a problem: how to explain an odd blunder which it contains—an error as to a passage of Scottish history that he knew particularly well, and an episode in that passage not easy to forget.

Johnson's interest in the reign of Mary Stuart can be traced back at least as far as 1760, when he epitomized, sympathetically, William Tytler's vindication of the Queen and denunciation of the Casket Letters as forgery, for *The Gentleman's Magazine*.[1] It should, moreover, be acknowledged that he was (for a man captious about historical writing) well read in the Scottish historians. That fascinating, though often misleading, document, the sale catalogue of his library, testifies to his possession of a number of their works; some were given him after his visit, and some he borrowed while he was composing the *Journey to the Western Islands of Scotland*. Many passed through his hands, especially in his latter years.

Now, among those histories which relate the Queen's reign, and which could have been known to Johnson, all that give any circumstantial account of her flight to England agree on a point which must indeed have been common knowledge: that, after the final defeat at Langside, she sought refuge in the Abbey of Dundrennan and, resolving to enter England, took ship at Kirkcudbright and landed at Workington on the Cumberland coast. Moreover, the episode is memorable for its pathos: that image of the Queen, with a remnant of her followers, going on board a fishing-boat to cross the Solway Firth is not easily effaced from the imagination. Nevertheless, this is how Johnson alludes to the episode, in a letter of 8 July 1784:

[1] William Tytler, *An Inquiry, Historical and Critical, into the Evidence against Mary Queen of Scots*, Edinburgh 1760. Johnson's *Account of a Book, entitled (etc.): Works* (1825), vi. 80–9.

When Queen Mary took the resolution of sheltering herself in England, the Archbishop of St. Andrew's attempting to dissuade her, attended on her journey and when they came to the irremeable stream that separated the two kingdoms, walked by her side into the water, in the middle of which he seized her bridle, and with earnestness proportioned to her danger and his own affection, pressed her to return. The Queen went forward.[1]

He was writing to Mrs. Thrale, whom he believed married or irrevocably committed to marriage with Piozzi, in an attempt to persuade her to settle in her own country, not her husband's. He was pleading urgently, but with small hope of success; and, with characteristic unselfconsciousness, likened her to the forlorn Queen and himself to her last true counsellor. Evidently, his mind sought an image of desolation and of a desperate endeavour to avert greater evil. But why did memory change the fishing-boat making out into the Solway Firth for the rider fording a stream? If the general tenor of the passage left any room for doubt, we might ascertain what was in his mind's eye from his choice of epithet: 'irremeable'—which Dryden had used to translate Virgil's 'irremeabilis'[2]—applied to the river that allows of no return, and which he had quoted from Dryden, to illustrate his *Dictionary*.

The explanation of this vagary of memory and imagination seems to lie in a train of events more intricate than has been hitherto recognized, and the disclosure may throw light on Johnson's mind—and also on an obscure passage in the growth of historical fiction.

George Birkbeck Hill,[3] remarking the historical error in Johnson's allusion, turned to the notable Scottish historians—Robertson, Hume, Keith, Anderson—in whose work it could not of course be found, and presently discovered 'J.'s story, or one like it' (as Dr. Chapman observes) in *Adami Blacvodoei Opera* (1644), p. 589. Blackwood, however, knew the course of Mary's flight, and though, as Hill notes, he or his printer was badly at fault in the spelling of place-names, there is nothing in his narrative to account for Johnson's error.

---

[1] *Letters*, no. 972.   [2] *Aen.* vi. 425.
[3] *Letters of Samuel Johnson*, ed. George Birkbeck Hill, Oxford 1892, ii. 408–9.

What I believe to have occurred may be most conveniently set out thus:

(i) As the wife of the Dauphin, with Poitou for her dowry, Mary Stuart befriended the young Adam Blackwood, a student in Paris, of ancient Scottish family but small resources; she obtained for him an appointment with her Parliament of Poitiers.[1] He repaid her bounty with lifelong devotion, writing in her cause (besides a Latin reply to Buchanan's *De Jure Regni*) a vindication in French of her life and conduct: *Martyre de la Royne d'Escosse Douariere de France*. This, which was published in 1587, probably in Paris but with a spurious Edinburgh imprint, was to be several times reissued and reprinted, and appear again, at the end of Blackwood's Latin works, in Paris in 1644.[2] In the *Martyre* he tells, as Birkbeck Hill noticed, the story of an attempt by the Archbishop of St. Andrews (John Hamilton) to dissuade the Queen from seeking refuge in England. Three particulars are worth remarking: the Archbishop is represented as old, experienced, and venerable;[3] he makes a long speech, alleging examples of English treachery, and, argument failing, tries to stay her fatal course by gesture:

> Quoy voyant ce venerable Prelat, & qu'elle se precipitoit en peril tout evidẽt & certain, comme elle se mettoit sur l'eau pour descẽdre en ceste terre fatalle se mit à genoux, la saisit au corps avec les deux bras, & avec larmes luy dit qu'elle auroit la peine de le trainer si elle passoit plus outre.[4]

Nevertheless,

> La Royne partant de Dundreuen descẽdit a Vvirkinton, premiere ville des frõtieres d'Angleterre. . . .[5]

---

[1] See the prefatory note to the 1644 *Opera*, and George Mackenzie's *Lives and Characters of the Most Eminent Writers of the Scots Nation*, Edinburgh 1708, 1711, 1722; iii. 487–8. See also (warily) *D.N.B.*

[2] See John Scott, *Bibliography of Works relating to Mary Queen of Scots 1544–1700*, Edinburgh 1896, nos. 144, **174**, 175, 180, 237.

[3] Hill comments on the far from venerable character of John Hamilton. This may explain why Walter Scott chose to transfer his gesture of remonstrance to another figure, in *The Abbot*: the right man would have evoked the wrong response, in Scottish readers.

[4] *Martyre* (1587), p. 182.

[5] Ibid., p. 183. The spelling of place-names varies from one edition to another of the *Martyre*.

Clearly, Blackwood knew it to be a sea-passage, but there were sources of possible misunderstanding in his account of it: the places, thus disguised, would not be easily discoverable by a foreigner.

(ii) In his later years, the Jesuit Nicolas Caussin augmented a work of which he had published the first version in 1624: *La Cour Sainte*. The fifth part, added in 1645, consists of exemplary lives,[1] Mary Stuart's among them.[2] This is wholly unhistorical, and the sole point worth remarking is that, in the episode of the flight to England, whereas the story follows the outline of Blackwood's *Martyre*, the narrator would appear to be perplexed by the Queen's *taking ship*. He makes her embark originally with the intention of seeking refuge in France; hesitate, bend her thoughts towards England, resist the entreaties of the Archbishop, and eventually take the fatal decision.[3]

Thus a Frenchman, writing after 1645 and drawing on these two French versions of the story, might well set a query against the sea voyage.

(iii) In Paris in 1674 appeared a remarkable precursor of the historical novel as it was to develop more than a century later: *Marie Stuart Reyne d'Escosse, Nouvelle Historique*, by 'le Sieur de G.B.'; that is, Pierre le Pesant, Sieur de Boisguillebert.[4] A prefatory leaf, presumably the author's, explains the character and intention of the work:

Ce n'est point icy un Roman, c'est une Histoire tres-veritable; non-seulement dans le general, comme chacun sçait; mais encore dans toutes ses circonstances que beaucoup de gens ignorent, puisqu'elles sont également éloignées des deux idées de Martyre & de Courtisane, que le zele du Pere Caussin & les calomnies de Bucanan ont répandu jusques icy de cette Reyne dans le monde.

---

[1] *La Cour Sainte Tome V, selon l'ordre ancien, contenant les vies et éloges des personnes illustres qui ont esté ajoustées et inserées dans l'ordre nouveau de la dernière édition*, Paris 1645.

[2] This life appeared also independently, in Italian as well as French. See Scott, *Bibliography*, and Catalogue of the Bibliothèque Nationale.

[3] *La Cour Sainte*, Paris 1645, seconde partie, tome ii, p. 1089. See also *The Holy Court*, London 1678, i.e. the 4th edn. of the English translation, by Sir T[homas] H[awkins], p. 817.

[4] Scott, *Bibliography*, no. 265. See also Freebairn's Preface to his translation, epitomized below.

'Cette Histoire', we are assured, has been drawn from fifteen or sixteen authors, and indeed it presently becomes clear that the writer has looked into a number of histories and memoirs, and has been at pains to gather particulars.[1] Blackwood is among the sources, named and recognizable, and I suggest that it was a Frenchman's reading of his narrative, probably clouded by the doubt implicit in that of Caussin, which yielded this version of the flight to England:

> Ainsi tous les efforts de l'Archevesque de Saint André qui la vouloit détourner de ce dessein, furent inutils; il eust beau apres mille raisons alleguées en vain, se jetter jusques dans l'eau pour arrester son cheval par la bride, lors qu'elle passoit un ruisseau qui separe les deux Royaumes; il falust qu'elle se precipitât elle mesme dans sa ruine.[2]

The unaccountable embarkation appears to have been omitted. True, de Boisguillebert presently gives the place-names 'Dundrenen', 'Vvirkinton', 'Cokirmont', and 'Carlei',[3] as in Blackwood's narrative, but he betrays no disquiet at this discrepancy.

(iv) In 1725 two versions of this *nouvelle historique* were published in this country:

(*a*) *The Life of Mary Stewart, Queen of Scotland and France. Written Originally in French, and Now done into English. With Notes illustrating and confirming the most material Passages of this History, collected from Contemporary, and other Authors of the Greatest Character and Reputation.* This was launched by the translator and editor, James Freebairn, in Edinburgh, with a list of Scottish subscribers.

(*b*) *Mary Stuart, Queen of Scotts: being the Secret History of her Life, and the Real Causes of all Her Misfortunes. Containing a Relation of many particular Transactions in her Reign; never yet Published in any Collection. Translated from the French, By Mrs. Eliza Haywood.*

I am satisfied that (*b*) is not derived from (*a*),[4] and suppose it to be indeed translated, in a slovenly fashion, from the original French.

[1] For example, the circumstances of the Queen's arrival in Scotland; see below, note 4. I have used the second edition (1675).
[2] ii. 110.   [3] ii. 117.
[4] For example, Freebairn corrects the place-names, but Eliza Haywood retains the French spelling. Moreover, describing the night after her arrival in Scotland, de Boisguillebert says that the Queen was kept awake by 'tambours de Basque' (i. 30). Freebairn, omitting the unaccountable proper name, has merely 'Tabors' (p. 21). Haywood has 'Biscayan Drums' (p. 11).

Both translators reproduce their author's claim to be considered as a historian, but Freebairn alone performs his task in this spirit. In a Preface of his own he gives the name and some account of the French author;[1] discusses the reasons that may have prompted him to give an historical work the title of novel, and defends his veracity.[2] His text, moreover, is heavily documented with footnote quotations from Scots historians. He gives the Archbishop's speech at length—not direct from Blackwood, but from Mackenzie's life of the Queen, avowedly drawn from Blackwood's *Martyre*.[3] Another note, attached to the passage in which de Boisguillebert mentions Dundrennan, Workington, Cockermouth, and Carlisle, indicates the scope of his translator's own knowledge of the circumstances of the Queen's journey:

> The Queen landed at Workintone in Cumberland upon the 17th of May, 1568, having taken Boat at Kirkudbright . . . Crawfurd's *Memoirs* p. 81.[4]

With such sources of information available, Freebairn can hardly have overlooked (as Eliza Haywood most probably did) the discrepancy between the two passages in which the journey to England is mentioned; yet he allows it to pass without comment.

In de Boisguillebert, Freebairn, and Haywood, we have three authors, all of whose versions of this story were available when Johnson was a boy, and in any of which he might have found the crossing of the 'irremeable stream'. In default of further evidence, I should suppose Freebairn the likeliest. The English versions would be more accessible than the French;[5] and, of these two, Eliza Haywood's seems the less likely to have remained in any reader's mind among historical associations, for she reduces *nouvelle historique* to tawdry romance. Freebairn's solidity of documentation might well associate his work, remembered at some distance of time, with

---

[1] He is here called 'Pierre le Pesant Sieur du Bois, Guilbert', author of *Le Détail de la France*. See p. x.

[2] See pp. xi–xxxvi.

[3] Freebairn, p. 159. Mackenzie, op. cit. iii. 307–8. Mackenzie acknowledges his indebtedness in his life of Blackwood: ibid. iii. 511.

[4] p. 163.

[5] He may, of course, have met it among the French romances said to have been read by his wife in her sickness; but there is no end to surmise.

authentic history. That the discrepancy between history and fiction, present in all three, is made more patent in his by this very documentation need be no impediment: there can surely be no doubt of Johnson's *knowing* how Mary Stuart came to England.

The interest of this little train of events lies, however, not in the particular book that Johnson read; given but the certainty that there was such a book, it lies in his way of remembering it. Memory can be a sly servant: what has once taken possession of the imagination may still haunt it, notwithstanding the dictates of reason. Johnson, when he wrote this letter, was old, sick, and unhappy. Shaken by an event that had diminished the sources of his own happiness, and appeared to him to threaten that of the woman to whom his was largely due, he sought to express wretchedness and foreboding. Memory presented him with an image, none the less poignant for being (as he knew, at the rational level of consciousness) fictitious. Any pause—a mere fortuitous delay—might have given reason the opportunity to challenge the power of imagination over memory, and efface its tell-tale imprint in this letter. Remaining, it allows us to discern the impetuosity with which he wrote, and the measure of his unhappiness.

JOHNSON AND JUVENAL

(1959)

To throw light on Johnson's two great poems by means of a comparison with the two satires of Juvenal which they were designed to recall is no new endeavour. Indeed, in respect of one of them, this good office of criticism has been performed afresh, and notably, within the last few years.[1] Nevertheless, taking heart from a characteristic remark of Johnson's—'Men more frequently require to be reminded than informed'[2]—I propose to lay the English alongside the Latin where significant likenesses and differences appear to me worth reconsideration, and to draw such general inferences as I may.

Of the place occupied by *London* and *The Vanity of Human Wishes* in the pattern of Johnson's life, it can be argued that with their publication he opened and closed his poetical career, though not his life as poet. When he assailed the citadel of English letters with his 'imitation' of Juvenal's third satire, he was, in the current phrase, writing for bread and reputation—for such reputation at least as should ensure that more bread would be forthcoming; and this poem declared his intention. The assault was not unsuccessful: Pope is said to have spoken cordially of the new poet, and those who were in sympathy with its politics applauded the poem. When he published his 'imitation' of the tenth satire, however, he was about to put to the proof his cherished vocation as tragic poet. In Johnson's own eyes, the reception of *Irene* did not vindicate this claim. He had had the taste of failure in his mouth for most of his forty years, and found it unmistakable. He seems to have put away his project for another tragedy, and never thereafter challenged public notice as a serious poet. Many years later, Mrs. Thrale was to record an occasion on which he had shown her some verses. ' "But Sir," said I, "this is not ridiculous at all." "Why no (replied he), why should I always write ridiculously?" '[3] True, the context may

[1] Henry Gifford, '*The Vanity of Human Wishes*', R.E.S., Apr. 1955, 157–65.
[2] *Rambler* 2.   [3] Piozzi, *Anecdotes* (1786), p. 66.

have prompted her to expect burlesque; but it is a curious exchange between the author of *The Vanity of Human Wishes* and a familiar friend.

My undertaking requires that I should characterize, however briefly and tentatively, the satires which Johnson is imitating and the eighteenth-century practice of imitation.

Juvenal's satires appear to be the work of an embittered and frightened man; a brilliant rhetorician; no philosopher; disappointed in respect of worldly ambition, professing to despise worldly success, perhaps despising himself. He was born about A.D. 60, probably in the small Italian town of Aquinum. Schooled in rhetoric, he looked for a splendid career, but was frustrated. Incurring the hostility of Domitian, he was exiled to Egypt. He returned after Domitian's death, and, under Hadrian's more liberal rule, published satires; but most of the illustrations (that is, references to particular persons and events) are drawn from the reign of terror in which he had grown up, and some from even earlier history. Perhaps he was still afraid to speak; perhaps the bitterness of that past experience would not be denied expression. By one of those strange turns that literary and social history may take, something in these nihilistic satires recommended them to Christian moralists, while the sombre phosphorescence of their style attracted writers and speakers.

Whether we ascribe to France the initial impulse, or allow merely that French prestige lent momentum, the art of 'imitating' an ancient author, as English poets were to practise it in the eighteenth century, seems traceable to John Oldham. He formulates it in the prose apology prefixed to *Some New Pieces* in 1681: he fears lest he may be censured for his boldness in offering a version of Horace's *Art of Poetry* (the first and biggest piece) after those of Ben Jonson and Roscommon: but 'it was a Task impos'd upon me' and

> being prevail'd upon to make an Essay, I fell to thinking of some course, whereby I might serve myself of the Advantages, which those, that went before me, have either not minded, or scrupulously abridg'd themselves of. This I soon imagin'd was to be effected by putting *Horace* into a more modern dress, than hitherto he has appear'd in, that is, by making him speak, as if he were living, and writing now. I therefore resolv'd to alter the scene from *Rome* to

London, and to make use of *English* names of Men, Places, and Customs, where the Parallel would decently permit, which, I conceiv'd, would give a kind of new Air to the Poem, and render it more agreeable to the Relish of the present Age.[1]

There is a difference between this and what Rochester had tried out some three years ago; small, but sufficient to justify a claim on Oldham's behalf to originality. Rochester, in his *Allusion to the Tenth Satire of the First Book of Horace*, had taken a piece of coterie-writing, framed his opening to recall that of Horace, but thereafter followed an independent course, playing the game with English poets and pretenders, careless as to their correspondence with Horace's Romans. Oldham, on the other hand, kept as many of the original 'men, places, and customs' as he altered, and, even in his alterations, aimed at finding recognizable equivalents. His experiment, therefore, may be said to have given rise to that train of 'imitations', 'allusions', and 'paraphrases'[2] which leads eventually to *The Vanity of Human Wishes*.

Thus in Oldham's work we may fairly look for the inherent possibilities and limitations of this way of writing as these presented themselves to his English successors. It requires of the reader just so much familiarity with the original poem as will make him quick to recall, when adroitly prompted, some memorable passage; of the writer, a knack of analogy: the art, or trick, of awaking such recollections. Oldham scores by his boyish ingenuity and sense of fun—as when he makes Juvenal's *Sapientia* into 'sound Divinity, and Sense', or substitutes this for the noise of ancient Rome:

> The restless Bells such Din in Steeples keep,
> That scarce the Dead can in their Church-yards sleep.[3]

To the writer who can avail himself fully of this interplay of likeness and difference, the imitation offers political opportunities, and risks.

---

[1] *Some New Pieces*, 'by the Author of the *Satyrs upon the Jesuites*'. *Advertisement*. Professor Harold Brooks has shown that primacy cannot be claimed for Oldham. See 'The *Imitation* in English Poetry, especially in Formal Satire, before the Age of Pope', R.E.S., Apr. 1949. I suggest, however, that Oldham set the pattern which was to prevail.

[2] The terms seem to be used indifferently, but it will be convenient to keep to the one which has grown familiar: imitation.

[3] Oldham, *Poems and Translations* (1683), p. 42 (Juvenal's thirteenth satire, l. 189); and op. cit., p. 200 (Juvenal's third satire, ll. 232 f.).

It allows him to direct attention towards the analogy between ancient and modern tyranny, or corruption; even, between dead and living perpetrators of such abuses; and to claim, with whatever inward trepidation, that his adversary will rather keep silence than admit, by reacting to insinuation, that the cap of Nero or Sejanus fits.

Johnson's choice of the third satire of Juvenal as a declaration of his poetic aspiration appears at first sight strange, for it had already been imitated by Oldham and translated (with an occasional preference of witty equivalence over exact correspondence) by Dryden, and he knew both versions well; but the tale of editions called for, contrasted with that of the *Vanity*, shows *London* to have been congenial to the time: it vented popular indignation with the Whig policy towards Spain. Even in his first choice, moreover, we may catch sight of Johnson's preference for taking the well-trodden way and walking in it with independent gait. The satire did not speak any the less forcibly to him because it had been long esteemed; and, sharing this esteem, he found encouragement to say something in his turn; for Dryden himself had, as he thought, caught the wit but missed the dignity of the original. 'The peculiarity of Juvenal', he was later to declare, 'is a mixture of gaiety and stateliness, of pointed sentences and declamatory grandeur'. One of these qualities was still to be recaptured. 'It is therefore perhaps possible to give a better representation of that great satirist, even in those parts which Dryden himself has translated, some passages excepted, which will never be excelled.'[1]

This, then, was Johnson's position: in imitating an ancient author, he was prepared to avail himself of the liberty which had already established itself among the conventions belonging to this literary newcomer; even to extend it. Thus he would tread freely in the footsteps of former imitators, deserting the course of the beaten track whenever his sense of the *intention* of their original required this of him. But how was this intention to be determined? Satire draws him to interpret by means of imitation; and to interpretation satire opposes certain difficulties, which the passage of time increases. It weathers queerly. I am not thinking of topical

[1] Life of Dryden, *Lives*, i. 447.

allusions; hard work and historical sense may come to terms with those. I mean irony. And what, in the last analysis, is irony, but a tone of voice? It is for this *intonation* that the imitator must listen; and who will claim that he has caught the tones of a dead man's voice—dead for seventeen centuries? If we could but hear the *tone* of Juvenal's references, say, to the satisfaction of simple living, in the third satire, or the proper worship of the gods, in the tenth, all other difficulties would surely yield; particular allusions could be cleared up, or would cease to matter. It may have been something of this sort that Dryden had in mind when he recalled Barten Holyday's opinion that, while it was difficult to find 'any' sense in Persius, with Juvenal the problem was to find 'the best sense'.[1]

If we try to characterize the kind of ironist with whom (I suppose) we have here to deal, we shall observe that, where he essays a self-portrait, he will represent himself as setting out gallantly, protected only by fool's motley, armed only with his dagger of lath, to assail the entrenched forces of society. To this it may fairly be retorted that disguise will hardly ensure protection if he gives such offence to powerful adversaries that they think it worth their while to silence him. Ambiguity is a far less effectual safeguard than luck or skill in timing: much can be risked when those in power cannot afford to notice his insinuations; nothing, when they cannot afford to ignore them. Thus we may suspect that some at least of the ambiguities which such an ironist attributes to the danger, and gallantry, of his undertaking are really shadows thrown by a conflict in his own mind. He both longs and fears to be understood, not merely by the little world of his friends—for their assent is given, not extorted at the point of his satire—but by the great world of hostile or indifferent readers. He longs to be understood, because otherwise he must confess himself ineffectual; he fears it, because understanding between the writer and the common reader proclaims an affinity which his satiric vision of mankind makes abhorrent to him. (He is indeed distinguishable from the generality of them in that he is by temperament more vulnerable than they; that is why his shafts go home only when he takes aim at fellow satirists.)

---

[1] 'Original and Progress of Satire,' *Essays of John Dryden*, ed. W. P. Ker (1900), ii. 96.

This, then, is our deepest difficulty with the ironist: a man who does not wish to be taken at his word may not really have made up his mind how he wishes to be taken.

Juvenal's third satire assumes the form of a dialogue between friends—if that can be called a dialogue in which one does all the talking and the other nearly all the thinking. Umbritius, playing the part of Juvenal's well-wisher, takes leave of him with the advice: 'Do as I am doing. Cut loose from Rome, and live by yourself in the country.' But we are sensible of an unspoken commentary. This counsel to seek happiness elsewhere is not offered all at once. Juvenal is too able a rhetorician for that; he knows how to weave to and fro, obtaining a cumulative effect. Besides, he cannot afford to be very explicit about advice that he has no intention of taking himself. His real theme is not country pleasures but the mingled attraction and repulsion exercised by the great cosmopolitan city, and Umbritius' leave-taking is merely an occasion for a denunciation of all that displeases him in Roman life. The two men are represented as going together to the point of departure from Rome, the gate on the Appian Way. There, Umbritius urges his friend to follow his example; but in much of what he says ironic overtones can be heard: in his allusions, for example, to the insignificant, depopulated village where he means to settle, or the even more desolate regions which Juvenal ought to prefer to Rome's tawdry splendour. These wry hints are surely but the echo of Juvenal's own thoughts: of his inmost certainty that, if life in Rome is disagreeable, dangerous, degrading, outside Rome there is nothing to be called life at all. A particular illustration of this pervasive tone may be discerned in the representation of the great gate as a scene of mere squalour: even an allusion to its legendary associations seems to point at the foreign squatters now encamped round it; for it was once the haunt of the Camenae—native spirits ousted, in the process of Hellenizing Rome, by the Muses; and the Camenae themselves are mentioned in a tone of strident flippancy. Like Housman, Juvenal will call up some half-belief which has charmed or comforted men, only to bring it down with a piece of well aimed ribald familiarity.

It is worth while to compare what Oldham and Johnson, and occasionally Dryden, make of this invitation to a country retreat.

Catching part of Juvenal's intention, Oldham sets the scene for his Timon's departure at Mile End, and exploits the opportunity for grotesque description; but Johnson chooses Greenwich, and makes his Thales gaze reverently at Queen Elizabeth's birthplace. True, any Elizabethan reference is an occasion for girding at the supposed policy of appeasing Spain; this, however, is but one of a number of passages in which Johnson summons up the shade of past greatness, in a tone which carries none of the vibrations of irony. When we reach the description of that retreat which Umbritius (Timon, Thales) proposes for himself and his friend, a sharper difference appears. Juvenal names little hill towns (romantic, perhaps, to us, but for him uncouth, cold, and dull); towns in which, for the price of a Roman garret, you can have the best house there is, with a little patch of kitchen-garden—a *very* little patch: there will be room enough merely to raise the vegetables on which you will have to subsist, with a lizard for livestock. Dryden gives the sardonic climax of the passage in a brisk couplet:

> 'Tis somewhat to be lord of some small ground,
> In which a lizard may, at least, turn round.   (ll. 374–5)

Oldham, with the freedom of an imitator and the rough playfulness of English satiric tradition, expands quip into conceit:

> Had I the smallest Spot of Ground, which scarce
> Would Summer half a dozen Grashoppers,
> Not larger than my Grave, tho hence remote,
> Far as *S. Michaels Mount*, I would go to't,
> Dwell there content, and thank the Fates to boot. (p. 199)

But Johnson turns *hortulus* into a country estate, and Juvenal's sour acceptance of a countryman's life into a little pastoral. His invitation begins bravely:

> Could'st thou resign the park and play content,
> For the fair banks of Severn or of Trent;
> There might'st thou find some elegant retreat,
> Some hireling senator's deserted seat;
> And stretch thy prospects o'er the smiling land,
> For less than rent the dungeons of the Strand. (ll. 210–15)

The climax bears out this promise:

> There ev'ry bush with nature's musick rings,
> There ev'ry breeze bears health upon its wings;
> On all thy hours security shall smile,
> And bless thine evening walk and morning toil.   (ll. 220-3)

Here indeed is *stateliness*. Professor Nichol Smith commented that this is a piece of idealization, which can never have expressed Johnson's real feelings about the country, associated as that was with the 'disappointment and failure' of his early years; what he had always believed in his heart about pastoral bliss was to find utterance in his dry enumeration of the rural delights Savage expected in Wales. It is with great hesitation that I differ, and urge the significance of that allusion to Trent and Severn. Johnson was always fascinated by water: it was the thing he noticed in landscape—alike with eye and ear; it gave him imagery, when he wanted to convey a sense of deep contentment. Lichfield, moreover, was, and is, a little country town built round a confluence of springs and streams feeding the Trent. He had spent the best part of thirty years there; they had not been happy years, but the beginning of his struggle to establish himself in London may well have been worse. The poem as a whole suggests that he was suffering from revulsion against his new surroundings.

In such a mood, he might perhaps miss the irony in Juvenal's tale of country pleasures, yet find the denunciation of Rome (to which they had been a merely conventional foil) heartily congenial. Rome, Juvenal says, is not fit for a decent man to live in. Poverty hurts a man nowhere so much as in Rome; and only the man who is without decency or scruple can be anything but poor there. Prosperity in Rome comes to the blackmailer, the rich man's slave, the immigrant, never to the freeborn Roman—thus he aligns humanity. Besides, to dwell in Rome is to suffer countless evils, whether of mischance—stench, fire, traffic; or of malice—at the hands of the cut-throat, the bravo, and the sot. And all these press most heavily on the poor man. (He means the man like himself, of limited means and disappointed ambitions.) These complaints are not set out in logical progression; the argument would hardly bear it. They are so ordered that, except in one passage (the diatribe against foreigners, where personal bitterness prevails), attention is kept always in motion.

Congenial though the general import of his original may be, the imitator of an ancient satire must here and there find its particulars intractable. Difference of time and place may lend enchantment to other literary forms, but a considerable part of satirical complaint has to do with the immediate: with the sting of to-day's vexation, or the sourness of yesterday's hope; with foul weather here and now. Thus, while there will be, in any great satire, passages which time cannot tarnish—passages that only await recharging with personal experience and the passionate affirmation 'I know—I have been there myself'—there must necessarily be others from which the force, the very meaning, has ebbed. Success in imitation will therefore be the reward of insight and boldness: the good imitator will keep no lumber—what he cannot either take as it stands or transform by a turn of his wit he will throw out. Some of Juvenal's grievances are peculiar to his world: those, for example, that relate to slavery and its ramified consequences. Here Johnson's firmness appears. Whereas Oldham had encumbered himself with all the references (direct or oblique) to the particulars of Roman life in his original, *he* cuts out those which refuse to be translated into English terms. He reduces Juvenal's 322 lines to 263; but those figures fail to show how much he eliminates; for, where he chooses to keep a passage, he will sometimes expand, contracting others to make room. He has two principal ways of reducing his original: by silent omission of what is inapplicable, and what is gross; and by drawing a number of details to a head under a succinct generalization—notably in a single couplet:

> Fate never wounds more deep the gen'rous heart
> Than when a blockhead's insult points the dart. (ll. 168–9)

There are indeed parts of Juvenal's imprecation which go home, anywhere, in any age: his evocation of the impenetrable indifference on the face of a big city, or the slights which must be endured by a man conscious of his own powers and promise amidst a society quite unaware that it needs, or he brings, anything of consequence.

Johnson knew all about this. On a plinth of personal experience, he set the monumental line

>   SLOW RISES WORTH, BY POVERTY DEPRESS'D.   (l. 177)

Compared with this, even Dryden's climax is weak:

>   Rarely they rise by virtue's aid, who lie
>   Plung'd in the depth of helpless poverty—   (ll. 275-6)

and Oldham's, amateurish:

>   'Tis hard for any Man to rise, that feels
>   His Virtue clog'd with Poverty at Heels.   (p. 194)

Between those passages which have become ineffectual, however, and those which need little more than vigorous translation, lie others which can be thrust home only by a skilful shift of aim: for example, Juvenal's gibes at the people with whom he, a Roman born, had to rub shoulders in an imperial city which was drawing provincials and foreigners, like wasps to a good plum crop. Here, Johnson's course is less clear, his sense of direction less sure. True, London was attracting men from other countries. The magnet, however, was not luxury but liberty: the freedom of the press sought by thinkers and writers. Then again, some of Juvenal's taunts might suit Johnson's London, but not Johnson. He *was* a provincial, his shabby clothes no more conspicuous than his Staffordshire speech. He obliterated the provincial; and Oldham showed him a way of dealing with Juvenal's abuse of foreigners— which was a pity; but it must in fairness be said that, when he converted the 'hungry Greekling' into a Frenchman, the result was caricature rather than calumny: Juvenal's graver charges had been left out.

Johnson's *London* has not the brilliance of its original, because it lacks the lightning flash of its irony. It has not the sparkle of Oldham's best passages, for want of his high spirits. But it says what Johnson believed Juvenal to mean, and says it with unflinching consistency.

Juvenal's tenth satire is built on quite another plan than his third, and Johnson's treatment tends to widen the division. The poet proposes to show the range of human futility and wrong-headedness as it must appear to the spirit of a philosopher, unconfined by bounds of space or time: the whole habitable world, past as well as present. His chosen symbol, repeated with variations throughout the poem, is the image of a man who would seem to have obtained what he asks of the gods—and is by so much the more wretched. This affords opportunity for two sorts of satiric picture: crowd scenes and portraits, not necessarily distinct; some of the portraits are, like the face of Chaucer's condemned man, distinguishable only by a significant trait from other faces in the crowd. These portraits may be historical (Sejanus, Hannibal, Xerxes), or typical (the old man who has outlived all that makes life worth living, the children whose ambitious parents obtain for them an unhappy eminence); and there are some betwixt and between: the would-be orator who is such a dunce that he misses the fame and escapes the fate of Cicero and Demosthenes.

Accepting this framework, Johnson handles what it contains even more independently than he had that of the third satire. His poem is, almost to a line, the same length as Juvenal's, but the proportions, and therefore the emphasis, are different. He leaves out what displeases him, and develops what he retains, as hitherto; and he avails himself of the full liberty traditional in imitation with regard to the illustrations: he substitutes Wolsey for Sejanus, Charles XII of Sweden for Hannibal, and the scholar's fate for that of the orator. Even where he keeps the man, or the type, he changes the tone; and he proceeds to a conclusion far removed from Juvenal's.

The most notable of the illustrations must suffice for comparison, and those that are least altered will best serve to open it. Johnson allows the figure of Xerxes to stand, as emblem of imperial vainglory. Juvenal has surely been betrayed here by his hatred of Greeks, or his profession of ironist, or both. He cannot mention the power and splendour of the Persian host without qualifying the impression of magnitude, even as it emerges, by hinting that Herodotus is a liar: the Greeks boasted that they had brought down a mighty tyrant—but, who knows? Thus he gives only the collapse of a half-mythical giant, the subject of tall stories—anticlimax proper to satire; Johnson, with tragic rather than satiric insight, the fall of a prince, powerful indeed, but himself the victim of tall talk, the talk of flatterers:

> Attendant Flatt'ry counts his myriads o'er,
> Till counted myriads sooth his pride no more.   (ll. 229–30)

Charles XII, taking Hannibal's place, runs true alike to the central purpose of both poems and to Johnson's lifelong conviction that war must be assessed in terms of its cost in human misery—together with the hope that it may be abolished by satirizing military ambition.[1] Yet, though they have so much in common, Johnson draws away from Juvenal even here. The Hannibal of the tenth satire is a bogey to frighten children: his campaigns are enumerated with a suggestion of grotesque bustle; each forced march brings him nearer his unpitied end. In exile, a 'mighty suppliant'—the epithet is loaded with irony—he must suffer at the whim of a petty oriental tyrant and at last become the theme of schoolboys learning the rudiments of rhetoric. 'Swedish Charles' had seized Johnson's imagination; he had written, and intended to write further, upon him. The passage given to him in the *Vanity* shows that no garish theatrical colours would have relieved the end of Johnson's tragedy:

> His fall was destin'd to a barren strand,
> A petty fortress, and a dubious hand;
> He left the name, at which the world grew pale,
> To point a moral, or adorn a tale.   (ll. 219–22)

The mood is not only sombre but stern. Nevertheless I hear no echo of the triumphant spite discernible in Juvenal's conclusion:

> i demens et saevas curre per Alpes,
> ut pueris placeas et declamatio fias!   (ll. 166–7)

If this is a true distinction, we may fairly ask: had Johnson taken to heart Armado's reproof to the sportive gallants—Hector 'the sweet war-man is dead and rotten; sweet chucks, beat not the bones of the buried; when he breathed, he was a man'?

With the third of these historical transformations, we enter a country of the imagination where such Shakespearian analogies are clearly permissible: here is not simply Sejanus into Wolsey, but, as attentive readers have long observed, Sejanus into Shakespeare's

---

[1] He would find warrant for this in the writings of Prior and Swift.

Wolsey. The two passages invite particular comparison. Juvenal's approach to the fall of Sejanus is tactically unsurpassable. He makes eavesdroppers of us: we listen sometimes to the nobles, sometimes to the populace, sometimes to the poet himself; we overhear fragments of whispered or muttered talk, scraps of eye-witness reports —rumours, hints, allusions, in the voices of those concerned in the final crash. This it is (the voices suggest) to be an emperor's favourite; yet who would have the resolution to refuse, or strength to abide the consequences of refusal? By comparison, Johnson's tale of Wolsey's fall is unimpressive: it proceeds as simple narration, in the single voice of the poet, and the tone of that voice is grave, compassionate, devoid of irony. The climax is reached in a question which carries no sultry reverberations:

> Speak thou, whose thoughts at humble peace repine,
> Shall Wolsey's wealth, with Wolsey's end be thine?
> Or liv'st thou now, with safer pride content,
> The wisest justice on the banks of Trent? (ll. 121-4)

I have given the last line as Johnson originally wrote it and restored it in 1755.[1] In finally preferring 'wisest justice' to the 'richest landlord' of the 1749 text, he was ostensibly bringing back the terms of the question to Juvenal's 'Would you rather be the man who was dragged just now through the streets, or a petty official in a provincial town, charged only with paltry decisions?' But it is the tone rather than the form of the question that sets the key for the expected answer, and in tone the version which represents Johnson's final preference is very far from Juvenal's mood.

The most significant of these comparisons is that between illustrations which carry personal overtones, for both poets. Juvenal gets his knife into the orator early in his poem; he turns it round in lines 114 to 132. The quip of which the first passage consists is caught by Dryden in a flippant triplet:

> With laurels some have fatally been crown'd;
> Some, who the depths of eloquence have found,
> In that unnavigable stream were drown'd. (ll. 11-13)

---

[1] The MS., now in the Hyde collection, shows that he had already altered the original 'wisest justice' to 'wealthiest landlord' before reaching the 'richest landlord' of the 1749 text. See *Poems*, ed. McAdam and Milne, in *The Yale Edition of the Works of Samuel Johnson*, 1964.

Johnson changes it into another key by the single word he chooses for the orator's fate—*impeachment*—a word of grave connotation through more than a century of English history. It is by his variation on Juvenal's second and fuller passage, however, that we may measure the difference between the orator of the one and the scholar of the other. Eloquence was the goal of Roman education; yet who, Juvenal asks, would not rather fail abjectly as a speaker than excel as Cicero and Demosthenes excelled, and end as they ended? Johnson's argument bears away in another direction. The scholar whom he substitutes for Juvenal's orator cherishes hopes which are not represented as ignoble, nor even unreasonable; yet the foregone conclusion is disappointment. Two possible courses are traced for him: first, the plain, hard way of ill success. Here Johnson draws as near as ever he will come (in English) to speaking of himself. Slowly, ineffaceably, the image forms before our mind's eye: a man conscious of intellectual power, ambitious of excellence, who—even if he is not thwarted of his aim by sloth, sickness, melancholy—will share the 'doom of man' and also know his own peculiar unfulfilment:

> Deign on the passing world to turn thine eyes,
> And pause awhile from letters, to be wise.   (ll. 157-8)

From this sombre self-portrait, and self-admonition, he reverts to Juvenal's theme of the consequences of success, but still with a difference. His subject is now the scholar who wins recognition, and even high office, only to fall, like Laud. Some objections have been raised to Johnson's choice of illustrious victim. It cannot indeed be quite dissociated from his royalist and Anglican sympathies, and his Oxford piety. But the force of this passage consists in the use rather than the choice of illustration: the meaning is to be inferred from the conclusion, and is not constricted by such sympathies or antipathies as Laud may excite. Why, asks Juvenal sardonically, had not Cicero and Demosthenes sense enough to remain obscure, and safe? This, however, is the turn given to his apostrophe in *The Vanity of Human Wishes*:

> Mark'd out by dangerous parts he meets the shock,
> And fatal Learning leads him to the block:

Around his tomb let Art and Genius weep,
But hear his death, ye blockheads, hear and sleep. (ll. 170-4)

It is not the fallen man who must meet the final challenge, as Johnson frames it.

This brief notice of divergent trends in some of the illustrations may serve to indicate a sort of *undertow*; but, if we are to understand the force of that big tide which is swinging Johnson's poem away to another conclusion than Juvenal's, we must now take Dryden for pilot. Johnson so valued his critical opinions that they became part of his own thought. (In *The Lives of the Poets* they are sometimes delivered as axioms.) He would, I surmise, have been prepared to maintain that Dryden was more faithful to Juvenal as critic than translator, and Dryden had said: 'Juvenal excels in the tragical satire, as Horace does in the comical'.[1] This epithet 'tragical' must presumably relate not to literary form but to the presence of some element in a work of literature; such an element as we may recognize intuitively, afterwards bringing critical analysis to the task of verifying intuition. Lacking space for such analysis, I venture to offer a rough and ready test by which we may decide whether or no this tragic element is present in a particular composition. The people of tragedy are playing for high stakes; and it is real money. (Contrariwise, in comedy the winners hand over their gains, and the losers are released from their forfeits, even as the end breaks that spell which held us together in imagination's magic circle.) Now, if we set side by side Juvenal's and Johnson's monumental effigies of the fools of hope and vainglory, we shall observe that, while both mark the end of the man who asks too much of life, Juvenal implies that to ask at all is folly, because life has nothing to give. He will not allow his victims even the credit of playing a poor hand with style, for they stand to lose nothing but worthless counters. But Johnson's response to the man who plays high and loses all is the Shakespearian—that is, the tragic—response. Shakespeare will often communicate to us the meaning of some event, in the tragedies, by an observation put into the mouth of a secondary character who understands what is happening to the principals. Thus Charmian,

---

[1] 'Original and Progress of Satire', ii. 96.

when she has inherited from the dead Enobarbus this office of interpretation, intimates the significance of the final defeat at sea:

> The soul and body rive not more in parting
> Than greatness going off.

This sense of a greatness whose authenticity is manifest in the very agony of *going off* underlies Johnson's treatment of downfall and defeat. We may discern it even in the terrible picture of old age, which he shortens and, at the last, tempers by changing Juvenal's repulsive dotard among a crowd of parasites into a solitary figure, not without dignity:

> Superfluous lags the vet'ran on the stage.   (l. 308)

All this must be borne in mind, that we may understand the explicitly Christian conclusion which Johnson imposes on his original. Can this be, as critics have alleged, a merely conventional *coda*? Juvenal has introduced his sole positive recommendation, the Stoic ideal of self-sufficiency, with a gesture of mock reverence towards the gods. They discern better than the suppliant what is good for him. (This is not to claim much for their sagacity.) When a man prays for wife or child, they alone know what he is getting. And (he continues), if you must force yourself on their notice with sacrifices, why, offer those delicious little sausages made from a white piglet, and ask only for a sound mind in a healthy body—no more than you can give yourself. Dryden's distrust of priestcraft leads him to overplay his hand a little here:

> Yet, not to rob the priests of pious gain,
> That altars be not wholly built in vain;
> Forgive the gods the rest, and stand confin'd
> To health of body, and content of mind.   (ll. 546–9)

He did not find all that in Juvenal; but he has come very close to Juvenal's superstitious man, with his cunning insurance policy of small offerings—a worshipper whose ingratiating air would discredit any divinity.

Johnson approaches the final question—'What may we then implore?'—without ironic overtones, as might have been expected;

but, beyond expectation, he proceeds to amplify the answer. We are indeed to ask for

> a healthful mind,
> Obedient passions, and a will resign'd— (ll. 359–60)

but, transcending all that this implies of philosophical equanimity, we are to pray

> For love, which scarce collective man can fill;
> For patience sov'reign o'er transmuted ill;
> For faith, that panting for a happier seat,
> Counts death kind Nature's signal of retreat . . . (ll. 361–4)

Not only is this in accord with a vein of thinking that runs through all Johnson's works (clearest in *Rasselas*); it is consistent with the course of his argument in this poem.

For Juvenal, it is a bitter jest that man, being finite, must for ever project his desires into infinitude. His eye rests always on the end; and for him *Respice finem* signifies: Look whether the end does not cancel all. But for Johnson this projection of our dream of fulfilment beyond the horizon is the proof of our immortality.

It appears that we may have to reckon with more sorts of irony than one. Whereas the ironist points the difference between what we are and what we would be thought, life admits of more various and subtle divergences than his art takes cognizance of. Thus, what becomes of us is separated from what we would attain, not only by the distance between our pretensions and our powers, but also by that between fair expectation and the unforeseeable event. An onlooker endowed with sensibility will recognize these ironies inherent in our condition. If he is a writer, he may seek to express them. Two such were among Johnson's favourite authors. It is a countenance not unlike his that Robert Burton sometimes turns upon the field of error. Sir Thomas Browne invokes illustrious victims in the very tones of the *Vanity*: 'Though the funeral pyre of Patroclus took up an hundred foot, a piece of an old boat burnt Pompey.'[1] This is not satiric irony, generated by a quarrel with

---

[1] *Urn Burial*, iii.

life; it is tragic irony, learnt in the contemplation of life. The awe and pity with which Johnson contemplates the spectacle of human unfulfilment makes of *The Vanity of Human Wishes* a great tragic poem. It is surely by an irony of circumstance that it was published in the year which saw the eclipse of his hopes as a tragic poet.

JOHNSON AND BOSWELL ON THEIR TRAVELS

(1965)

JOHNSON had been curious to visit the Hebrides—so he told Boswell in 1763, the first year of their friendship—ever since 'his father put Martin's Account into his hands when he was very young, and ... he was much pleased with it'.[1] Boswell, for his part, had been at pains to keep alight the embers of this curiosity—not unsuccessfully, as various references show. Writing to him in 1771, Johnson quotes Horace on the innocent man's safety even in perilous enterprises— '... whether we climb the Highlands, or are tost among the Hebrides ... I hope the time will come when we may try our powers both with cliffs and water'—and assures Boswell of his constancy.[2] In 1772 he reafirms his purpose: 'I ... have not given up the western voyage.'[3] If a precipitant were needed, there was the activity of Thomas Pennant. He had traversed a considerable part of the mainland of Scotland in 1769 and published his account of it in 1771. On his second journey, in 1772, he bore to the north-west and visited the Inner Hebrides. His report of this region did not appear until 1774, but Johnson may have known that it was expected, for Pennant was acquainted with the Thrales.[4] Such a conjunction of forces may account for the studied imprecision of Johnson's opening sentence:

I had desired to visit the *Hebrides*, or Western Islands of Scotland, so long, that I scarcely remember how the wish was originally excited; and was in the Autumn of the year 1773 induced to undertake the journey, by finding in Mr. Boswell a companion, whose acuteness would help my inquiry, and whose gaiety of conversation and civility of manners are sufficient to counteract the inconveniences of travel, in countries less hospitable than we have passed.[5]

---

[1] *Life*, v. 13. [2] *Letters*, no. 250. [3] Ibid., no. 274.
[4] See L. F. Powell, 'The tours of Thomas Pennant', *Library*, 4th Ser. xix (Sept. 1938), 131–54. [5] *Journey*, pp. 1, 2.

Thus, in a single stately gesture, he refers to the consummation of a purpose negligently cherished by himself for over half a century and diligently fostered by Boswell for some ten years, whilst acknowledging his obligation to all his hosts, among whom he rightly gives Boswell pride of place.

There can be no question as to Boswell's position. But for him, events would have taken another course: Johnson, if he had ever set out (which is unlikely), would have fared altogether differently; Boswell was in some sense his host not only in Edinburgh but also throughout the length of their hundred days together. The force of this relationship, as it was felt on both sides, may be measured by two incidents: the passionate and (as it seemed to Boswell) unaccountable vehemence with which Johnson accused his companion of 'leaving him on the road' at the approach to Glenelg,[1] and his own reaction, likewise intemperate, to the meagre hospitality of Sir Alexander Macdonald, who then awaited them in 'a small house on the shore [of Skye], as we believe, that he might with less reproach entertain us meanly'.[2] Johnson, though he wrote freely to Mrs. Thrale of the Macdonald household, said nothing of it in his book—but the silence can be felt. Boswell, less ceremonious and far less discreet, betrayed his own disappointment and recorded the boyish jokes in which both travellers indulged whenever Sir Alexander's name recurred in talk between them. His first published account cost him much vexation,[3] but he could not desist from offering further provocation: his repeated allusions in both *Tour* and *Life* are a measure of his disappointment and chagrin. From their first host in the Isles, a man with whom they were both acquainted and with whose wife he himself claimed kinship, he had expected more than common cordiality,[4] and he reacted to the want of it as though he had been put to shame in his own house.

Boswell was, moreover, interpreter as well as host. Johnson's deafness made the Lowland Scottish voice troublesome to him, and his companion would interrogate for him those who awakened his curiosity: the old woman (for example) living in the crypt of the ruined priory at St. Andrews and claiming royal alliance. It is a

---

[1] *Life*, v. 145–6. [2] *Letters*, no. 326.
[3] *Life*, v. 578. [4] Ibid. ii. 157; iii. 540; v. 149.

proof of Boswell's readiness and care and of the good understanding between the friends that such talk as the *Journey* preserves, in Johnson's favourite medium of *oratio obliqua*, always rings true. His ear was likewise at fault with names, and these are amongst the most useful corrections offered by Boswell, who was besides a gatherer of information.

There was in the *Journey* one error big enough to occasion some trouble. Boswell did not offer to correct this, perhaps because it had been initially his own. The Macleods derived from the Outer Hebrides; but those whom he and Johnson met were the Lairds of Raasay and of Dunvegan in Skye, with their respective kindred. While staying on Raasay, Boswell walked and talked alone with his host, John Macleod, and recorded in his *Journal*: 'He does not contest the chieftainship with the Laird of Macleod'[1]—that is, with Norman MacLeod of Dunvegan. Passages in the journal-letter for that week which Johnson presently wrote to Mrs. Thrale show that Boswell had passed on to him this item of misinformation—for such it turned out to be: 'The Laird of Raasa has sometimes disputed the chieftainry of the Clan with Macleod of Skie, but being much inferior in extent of possessions, has I suppose, been forced to desist.'[2] Consequently a passage on Macleod of Raasay, in the *Journey*, concludes with this sentence: 'He acknowledges *Macleod* of Dunvegan as his chief, though his ancestors have formerly disputed the pre-eminence.'[3] With the arrival of a copy of his book on Raasay the storm gathered. John Macleod remonstrated, courteously but firmly. He admits no such subjection: 'I acknowledge, the benefit of being chief of a clan is in our days of very little significancy'; it is 'but an ideal point of honour'—yet one 'not hitherto . . . disregarded in our country', and he is concerned about the effect of this 'misinformation' on friends and 'rival clans'.[4] This protest was addressed to Boswell who, assiduous as an intermediary, seems to have kept silence as to his own share in the misunderstanding.

---

[1] *Boswell's Journal of a Tour to the Hebrides with Samuel Johnson 1773*, ed. F. A. Pottle and C. H. Bennett, New York 1936, revised 1962, p. 135. I quote always from the revised edition, and distinguish this *Journal* on the one hand from the published *Journal of a Tour* . . . (henceforth called the *Tour*), and on the other from the rest of Boswell's journals, published in the *Private Papers*.

[2] *Letters*, no. 327.   [3] *Journey*, p. 133.   [4] *Life*, v. 410.

Johnson accepted responsibility and apologized for his error. In a conciliatory letter to John Macleod, which passed through Boswell's hands, he said that he had not meant to suggest anything beyond the 'superiority'[1] of the house of Dunvegan.

> Even this I now find to be erroneous, and will therefore omit or retract it in the next edition.
>
> Though what I said had been true, if it had been disagreeable to you, I should have wished it unsaid; for it is not my business to adjust precedence. As it is mistaken, I find myself disposed to correct it, both by my respect for you, and my reverence for truth.[2]

The error was acknowledged in the Edinburgh papers, through Boswell's good offices[3]—so much he records in his *Tour*, from which he has deleted the tell-tale passage;[4] but to correct the *Journey* was not so simple. The 'next edition' (1785) appeared posthumously, and after the death of Johnson's printer, William Strahan. Someone (perhaps Andrew Strahan, who inherited his father's business) had taken prompt note of Boswell's published narrative 'since this work was printed off', and was careful to record the apology and promise of amendment sent to the Edinburgh papers; but fulfilment of the promise would presumably have required a cancel, and Johnson was no longer there to insist on such measures. Subsequent editions were to pursue an erratic course: two omitted the offending passage; others retained it together with the apology (thus copying the 1785 edition parrot-wise); others again took no pains at all about the matter, neither correcting nor apologizing.

Johnson spoke of his own 'reverence for truth'; but had he failed here to ensure its transmission? And was this but one of the opportunities he let slip? I have formed the impression that Boswell suffered a succession of disappointments over the *Journey*, whose shadows may be traced in the following references. He wrote on

---

[1] 'Superiority' can signify merely 'magnitude'. See *Dictionary*.
[2] *Letters*, no. 389.
[3] A draft in Johnson's hand survives among the Boswell papers at Yale. See *Journal*, p. 451. The corrections show Johnson's concern that the apology shall be ample. The final version is given in the *Tour* (*Life*, v. 412).
[4] It could have been inferred from Mrs. Piozzi's *Letters to and from the late Samuel Johnson* (1788), i. 144–5; but Boswell had by then given his own account of the affair, and John Macleod was dead.

24 June 1774 to remonstrate with Johnson on his failure to acknowledge 'various packets'.[1] Next day he recorded[2] the arrival of a letter crossing his: on 21 June, Johnson had written to tell him that the first sheets of the *Journey* had ('yesterday') gone to press, and to assure him: 'I have endeavoured to do you some justice in the first paragraph'[3]—but not to acknowledge his 'packets'. For that he had to wait until 4 July, when Johnson, on the eve of departure for Wales, wrote: 'I wish you could have looked over my book before the printer, but it could not easily be. I suspect some mistakes; but as I deal, perhaps, more in notions than facts, the matter is not great, and the second edition will be mended, if any such there be.' He concluded this letter: 'I am obliged to you for all your pamphlets, and of the last I hope to make some use. I made some of the former.'[4] This, it may be supposed, was all the satisfaction Boswell would get for his pains. Johnson's 'it could not easily be' has a negligent air. Moreover, he was not usually sparing of corrections in proof. Nevertheless there is substance in a later apology: on 1 October he repeated his wish that Boswell might have 'read the book before it was printed', continuing 'but our distance does not easily permit it'.[5] He had been travelling with the Thrales, and between Edinburgh and a coach on the roads of England and Wales there could have been no communication. On his return[6] he found that the printing had been held up, and became eager to press on with it. He must have worked, and urged others to work, quickly: by 20 October he could tell John Taylor that, with 240 pages already printed, he hoped 'to have the book out in a Month',[7] though it was after all 26 November before he could report to Boswell that he had 'corrected the last page'.[8] True, he was still to ask Strahan (four days later) for a major alteration, the celebrated cancel of D8; but this, like John Macleod's 'ideal point of honour', would belong to the category of *notions*: self-examination led him to question the spirit in which he had denounced (though without naming) the Dean and Chapter of Lichfield; he offered to meet the cost of cancelling the leaf and promised that he would 'write something to fill up the

[1] *Letters* [Boswell], i. 204.
[2] In his journal: see *Private Papers*, ix. 128.
[3] *Letters*, no. 356.   [4] Ibid., no. 357.   [5] Ibid., no. 360.
[6] On 30 Sept.   [7] *Letters*, no. 360. 1.   [8] Ibid., no. 363.

vacuum'.[1] The death of Col was indeed a fact; yet I doubt whether Johnson would have inserted it (in the last set of proofs to be corrected) unless he had wished to couple it with a tribute of gratitude and affection. Sir Alexander Macdonald's death, had it occurred in that autumn, would not have impelled him to tax the patience of Strahan's printers. The change in Strahan's own plans,[2] which was incidentally to halve the list of *Errata* and permit small stylistic improvements and printing-house corrections in one of the sheets, cannot have been envisaged as an opportunity for general revision. I therefore judge it fair to say that, if Johnson's response to Boswell's earlier offers of help wanted alacrity, it was not lacking in candour.

Traces of a second advance and retreat may be discerned—this time in Boswell's private journals and his letters to Temple rather than in his correspondence with Johnson, or any remonstrance that the *Life* records. Scattered allusions bear witness to a thwarted purpose, or purposes. Throughout the greater part of their travels together Boswell had allowed Johnson to read his Journal,[3] and had been gratified by his reaction. He quotes, for example, a passage of talk between them on 19 September concluding with Johnson's words: 'It might be printed, were the subject fit for printing.'[4] Perhaps he underestimated the weight of the reservation: when he said that it might be printed, Johnson was merely assuaging Boswell's doubts as to the style. On New Year's day 1775, alight with expectation, he showed this Journal to Sir William Forbes, 'to prepare him for Mr. Johnson's Book. He was much entertained, and I left him my three volumes.'[5] A fortnight later, Johnson wrote that his copy was on its way, and adjured him to 'let me know if any mistake is committed, or any thing important left out', reiterating his wish that Boswell might have 'seen the sheets'.[6] When it arrived on the 18th (the very day of publication), any disappointment he may hitherto have felt was swallowed up in elation, as his letters and journals alike testify.

[1] *Letters*, no. 364. He rewrote p. 48.
[2] See W. B. Todd, 'The printing of Johnson's *Journey* (1775)', *Studies in Bibliography*, vi, Charlottesville, Virginia, 1953, 247–54.
[3] From 18 Aug. to 26 Oct., according to Boswell's own notes in the *Tour*. See *Life*, v. 58, n. 2, and 360, n. 4.
[4] *Journal*, p. 188; *Life*, v. 227, with Boswell's exultant note.
[5] *Private Papers*, x. 75.   [6] *Letters*, no. 371.

JOHNSON AND BOSWELL ON THEIR TRAVELS 161

For some two months he basked in happiness among his Edinburgh friends. Meanwhile, Johnson showed a flattering deference to his opinion,[1] enjoining him to note corrections in his copy and bring it to London, where first reports of the rate of sale were satisfactory.[2] By 18 March Boswell was on his way south, and writing from Grantham to Temple: 'I am pleased with Lord Lisburne's fancy that he should like my Remarks.'[3] Since Lord Lisburne had evidently heard of the Remarks in London,[4] it is clear that Boswell had not waited to bring these with him. Three days later he arrived and called at once on Johnson. Thenceforward we have to reckon with allusions not only to what Boswell had written but also to what he intended writing—and a sanguine temperament does not always distinguish these two categories. In the first comes the famous Journal, which we now know to have been (so far as it went) a work but little short of readiness for publication,[5] and the Remarks. A copy of these survives,[6] consisting of eleven folio pages in the hand of Boswell's clerk, John Lawrie.[7] The comments, queries, and corrections composing them are keyed to the printed text, and the pervasive excitement, together with the presence of afterthoughts which sometimes disturb the order, suggest that they were written down while the book was still fresh in Boswell's mind. One reference ('My Journal stops at Lochbuy's... But I am continuing it, and you shall read it when we meet') is an indication rather of mood than of date, for he never did complete it.[8] In default of evidence to the contrary, we can only assume the version sent to Johnson to have been a fair copy.

In London Boswell began to taste the new wine of celebrity. Lord

[1] Ibid., no. 374.   [2] Ibid., no. 380.
[3] *Letters* (Boswell), i. 212. This and subsequent references to his Remarks in Boswell's letters are noted by Professor Pottle (*Literary Career of James Boswell*, Oxford 1929) under 'Projected Works': see p. 303.
[4] For Lord Lisburne's presence in London, see *Letters* (Boswell), i. 110. He was Temple's patron.
[5] See Professor Pottle's Preface to the revised edition of the *Journal*.
[6] In the Hyde Collection, where I enjoyed the privilege of reading it. A transcript (not quite accurate) is printed in the *Catalogue of the Johnsonian Collection of R. B. Adam*, Buffalo 1921, and a photographic reproduction appears in *Adam Library*, ii, following p. 45.
[7] An interpolated correction is in Boswell's hand.
[8] For Boswell's failure to complete his Journal, see F. A. Pottle, *The Private Papers of James Boswell: a Catalogue* (1931), under item 33.

Mansfield received him with the flattering assurance: 'We have all been reading your travels'.[1] At Sir John Pringle's 'learned levee', he gave the company 'some lively Anecdotes'.[2] Both visits were paid on 26 March 1775; the following day surpassed this. Leaving Strahan's (where he had been encouraged in his project of removing to London) with Johnson, he called on Reynolds. Although the Journal reverses (inadvertently, I suppose) the order of events, what happened is clear.

> As Mr. Johnson and I came along in the hackney coach, he advised me not to show my Journal to any body but bid me draw out of it what I thought might be published, and he would look it over. This he did upon my telling him that I was asked to publish; but he did not seem desireous that my little bark should 'pursue the triumph and partake the gale'.[3]

On arrival they separated, Johnson (Boswell surmised) to sit to Miss Reynolds, while he called on her brother. 'I had a very pleasing reception from Sir Joshuah, and read him some passages of my Journal on the Tour with Mr. Johnson, and he said: "It is more entertaining than his." '[4] However favourably Boswell might have reacted to Johnson's proposal a month or two earlier, he would hardly be in a mood now for submitting to tutelage; nor would the knowledge that he had both shown and read from the Journal make it easier to open the subject between them. Perhaps this is why his thoughts seem to have turned towards another project. By 4 April he was telling Temple: 'Mr. Johnson has allowed me to write out a supplement to his *Journey*. But I wish I may be able to settle to it.'[5] It is clear that he did not 'settle'. On his return to London after visiting Temple at Mamhead, he is launching yet another paper boat on the stream of fancy. 'I have not written out another line of my *Remarks* on the Hebrides', he tells Temple on 10 May.

> I found it impossible to do it in London. Besides Dr. Johnson does

---

[1] *Private Papers*, x. 149.   [2] Ibid. x. 150.
[3] Ibid. x. 154–5. R. W. Chapman doubted whether Boswell could have contemplated publishing his Journal in Johnson's lifetime. See *Johnson's 'Journey to the Western Islands of Scotland' and Boswell's 'Journal of a Tour to the Hebrides'*, ed. R. W. Chapman, Oxford 1924, p. xvi; but this was before the recovery of Boswell's private papers.   [4] *Private Papers*, x. 154.   [5] *Letters* [Boswell], i. 218.

JOHNSON AND BOSWELL ON THEIR TRAVELS 163

not seem very desireous that I should publish any supplement. Between ourselves, he is not apt to encourage one to *share* reputation with himself. But don't you think I may write out my remarks in Scotland, and send them to be revised by you, and then they may be published freely? Give me your opinion of this.[1]

Apart from the aspersion on Johnson (to be considered presently), this letter raises the question: was Boswell's proposal made in sheer petulance, or did the suggestion that he might *write out his remarks in Scotland* imply an illusory hope of developing the manuscript he had sent Johnson into a pamphlet—approximating to the 'supplement' he had formerly projected, but written in the comparative quiet of Edinburgh, under an easier supervisor, and perhaps with more freedom to draw on the Journal than Johnson would have allowed? In Edinburgh, Boswell came to terms with his situation. 'Dr. Johnson', he tells Temple on 6 November,

has said nothing to me of my *Remarks* during my journey with him, which I wish to write. Shall I task myself to write so much of them a week, and send to you for revisal? If I do not publish them now, they will be good materials for my *Life of Dr. Johnson*.[2]

This seems to be the first intimation that he is taking the long view: waiting for the death of the lion. More than a year afterwards, however, an earlier project flickered into momentary life. In a letter of thanks for further copies of the *Journey* (8 February 1777), he sounded Strahan: 'I think . . . that I could write notes upon it, which would improve it. I put into the Dr.'s own hands a copy of the notes by Lord Hailes and Sir Alexr. Dick. I wish you could get him to write more.'[3]

Since Johnson lies under a double charge—failure to encourage Boswell's endeavours to write on their travels,[4] and failure to make use of what he had already written[5]—we must assess the possibilities that really lay open to him. Boswell's wish for immediate publication of his Journal in its entirety may be dismissed as chimerical.

[1] Ibid. i. 222.   [2] Ibid. i. 246.
[3] Ibid. i. 256. (I take this to mean: Get Johnson to write more notes, to be published with those already given him.)
[4] He 'took no interest in the plan' of a supplement (C. B. Tinker in Boswell's *Letters*, i. 212, n. 3).
[5] Mistakes pointed out by Boswell 'remain uncorrected' (L. F. Powell in *Life*, ii. 291, n. 4).

As Professor Pottle has said: 'Boswell ... in his first drafts ... thinks and writes more like a twentieth-century author than do any of his contemporaries'.[1] Even Malone's editing could not avert their censure. Johnson cannot be held to account for discouraging a project which he is unlikely to have taken seriously; and the charge of indifference assumes that he knew what was in Boswell's heart. Three ways therefore presented themselves: he could have corrected his own text with Boswell's help; he could have furthered Boswell's plan of writing a 'supplement' for present publication; he could have accepted his proffered notes and preserved them against the time when his own book should be republished. Looked at more closely, however, these possibilities seem less distinct.[2] They prompt the question: might not Boswell's eagerness have prevailed over Johnson's inertia, if he had but determined on a single objective? He surely had too many irons in the fire.

The projected 'supplement', being the most distinguishable enterprise, may best be considered on its merits. An allusion in a defence of Boswell's *Tour* ('In Mr. Boswell's Journal, some expected a second part of Dr. Johnson's "Journey" ')[3] suggests that he had spoken at large of the plan; but he had better have taken to heart the tale of Wheler and Spon. Sir George Wheler and Dr. Jacob Spon travelled together, in Greece and the Levant, in 1675 and 1676, and when Spon published an account of their journey[4] Wheler, though he read it 'with great satisfaction', felt obliged to counter an impending English translation by giving his own version of what they had seen; and this he proceeded to do with portentous ceremony and particularity. 'When I met with any things to be mistakes, I have ... freely corrected them, and in dubious Criticisms I have given my own Opinion and Reason.' Thus, one particular after another is subjected to such comment as 'Three Gates, and with Mr. Spon

---

[1] *Journal*, Preface, p. xi.
[2] It must be remembered that, in these and other references, nomenclature is confusing. Thus, Johnson kept a 'book of remarks' (*Letters*, no. 329); Boswell refers to Johnson's forthcoming work as 'remarks' (*Letters* [Boswell], i. 202), and speaks of his own 'Remarks' as a work yet to be written, in Nov. 1775 (*Letters* [Boswell], i. 246).
[3] [? (Sir) Walter James James], *A Defence of Mr. Boswell's Journal of a Tour to the Hebrides; in a letter to the author of the Remarks signed Verax* (1785), p. 41.
[4] Jacob Spon, *Voyage d'Italie, de Dalmatie, de Grèce, et du Levant*, Lyon 1678.

favour no more'—or (of two streams) 'This I guess to be *Ismenus*, and the other *Dirce*, as I said. I know not why my Comrade seemeth of the contrary Opinion.'[1] His behaviour had evidently amused Johnson, who excused his own 'dilatory notation' of the dimensions of a cave by reflecting on the fallibility of memory and citing as example these two travellers, who 'described with irreconcilable contrariety things which they surveyed together, and which both undoubtedly designed to show as they saw them'.[2] Boswell could, of course, be likened to George Wheler only in so far as he too offered to superimpose his own recollection on an already published narrative; but from Johnson's pleasantry we may infer that he had little use for this kind of *supplement*. It is sometimes forgotten that his critical opinions on books of travel had been proclaimed even earlier than those on biography: in the Preface to his *Lobo*. The culminating assertion of *Idler* 97—'He that would travel for the entertainment of others, should remember that the great object of remark is human life'—is no mere aphorism but the condensed expression of his constant theory and practice. It would surely have pleased him to learn the terms in which Gilbert White described his travel-book: 'It is quite a sentimental Journey, divested of all natural history and antiquities; but full of good sense, and new and peculiar reflections.'[3] This, and not the enumeration of particulars, had been his aim; and with such enumeration the *supplements* to contemporary travel-books were stuffed.

Failure to correct such mistakes in his own text as Boswell had brought to his notice would be another and a graver matter. Here it might be permissible, and even justifiable, to demand the Scottish verdict of 'not proven' rather than 'guilty'. Johnson *may* have preserved some record of factual errors awaiting correction—we can hardly believe that he would *not* have wished to correct the two faulty dates about which Boswell took particular pains in his Remarks,[4] and which, though patently nonsensical, clung obstinately to the text.

[1] George Wheler, *A Journey into Greece* (1682), pp. a, ii, iii, 16, 331.
[2] *Journey*, p. 343. Johnson was ill served by his printer, in respect of the travellers' names: they appear as Wheeler and Spen.
[3] *The Life and Letters of Gilbert White of Selborne*, ed. Rashleigh Holt-White (1901), i. 277 (a letter to his brother).
[4] He corrected *twentieth* to *second* in his own hand (p. 107), and dictated the correction of *thirteenth* to *thirtieth* (p. 60).

He may even have given instructions to William Strahan.[1] The 1785 edition of the *Journey* which Andrew Strahan brought out after his father's death could—for any evidence to the contrary—have been prompted by the success of the *Tour*, and would in that case be what indeed it appears: a hasty production. Material for correction may have lain unused in the printing-house. Yet, wanting even such evidence as could change 'possible' to 'probable', I would rather concede that Johnson seems to have taken no steps to ensure a good text for any future edition. In promising Boswell that mistakes would be corrected in a 'second edition . . . if any such there be',[2] did he mean to question the likelihood of the mistakes or of the edition? The informal syntax of a letter admits either possibility. What reason had he to expect such an edition? William Strahan could give him a sober estimate of the book's prospects: although the event had justified his decision to print a second thousand, any surviving demand must have been offset by the unauthorized reprints.[3] There was, as we know, to be no other edition within the lifetime of either man; and it was some while since Johnson had cherished confident hopes of publishing his collected works.

Ought he then to have taken Boswell into partnership and invited him to prepare a revised, and perhaps annotated, edition ready for the day when it should be required, however distant? Perhaps; but here again essential evidence is wanting. Unless—or until—the marked copy which Boswell 'put into the Dr.'s own hands' comes to light, we have nothing on which to build an estimate of this contribution, except the Remarks. It is therefore time to characterize these—for they forbid exact analysis. They are spontaneous, impulsive; Boswell frequently advances a proposition only to retract it. On the other hand they are painstaking: a place-name misspelt will be corrected wherever it occurs. Thus, if I say that they fall not far

---

[1] Johnson sold the copyright to Strahan on 22 Jan. 1784 (for £150). See J. D. Fleeman, *Documents and Manuscripts of Samuel Johnson*, Oxford Bibliographical Society, Occasional Publications no. 2, 1967, item 211. Johnson's MS. note of this transaction was sold by Sotheby on 30 Nov. 1970, lot no. 194.   [2] *Letters*, no. 357.

[3] In Professor Todd's view, Strahan's four thousand copies fully satisfied the demand (op. cit., p. 253). Johnson told Boswell in 1778: '. . . the "Journey to the Hebrides" has not had a great sale' (*Life*, iii. 325). Boswell, recording this, demurs: the first edition had sold briskly; 'a new edition has been printed since his death, besides that in the collection of his works' (n. 5). He does not, however, reckon with the success of his own *Tour*.

short of a hundred this must be taken as an approximate reckoning. Attempts at arrangement are likewise baffled by the composition of the several notes, any one of which may range in content from general to particular, from fact to opinion. They may, however, be sorted into some such pattern as this: names of persons and places and particular facts relating to them corrected; geographical and historical circumstances established; personal details (Johnson's feelings and behaviour on such and such occasions) challenged; all these, together with a few such corrections as a careful proof-reader might make, amount to about forty. Out of this number, notes concerned with names, with geographical and genealogical fact, and with printing errors are useful, though not all of them are important —but they make up no more than half the sum. The rest include some trivialities[1] and some particulars which Johnson would regard as trivial even if his biographer did not;[2] and Boswell himself withdrew a few on reflection. Another seventeen or so relate to matters of such general interest as Johnson would reckon admissible: they all have something to do with Scottish social life—but very few of them attempt either to correct or to supplement Johnson's account. At least ten are expressions of unreserved approval; three or four are tentative queries which Boswell himself withdraws. Thus only three or four invite Johnson to reconsider his opinions. Another group of Remarks, amounting to fifteen, consists of praise, most of it given to descriptive passages. There remains, apart from miscellaneous comments of small weight, one surprising category: stylistic criticism. Boswell challenges sixteen passages on a suspicion of ambiguity or awkwardness; and he is almost always wrong. Thus he will fail to discern the purpose of a change of tense, or miss a pleasantry, or a point. When Johnson compares the welcome he has found on Raasay with that which King Alcinous offered to another sea-borne traveller, he is careful to mark the limits of the comparison: 'In *Raasay*, If I could have found an Ulysses, I had fancied a *Phaeacia*';[3] but Boswell, lost in the maze of this stately compliment, inquires anxiously whether the reservation will not

[1] e.g. on p. 40: (J.) 'Ladies come hither . . .' (B.) 'Should it not be Ladies & Gentlemen? Ladies do not come alone to the Buller.'
[2] e.g. on p. 277: (J.) 'We, being no seasoned sailors, were willing to call it a tempest.' (B.) 'You treat the storm too lightly . . .' [3] p. 149.

give offence. Mrs. Boswell, as he candidly records, saw no fault here; perhaps she had the finer ear for tone. When they discussed another passage, one which needed clarifying, it was she who suggested the appropriate word. In this, as in other sorts of Remark, Boswell is quick to acknowledge excess of zeal.

On my reckoning, therefore, not more than a quarter of all these queries would be recognized by Johnson as calling for reconsideration; and, if we add a handful of personal details which he would rate lower than Boswell—lower, perhaps, than they deserved—the total is still not great. It is indeed a pity that he failed to ensure the correction of dates, names, and a few particular facts; but we are in danger of magnifying this failure merely because R. W. Chapman recorded, as his purpose required, every Remark which detected error—and samples only from among the rest. These latter have for the most part a positive significance: Johnson's deprecating 'I deal, perhaps, more in notions than facts' will be misunderstood if its frame of reference is overlooked. Notions unrelated or even opposed to facts would be worthless or pernicious. He assumed that, both as to general observations and the opinions he derived from them, he and Boswell were of one mind; and this assumption the Remarks nearly always bear out. His opponent in the major issues canvassed by the *Journey* is not Boswell but Pennant, to whose whole scale of values it offers a formidable challenge. But that is another and a far longer story.

Whatever conflict of wills developed between the two travellers as to the particulars of their tale seems to have resolved itself— much as the entanglements of a fourth act yield to the happy ending. Boswell had only to wait for the time when his peculiar genius, his vivid narrative gift and concern with particular persons and events, would find much fuller scope than supplement or annotation could have afforded. It was surely with a sense of triumph that he set on the title-page of his *Tour* those lines from Pope which had once expressed his disappointment and frustration:

> O! while along the stream of time, thy name
> Expanded flies, and gathers all its fame,
> Say, shall my little bark attendant sail,
> Pursue the triumph and partake the gale?[1]

[1] *Essay on Man*, iv. 383–6.

Was he quite oblivious of the vein of comedy in his choice of epigraph: Pope's acknowledgement of indebtedness to his 'guide, philosopher, and friend' for the intellectual content of a poem which Johnson had found intellectually meretricious?

Meanwhile, Johnson's *Journey* preserved its original form intact: massive yet spare, like early masonry which has escaped the restorer's hand. Its errors of fact have (with very few exceptions) been set right by R. W. Chapman, often with Boswell's help—and that of his editor.[1] For its implications (fold within fold of meaning), we must read it attentively—and then it will be no loss that we cannot seek hither and thither in supplements and commentaries. Like *Rasselas* it must be taken on its own terms; for, like *Rasselas* in this respect at least, it is a singular compound of narrative and argument. Such integrity would be destroyed by any interference, however well informed or well intentioned.

It may be inferred that I am not altogether disposed to 'think like a twentieth-century author'; and indeed I hold with James Ramsay that, while 'the name of Samuel Johnson will never be mentioned without recalling that of James Boswell . . . the latter bears the same relation to his revered friend that a pinnace does to a first-rate man-of-war'.[2] If this metaphor was (as I surmise) prompted by the lines on Boswell's title-page, we might well see it as a flourish set on that little comedy of cross-purposes whose course I have endeavoured to trace.

[1] Private correspondence between R. W. Chapman and Dr. L. F. Powell.
[2] *Scotland and Scotsmen in the Eighteenth Century from the MSS. of James Ramsay Esq. of Ochtertyre*, ed. Alexander Allardyce (1887), i. 174. This passage was written in the late eighteenth century.

REVIEW

(1954)

The Letters of Samuel Johnson. With Mrs. Thrale's Genuine Letters to Him. Collected and edited by R. W. Chapman. Oxford: Clarendon Press, 1952.

THIS is a work to be compared, for the triumphant use of experience in surmounting former difficulties, with nothing less than the Skerryvore lighthouse. It has gone up stone by stone: merely to enumerate the articles in which Dr. Chapman has from time to time reported progress—scrutinized sources of information, established credentials of witnesses, and so on—would take too long. Moreover, it has been, and continues to be, in some degree, a work of collaboration, offering itself for comparison with eighteenth-century Shakespearian studies at their happiest, as to community of intellectual goods. The acknowledgements of willing and serviceable aid—of the courtesy and insight of American owners of manuscripts, of the labours of fellow scholars, especially other editors of Johnson and Boswell—these also are too numerous for mention; it must be enough to say that lovers of Johnson in Oxford, in notable American universities and libraries, and in his native place, are nobly represented in this edition; and it is pleasant to think that A. L. Reade lived to see it appear. Experts in many fields have contributed various information; the editor might well have taken for his motto Johnson's words to Thomas Warton: 'A commentary must arise from the fortuitous discoveries of many men, in devious walks of literature' (letter 114).

In measuring the scope of this undertaking, comparison with G. B. Hill's edition of the *Letters* must be the first instrument. His numeration is preserved (as his pagination was in Dr. L. F. Powell's revised edition of the *Life*)—even, occasionally, at some cost. The scale is much enlarged. Apart from the inclusion of the Thrale letters, there is the very considerable number of Johnson's own

letters recovered since Hill published his two volumes in 1892—
including some he was able to include in his subsequent *Johnsonian
Miscellanies*; and the plan of his edition had been selective: it excluded those letters which he had already edited in the *Life*. Moreover, a great deal of illustrative material, having been gathered since
his day, awaited organization. And to all this Dr. Chapman is able
to add unpublished letters and fresh information: his total of letters
is nearly a third as much again as that of Hill's *Life* and *Letters*
together; his commentary is at once fuller and more elaborate, thus
carrying exploration a day's march beyond even the Hill-Powell
Life and *Tour*. Expansion to three volumes is easily accounted for;
the marvel is that these three are made to hold so much. The
establishment of the text likewise has advanced beyond calculation:
it represents a lifetime of Johnsonian scholarship, of *literature*, in
Johnson's own large sense of the word, of lying in ambush for the
reluctant witness and pursuing every piece of evidence to its last
retreat.

The serious reader, intent on availing himself of the full resources
of this edition, must address himself to it sturdily. He must famili-
arize himself with the system of numeration: thus, if several letters
have come to light since Hill's count, one may be, e.g. 264. 3, and,
if more than one of the Thrales reply, the figures may reach 264. 3*b*.
Then, where Hill's dating was at fault, he will see, for example,
instead of the letter formerly placed 29th, a reference carrying him
to the interstice between 36 and 37. In a very few instances, he must
reckon with the emergence of a letter at a late stage in the preparation of this edition: thus, 229. 2 appears in the Addenda but has
not been recorded in the text. Moreover, having so much fresh and
important material, Dr. Chapman must sometimes refer the reader
to a note in Hill's *Letters* or the Hill-Powell *Life*, for an illustration
he has not chosen to use himself. (Computation, not supported by
common sense, suggests that the careful reader might find himself
pursuing cross-references with eleven volumes propped open at
once.) And, where the matter is so rich and intricate, there must
be a system of abbreviations and distinctive variations of type.
(In this, as in other respects, the editor is of course well served by
that press which has been responsible for so many Johnsonian

undertakings.) All these devices, like a long list of *dramatis personae*, must be memorized at the outset.

Once the plan is mastered, however, the reader will find himself sustained and even exhilarated by its consistency. The cross-referencing will mean much more than a mode of finding his way about; it enables him to form candid judgements, with all available evidence in view. Thus, Mrs. Thrale's treatment of Boswell is seen to be petulant, not deliberately malicious: she printed Johnson's praise of him in 337, but suppressed that in 408; and Johnson's brief notes to Nichols are shown to form a pattern illustrating his progress in the work we know as the *Lives of the Poets*. The map of many transactions is fairly spread before our eyes.

It will, of course, be in everyone's mind that a principal reason for the complex plan of this edition is the chance that brought the Malahide and Fettercairn deposits to light within recent years and governed their gradual publication. These events—hardly less disturbing than earthquakes—have given rise to Addenda, Postscripts, and Further Addenda; most numerous, naturally, in Volume I. The editor explains his method of dealing with such exigencies: 'I should perhaps apologize for having intercalated notes on the latest Malahide finds by way of postscripts. My excuse is that this form of statement exhibits the process of trial and (sometimes) error, which does not lack edification' (iii. 309). These circumstances, however, are also to be thought of as forcing upon our notice something latent in the very nature of the undertaking. When a man inspires such intensity of editorial and biographical devotion as Johnson (and when, unlike Shakespeare, he leaves us substantial means for the satisfaction of our curiosity), finality is not to be looked for. The greatest edition, whether of *Life* or *Letters*, must still be growing: as Dr. Chapman and Dr. Powell receive and give mutual help—as one carries a step further his elucidation of the famous *impransus* letter (10), or the other supplies fresh clues to problems posed by Boswell's narrative—so lesser men will still be finding or surmising answers to questions raised by these two, at least so long as the issue of Boswellian papers continues.

What is achieved by *this* edition may best be considered under the heads of comprehensiveness, correctness of text, and fullness of illustrative commentary—even though these cannot always be kept apart.

The most immediate and solid satisfaction, for its possessor, consists in having all the hitherto known letters together. The scope of its plan is indeed so wide that room is found for some letters which Johnson wrote, and some which he is reputed to have written, on others' behalf: not merely for that by which Frances Reynolds hoped to reconcile herself to her brother (1149), but also formal pieces differing not much from the dedications he wrote on behalf of needy authors. The question must arise, whether it was prudent to swell so considerable a bulk by including letters from the Thrale household—all but a very few, of course, being Mrs. Thrale's. That, if any of Johnson's correspondents were to be chosen for this perilous honour, she had first claim, we must agree. Against the decision to include them it might still be urged that they are significantly incomplete. From the evidence, Dr. Chapman infers that, in the first grief and anger of estrangement, Johnson may have destroyed those that he could lay hands on—the most recent; while it was tenderness that led him to do away with her eldest daughter's letters written at the time of the quarrel and probably bearing on its cause. Thus, the argument for inclusion—that the two sides of a correspondence with a family so important in Johnson's life complete the story of that life—is qualified by the consideration that the other side fails at the crisis of this very story. Yet Mrs. Thrale by her manipulation of her own letters had posed a textual problem: Hill's distrust of her as a witness had to be reconsidered. The labours of Professor Clifford and Miss Balderston had shown that she deserved a hearing; and, unless a separate volume were to be devoted to those of her letters judged genuine, they must be intercalated here.

The Thrale letters apart, we have here, in addition to what Hill knew, not only those little windfalls which may usually be gathered even after the appearance of an edition supposed complete, but also more than one substantial series (to 'Queeny' Thrale, to Robert Chambers); and, amongst single acquisitions, many of importance. Following Hill's plan, Dr. Chapman gives a scrupulous record of letters reported but not extant, or not obtainable, 304. 2 being perhaps an extreme instance of this scrupulosity. His own happy find of 42. 1 suggests that a few unrecorded letters may still await discovery. To conclude, of the 472 items by which Dr. Chapman's total exceeds Hill's, many are valuable in themselves, many help to set others in perspective, and not a few are new.

The text has been established by various means: wherever the original of a letter already printed is extant, by collation. Sometimes Hill had to rely on a transcript, and even a careful and skilful scribe might fall into one of the snares set by Johnson's handwriting—e.g. yet/got. Dr. Chapman has shown that an editor of Johnson's own day did not reckon it his business to correct printed copy in this way, even when he had the means, but merely to scan it with an eye to the sense and general probability. (It was, however, a common practice to send the originals to the printing-house, and the standard of fidelity there was high.) Where there is no manuscript, he brings to bear on the printed text his experience in textual criticism and his knowledge of what Johnson is likely to have written: of his idiom and that of his age, together with its social usage; and can say, from familiarity with his handwriting, how a corruption may be inferred. (The present reviewer tentatively hazards the suggestion—if Johnson's hand allows it—that, when he playfully remonstrates with Edmund Hector for his love of giving, he must surely have continued, or intended to continue: 'Your friends [not 'your minds'] ought to learn how to refuse.' 376. 1.)[1] Moreover, he can discount apparent irregularities, knowing that Johnson was sometimes careless as to small words, or the punctuation of a passage whose close coincided with a visual pause: the end of line or page. Such an intricate system of detection calls for help from persons so various as dignitaries of the Church and the Edinburgh police (this would surely have pleased Boswell).

Another sort of correction—that of the dating of these letters—has brought into play the editor's familiarity with eighteenth-century life and with material objects surviving from that age—the postal system, for example, and the varying aspects of letters transmitted by various means. 'I do not apologize', he observes, 'for my insistence on these postal minutiae: a neglected part of epistolary

[1] Dr. Chapman referred this problem to Mrs. Hyde, who confirmed that the reading of the MS. is clearly *friends*.

editing, and one that is sometimes not unimportant' (i. 378). He is often able to cite evidence not recognized by Hill—though it may not prove conclusive, and can be extremely minute. Johnson, who was insistent with Mrs. Thrale on the value of exact dating, deserves this care, though he seems to have been capable of occasional odd blunders.

To the *illustration* of these letters, the editor comes furnished with experience that Johnson himself would have relished—of the whole process of putting works of literature through the press. By this means, and in collaboration with Professor Nichol Smith, such allusions to contemporary publications as those in 15 and 64 are elucidated; and, by the light of ancient and modern studies, many of Hill's instances are considered in a wider context. (Where ancient authors are concerned, as in the tags with which Johnson teased and flattered Mrs. Thrale, Dr. Chapman prefers to offer the modern reader those translations which Johnson himself would have approved.) Besides the recognizable, if not always identifiable, quotations, there are many passages that ring allusively. A list of unsolved problems therefore remains, to challenge diligence and ingenuity. For all this width of illustration, however, there is no dispersion. From the anecdotal discursiveness of Hill's notes, we are brought steadily back to the main theme, sometimes with a hint that Hill on Johnson's Oxford, or Johnson's London, makes good reading; more often, the substance of his account is given in smaller compass. Very rarely, a topic which might have invited attention is curtly dismissed: it is surely the *mixture* of sense and nonsense in Charlotte Lennox's *Shakespear Illustrated*, and in Johnson's dealings with her and her books, that pricks curiosity. But this edition is (like Johnson's *Dictionary* itself), as to all debatable decisions, one man's work; and who—given the chance of such an editor—would have preferred a Committee and a Variorum? It is time to leave particular instances and turn to remark that insight into Johnson's mind and heart which subtly pervades these illustrative notes, finding explicit utterance only here and there, as in the pungent retort to idle talk of hypochondria in a comment on 309, or this on a quotation from the Psalms in 465: 'J. read the Bible in many tongues, and quotes or translates indifferently.'

(Surely, of deliberate and positive Anglicans, Johnson was the least typical.)

The subdivision of the Index may perhaps be thought too curious. Persons and Authors, for example, occupy separate categories; and, while careful cross-reference saves the reader from error, he may sometimes wish that, of the two distinct classes of authors, the Ancients had been left standing alone, and the Moderns allowed to mingle with Persons. Index VII, 'Johnson's English', seems to hint at a compromise between a glossary of contemporary usage and an analysis of Johnsonian idiom. If knowledge of eighteenth-century English had been taken for granted, there would have been room to consider (for example) the extension of meaning which pleasantry and intimacy allow to such words as *genius* and *image*, in the letters as contrasted with the published writings. But perhaps it may already be too late to count on such knowledge even among those likely to use this edition, and the time be not far distant when the Clarendon Press must appoint fit persons to compile an eighth index, of Dr. Chapman's English, for a barbarous generation.

In so big and intricate a work, some small errors must necessarily elude vigilance;[1] besides those mentioned in the Errata list, a few are acknowledged where they occur. So far as the present reviewer can tell, one alone for which any importance could be claimed has escaped both meshes: for 890. 3 we are referred to the Addenda, from which this letter seems to have slipped.

It remains to be asked, what is the gain to our knowledge of Johnson from having thus gathered and set out all of his letters known to survive? To one reader at least, steady progress through the collection has made it even more evident than before why Johnson was so much loved. Few men can have stood to lose less by total exposure. As the curiosity of survivors had demanded a version of the

---

[1] The following few and unimportant corrections are offered as the reviewer's contribution to subsequent editions:

47, n., 'the' Barbados wrongly suggests a group of islands.
154, n. 2, for Index III read V.
196, n. 1, for H.L.D. read H.L.P.
574. 1, reference to Addenda: for p. 530 read p. 529.
610. 1, reference to Addenda: for p. 529 read p. 530, and, in this passage of Addenda, for I. 442 read I. 432.

In Appendix E. II, § 5. d, the reference to Porter should read § 2.

'rough' letter in which Johnson answered Mrs. Thrale's announcement of her second marriage (970), so the rigours of modern scholarship have exacted the publication and analysis of the enigmatic letter (in French, but not singular in this respect) in which he confessed to her his fears of insanity (307. 1). Both she had rightly withheld but pardonably preserved. Boswell likewise suppressed some part of the letters in which Johnson reported his case to his physicians; but anything from his hand in these latter years was too precious to be destroyed. Any collection of Johnson's letters we are ever likely to possess must prompt the wish that more had been preserved from his youth and middle age: one alone survives in which he uses 'thee' and 'thou' (12, to his wife)—a usage he seems to have kept, in talk, for particular friends and occasions. This is the category least likely to increase, but even the few early letters that we have help to redress the balance of the *Life*. The brief notes which show him dealing with a business in straits serve to correct Boswell's picture of the philosopher making himself ridiculous in the part of Thrale's executor. 'I was bred a Bookseller' (609). One trade at least was no mystery to him.

To the mingled influences of pride, self-interest, and affection which safeguarded the letters of Johnson's later years we owe the evidence of his wise and tender counsels (as in 338); of his insight and sympathy (as in 306); his delicacy in acknowledgements of kindness and in the conduct of his 'vicarious charities'; the ceremonious politeness of which he was justly proud, and the powerful mind that, even when his horizon was narrowed by sickness and confinement, could still order his ideas. Judged by the standards of their age, these are not letters of art. When Johnson rises to an epistolary set piece we may suspect irony—and, sure enough, the rocket presently explodes and comes down in a shower of sparks: 'Now you think yourself the first Writer in the world for a letter about nothing. Can you write such a letter as this? So miscellaneous, with such noble disdain of regularity, like Shakespeare's works, such graceful negligence of transition like the ancient enthusiasts' (657). The most entertaining, written to Mrs. Thrale from the Hebrides, and pointed by a sense of place and time in which the rest are wanting, register the exceptional stimulus of that propitious journey, and of his best correspondent; for such she seems to have been in the years when he could refer to her house as 'home' (206); on Tuesday speak of his 'love and reverence' for her and on Wednesday call her 'a goose' (401 and 403). He wished her to preserve these letters; not (I surmise) merely as memoranda for his book.

Although Johnson would certainly not have acquiesced in this project—the publication of all his surviving letters—he would surely have been pleased with the way in which it has been carried out. 'I like that *muddling* work',[1] he is reported to have said of his own Dictionary, and here also Dr. Chapman is in sympathy with him: unperturbed, in this labour of love, by detail as by magnitude. He could not but value a memorial strong in that very union of qualities for which the great lighthouse itself is celebrated: mass and elegance.

[1] *Life*, ii. 203, n. 3.

THE SIR WALTER SCOTT LECTURES
FOR 1960

Delivered at the Old College on 9th and 10th May
(Revised 1971)

I. SCOTT AND SHAKESPEARE

[*This lecture, when it was delivered, opened with a tribute to those of my teachers who came from Scotland: Janet Spens, Walter Raleigh, George Gordon, David Nichol Smith.*]

APOLOGIES make a dull opening, but some of those I owe you cannot be passed over in silence. The pleasure of speaking about a favourite author consists largely in quotation, and the best part of this I must forgo. I cannot hope to quote from Scott's finest passages of dialogue without offending your ears. (Even for my pronunciation of proper names, I must beg your indulgence: like Edward Waverley when instructed in the alternative modes of addressing Fergus MacIvor, 'I am afraid I shall never bring my English tongue to call him by either one or other', correctly.) I am thus in the pitiful situation of someone lecturing on opera, who hears a whisper in his ear: 'No musical illustrations, please'. For this shortcoming I hope there may be some small compensation. The splendours of Scott's eloquence—as, for example, in Jeanie Deans's appeal to the Queen, or Edie Ochiltree's reflections in the storm—must be well known to you; those lesser matters towards which I hope to draw your attention may perhaps have slipped your memory, or even observation; and yet they have something to contribute to our understanding of the whole of Scott.

I have, besides, to confess that I am not well read in criticism, although I have derived great benefits from Dr. J. C. Corson's bibliographical work; pleasure, also, from others who have delivered the Scott Lectures before me.[1] In some directions, I have travelled

[1] I have gained much, also, from talk with Dr. Ian Jack, and, in the years between printing and revision, with Professor W. L. Renwick.

far enough along the dusty road of criticism to discover that I have no wish to offer—nor you, I suppose, to hear—what lies in that quarter. Those who have read Wilmon Brewer's book, *Shakespeare's Influence on Scott*,[1] may wonder why I should choose a subject associating those two names yet again; but I do not mean to emulate such a statistical feat, nor even the more selective work of R. K. Gordon.[2] Influence is a questionable term in imaginative literature: try to assess it, as though in the columns of a ledger, and there may be cause for the expostulation which Sheridan gives to Puff, in *The Critic*: 'All that can be said is, that two people happened to hit on the same thought—and Shakespeare made use of it first—that's all'. The occasion required a particular turn of plot or dialogue; Scott may or may not have derived assurance from Shakespearian precedent—there is no telling. Neither shall I attempt any parallel, or comparative estimate. This has been a commonplace of criticism, at least from 1817 and that curious review of *Tales of my Landlord* in the *Quarterly*. These comparisons are most of them quantitative: they are grounded in the belief that, for a scale to measure Scott by, you must go back to Shakespeare. One exception deserves mention, and (presently) brief illustration: a little volume called *A Parallel of Shakespeare and Scott*, and consisting of addresses delivered by an unknown gentleman to the Literary and Philosophical Society of Chichester in 1833 and 1834. They are lit by candour and that none too common quality in criticism, common sense. They are not great, but there is no extravagance in the admiration nor rancour in the censure. They were written before the volumes of Lockhart's *Life* had begun to appear, and they stick close to the *writings* of Shakespeare and Scott.

With a like aim in view, I shall set out from this assumption: I believe that the only *comparative* question worth asking, about these two, is this—how did they respond to comparable opportunities?—and the only influence, the only impact of one great, original mind on another, that is worth trying to measure, is a liberating influence: one by which the first-born releases latent power in his successor,

[1] Boston 1925.
[2] 'Shakespeare's *Henry IV* and the Waverley Novels', *M.L.R.*, July 1942; 'Scott and Shakespeare's Tragedies', *Transactions of the Royal Society of Canada*, 1945.

frees him from false or usurped authority, and teaches him to go away and make something of his own. For he must *go away*. Greatness has to be paid for at a fixed rate. Shakespeare's greatness made it impossible that the very kind of drama he wrote should ever be written again. Dryden admitted this—even in the act of tampering with *The Tempest*. (We sometimes speak truer than we know.)

> But Shakespeare's Magick could not copy'd be;
> Within that Circle none durst walk but he.

It was Scott's achievement to discover a channel for some of the hitherto pent-up forces of romantic drama, in the romantic novel.

The discovery may well have been rather intuitive than deliberate: it was the outcome of a deep familiarity with those elements in Shakespeare's plays to which his imagination most keenly responded. (The non-dramatic poetry he seems scarcely to have known.) For this kind of familiarity Scott himself found words, in his *Journal*. After quoting a stanza from Burns, he exclaims: 'Long life to thy fame and peace to thy soul, Rob Burns!. When I want to express a sentiment which I feel strongly, I find the phrase in Shakespeare or thee. The blockheads talk of my being like Shakespeare —not fit to tie his brogues.'[1] Let this be our clue through the labyrinth of Shakespearian quotations—and misquotations—and allusions, with which all his writing is riddled: not the novels alone but also the miscellaneous pieces, the letters, and the journal. Enumeration would yield nothing but a concordance—work which (we are told) is now better done by a machine; yet Wilmon Brewer's list may help us to frame a working hypothesis as to Scott's bias of preference. On his computation, there are but two of the Waverley novels which contain no single quotation from *Henry IV*; and these exceptions weigh light against the rule. One, *Count Robert of Paris*, may be discounted as of small importance. The other, *The Heart of Midlothian*, sustains deliberately a train of allusion to a particular play, *Measure for Measure*, and thereby preserves a mood in which Scott's favourite quotations from *Henry IV* would sound discordant. For the greater part of these are taken not from the scenes at Westminster but those at Eastcheap, or Gadshill, or

---

[1] *Journal*, 11 Dec. 1826, p. 252.

Windsor, or in Gloucestershire; and the speakers are those who recur (they or their like) in *Henry V* and *The Merry Wives of Windsor*: Falstaff and his associates.

The qualities that drew Scott to Falstaff are easily discernible: not merely his wit and sheer gaiety, but also what is implied in Johnson's comment: 'Falstaff speaks like a veteran in life.'[1] His heart warms rather to the wary retort 'Indeed, I am not John of Gaunt your grandfather; but yet no coward, Hal',[2] than to the more dazzling sallies of effrontery. The rugged imperturbability of Corporal Nym likewise furnishes him with a favourite phrase: 'Things must be as they may.' But, if we hope to understand why it pleases him to assume the piping tones of Shallow, or Slender, we must ask in general terms: what indeed is it that makes someone—anyone—interject into his own prose a remembered line of poetry? A sudden glory?—the sense that a vivid experience or impression is heightened when it is matched with fit expression, and that, to this expression, reading and memory together hold the key? This is certainly possible, and may perhaps account for one or another of the occasions on which Scott uses a Shakespearian quotation to heighten the mood of some episode in his story, and fix our attention. *Lear* was a favourite play, and character, with him when he sought to express the pathos of a situation. ' "The little dogs and all!" ' Henry Morton murmurs, when he returns to find himself a stranger even to his own spaniel.[3] Sometimes the passage will call up a whole context of which the speaker seems unaware. There is irony of this sort in Redgauntlet's words to his nephew: ' "We have that before us which will brook no delay from indisposition—we have not, as Hotspur says, leisure to be sick." ' Words spoken by the rebel leader before Shrewsbury ('How has he leisure to be sick In such a justling time?'[4] he asks, of his father, whose holding back is to cost him the battle and his life)—these wake disturbing echoes; and, in the event, the hesitancy of his allies will prove fatal to Redgauntlet's attempt.

Examples such as these can be multiplied, but they will still remain in a minority. For a more numerous, and (I think) more

[1] Note on *2 Henry IV*, IV. vii (IV. iii. 85).
[2] *1 Henry IV*, II. ii. 64.
[3] *Old Mortality*, iv. 223 (Chapter XXXIX). *King Lear*, III. vi. 61.
[4] *Redgauntlet*, iii. 106 (Chapter XVII). *1 Henry IV*, IV. i. 17.

characteristic use of Shakespearian line or phrase some such explanation as this may be required. We are brought up to think shame of explicit reference to ourselves, but some particular occasion may call for it, and, against this need, most of us adopt a protective device—the use of a 'little language', reversion to an idiom which passed current when we were young and our world was smaller. At its worst, this deprecating use of language can be very awkward. At its best, it may fairly be described as a sort of delicate clowning. Now, Shakespearian quotation seems to have been a currency used by the young Scott and his friends, and it remained for him the 'little language' with which he guarded references to himself. As early as *Marmion*, he was writing (in an Introduction to the sixth Canto):

> How just that, at this time of glee,
> My thoughts should, Heber, turn to thee!
> For many a merry hour we've known,
> And heard the chimes of midnight's tone,
> As boasts old Shallow to Sir John.[1]

And the habit grew on him. A favourite way of curtailing an expression of poignant feeling (whether his own or that of one of his characters) was Edgar's aside, prompted by his father's misery: 'I cannot daub it further'. Inclination and custom were reinforced by circumstances. Every writer of fiction must surely look from time to time in a glass which shows him a double image: the man who passes among his fellows for a candid, single-minded companion—and the man who can assume many masks, and voices so different as those of Chaucer's Prioress, and Wife of Bath, and Pardoner. Scott liked to contrast his own character and course of life with those of the wayward, eccentric, even lawless people to whom his imagination was drawn. 'After all,' he somewhere observes, 'scribbling is an odd propensity.' It is no surprise, therefore, to come upon Prospero's wand as his chosen image for his own endowment. He was, moreover, increasingly aware of the sheer volume of what he published, and liked to shrug off uneasy consciousness by borrowing, again and again, from Dogberry: 'Truly, for mine own part, if I were as

---

[1] This line, present in the MS. but omitted from the printed text, makes the allusion explicit. (See *Miscellaneous Poetical Works*, 1834.)

tedious as a king, I could find it in my heart to bestow it all of your worship.'[1] Sometimes it amused him to give an opposite direction to a familiar passage. Thus, he has his own variation on poor Slender's answer to the question whether he can love Anne Page: 'I will marry her, at your request; but if there be no great love in the beginning, yet heaven may decrease it upon better acquaintance, when we are married and have more occasion to know one another.'[2] This he turns one way and another until Slender would hardly recognize his own words. Every variation on the passage carries a suggestion of rueful self-mockery. Scott knew himself for a man who, despite his good-nature in society and professed esteem for the opinion of his readers, would go his own way, and pay the price. Add to all these circumstances his pretence of anonymity, throughout the years 1814 to 1827, and the consciousness from January 1826 to the end of his life that many eyes were upon him, and it is easy to understand why he developed this 'little language', drawn for the most part from Shakespeare's ludicrous or disreputable characters, for use in referring to himself. But it was not only when he stood before others that he resorted to it. The *Journal* contains many such passages as this: 'Went over to Galashiels and was busied ... about a petty thieving affair and had before me a pair of gallows birds to whom I could say nothing for total want of proof except like the sapient Elbow, thou shalt continue, thou knave thou, thou shalt continue.'[3]

You cannot treat even a favourite author thus without knowing him in a particular way. I will not claim uncommon critical insight for Scott. His general views on drama were not remarkable, unless for remoteness from the theatre. Some of those on Shakespeare may surprise us: he surmised that Hamlet must be a very unsatisfactory part for an actor.[4] Though he pleaded gallantly and generously for toleration of the theatre, it is clear that he regarded play-going as a youthful taste and came to prefer reading the plays to seeing any performance. Nevertheless, his love of Shakespeare (which, he tells us, went back to his childhood) was deep, and his memory of what

---

[1] *Much Ado*, III. v. 20. [2] *Merry Wives*, I. i. 224–8.
[3] *Measure for Measure*, II. i. 181. *Journal*, 9 Jan. 1831, pp. 623–4.
[4] Review of Boaden's *Life of Kemble* for the *Quarterly*, Apr. 1826 (*Miscellaneous Prose Works*, xx. 176–7).

he loved was firm; and the kind of knowledge that these gave him proved a liberating force.

If we ask what it was that Shakespeare set Scott free to do for himself, the first thing that will come to mind is likely to be a commonplace of criticism: he taught him to ally history and romance. This will bear looking into. Has it ever been remarked that Scott may be said to reverse the usual process—that his history is romantic, his romance as scrupulously documented as other men's history? Historical figures—public personages known to all his readers—are handled very freely, made responsible for events that happened before they were born, and so on; but those persons who never appeared in history, who came to him from recollections gathered by word of mouth, or out of his own imagination, are minutely circumstantiated in the notes. What the two men had in common is best expressed in these phrases from the Chichester *Parallel*: a 'happy use of the scattered materials of history and tradition', of 'chronicles, tales, songs and popular works of the day', a 'power of appropriation'. In Scott these were conditioned by his antiquarian studies—the antiquary has always stood high in Scotland; but for him as for Shakespeare the historical theme took precedence of particular fact.

If I say that, under Shakespeare's protective shade, Scott, as writer of romances, learnt to *think historically*, the phrase may sound inflated—and, from one who is no historian, hollow. I can but hope to bring out the meaning little by little. First, it was urgently necessary that anyone who proposed to set his story in the past should be freed from the toils of false romance. When Diana Vernon warns Frank Osbaldiston that his jealous love is the mere stuff of 'playbooks and romances',[1] she conveys Scott's sense of the spurious conventions governing a whole realm of imaginative literature—one far removed from Shakespeare's plays. The most questionable alliance of history and romance, in the years before *Waverley*, was to be found in the so-called Gothic novels. To take their influence seriously may seem absurd, but the truth sometimes *is* absurd, at least in literary history. What is manifest tinsel, when seen in perspective, may well have appeared true gold to those who saw it for

[1] *Rob Roy*, ii. 79 (Chapter XVII).

the first time, and close at hand. So late as 1827, George Richmond could record, on a drawing he made of Samuel Palmer, that the group of young artists then gathered would, while they worked together, take turns to read aloud from 'Mrs. Radcliffe romances, Shakespeare, Milton, etc. . . .'—yes, in that order. Now, to set your story in the past should release reflective curiosity, prompt conjecture as to the *working* of time, its ferment and movement; but throughout these tales time stagnates. Everyone knows and laughs at the simplicity of Ann Radcliffe and her followers in making their heroines inhabit ruined castles and abbeys, and can point out that these must have been defensible, weatherproof—even garishly new —in the age supposedly represented. This is a blunder from which Scott's antiquarian knowledge alone would have preserved him. But there is a graver and more insidious error into which the want of historical thought and imagination betrays these fabricators of romance. It is not only in respect of the trappings of their tales that time stands still, as in a picture. To think historically, you must be curious about a process, that by which the past has given birth to the present. (I do not, of course, mean that you should seek for analogies and parallels—far less, force them.) These novelists point the danger of turning your back on your own age when you look at the past. Events in France had laid open before them the mingled ignominy and splendour of the European heritage—had brought to their very door the witnesses of these events, in the persons of refugees, members of the dispersed religious orders—as Scott reflects, in his Introductory Epistle to *The Monastery*. But they had contrived for themselves a peculiar combination of continental anti-clericalism with insular Protestantism, and, thus guarded against historical curiosity, saw the past as a sort of interlunar darkness as single and indivisible as that mysterious place, *abroad*—in which (for example) Roman Catholicism was endemic. Anything might happen; but nothing could ever grow, or develop.

Against such patent folly Scott was protected alike by upbringing and education, by antiquarian curiosity and a lawyer's sense of evidence. Nevertheless, to have recognized that the position of these writers was intellectually disreputable was not enough. It might have diverted him from the way they took; it could not have opened another road for him, and made him a great historical novelist. To foster greatness, something is required that can force upon the imagination a tremendous exertion; the impulse to call up a true image which will annihilate the false. It is by virtue of this powerful imaginative activity that Scott can show us—even in a medieval setting, where he is least at home—men who confront one another across a barrier of living issues. Where he is on his own ground, in *Waverley, Guy Mannering, The Antiquary, Old Mortality, The Heart of Midlothian*, and *Redgauntlet*, he can convey such a sense of the undertow of time and change as we shall find nowhere else but in Shakespeare's English history plays. His own acknowledgement of this kinship is so explicit that I am at a loss to choose among the many possible illustrations. I shall instance the first and last of the novels I have just mentioned, which may be seen as pendants or companion-pieces one to the other. Waverley, perplexed as to his allegiance, adapts a quotation from *King John*:

> 'Why did not I
> Unthread the rude eye of rebellion
> And welcome home again discarded faith,
> Seek out Prince Charles, and fall before his feet?'[1]

Redgauntlet, a man of opposite temper, asks his nephew whether he supposes any crucial event in history to have been willed by the participators. 'In doing and suffering, we play but the part allotted by Destiny, the manager of this strange drama, stand bound to act no more than is prescribed, to say no more than is set down for us; and yet we mouth about free-will, and freedom of thought and action, as if Richard must not die, or Richmond conquer, exactly where the Author has decreed it shall be so!'[2]

This kinship was not simply intellectual. Many critics have claimed to discover an affinity of temperament between Shakespeare and Scott, and certainly there is one epithet applied to both by those who knew them well. Ben Jonson more than once qualifies his censure by this same word 'gentle'. Lord Cockburn, outspoken and severely critical of his friend's opinions and transactions, concludes a tribute to his temper in this way: 'No man was so uniformly

---
[1] *Waverley*, ii. 169 (Chapter XXXIII); *King John* V. iv. 11–13.
[2] *Redgauntlet*, ii. 180 (Chapter VIII).

gentle.'[1] Allowing for some slight variation of meaning, this epithet is surely applicable to a man whose sympathies far outnumber his antipathies, who is able to enter into others' thoughts and feelings, even where these are mutually opposed. Neither Shakespeare nor Scott, we may surmise, liked an extremist, but the writer of the *Parallel* is on firm ground when he allows to both a capacity for putting a fair construction on opposite religious views, and finds but one frame of mind that antagonized Scott: 'dark, heartless and withering scepticism.' (If he had known the letters, he might have added the significant word 'misanthropy'.)

The circumstances of these two, superficially unlike, had indeed something in common. Scott, in the aftermath of civil disturbance, confessed to a divided heart. 'I became a valiant Jacobite at the age of ten years old,' he told Robert Surtees (in 1806), 'and, even since reason & reading came to my assistance, I have never quite got rid of the impression which the gallantry of Prince Charles made on my imagination'.[2] But in *Waverley* his hero reflects soberly on the disputed claim, and, even when his sense of ill-usage is sharpest and his love for Flora at its height, comes down on the side of established government.[3] (Waverley himself is surely as innocent as an American confronted with a dynastic crisis—or, I dare say, an Englishman with a Presidential election. We may therefore take much of what he learns as interpolated explanation by the author.) Of Shakespeare far less is known, but some things we dare affirm, and some we may fairly conjecture. With civil wars of factious nobles hardly left behind, and civil wars of religion just across the narrow seas, his generation cherished one resolution: that Englishmen should no longer engage in killing one another. It was not censorship alone, but also the temper of audience and players that determined what degree, and what kind, of provocation could be allowed on the stage; and that allowance was small, at least in respect of religious divisions. It is evident that few of the great nobles, who were the players' most effectual defence against Puritan zeal, or the Inns of Court men, who were their keenest and most articulate critics,

---

[1] *Journal of Henry Cockburn, being a continuation of the Memorials of his Time, 1831–1854*, 1874, i. 176.
[2] *Letters, 1787–1807*, p. 343.
[3] *Waverley*, ii. 87 (Chapter XXVIII).

wished to hear the old religion abused. (Papal interference, yes; but the plays are almost devoid of aspersions on individual members of the religious orders—which is remarkable in view of the ribald Italian tales from which so many were derived.) On the other hand, it was plainly unwise to antagonize popular sentiment and give occasion for the civic powers to intervene. Shakespeare's allusions to the overbearing ways of righteousness in office are not offensively particularized. This, it may be objected, tells us little about Shakespeare—unless, that he was a prudent man, and at pains to stand well with those on whom his livelihood depended. We can never hope, now, to separate those two unknown quantities, Shakespeare and his audience; but we have learnt, latterly, to desist from trying too hard, at least in one respect: we no longer charge them with all that we dislike in the plays. Why should we not assume substantial unanimity about some of the things we like—notably, this forbearance? I cannot believe that a man who had no thoughts in his head beyond supply and demand—or, if he had any, forced himself to suppress them—would have written the plays he wrote; for he would have been a dull man, or an unhappy one, hating himself for what he was about; and hatred is a sterile passion. I shall therefore take the liberty of supposing that the temper of his plays reflects his accord with the Elizabethan settlement and (if a bias is perceptible) a tenderness for some of the loyalties it replaced. There is no need to labour this parallel with Scott.

Now, if we believe that Scott found in Shakespeare a congenial temper and point of view, we have yet to ask what impetus the discovery gave to the development of his art. It seems probable that his reading, or misreading, of the plays, in the light of a critical theory that was already old-fashioned when he wrote his essay on *Drama*, lent boldness to his preference for improvisation. 'I hate the re-writing,' he confesses in the person of Chrystal Croftangry, 'as much as Falstaff did the paying back.'[1] And I have little doubt that he suspected Falstaff's author of this very disinclination. Incurious as to Elizabethan stage conditions (he seems to have been impatient of the work that went into Malone's *Variorum*), he was willing to attribute the alien structure of the plays to unpremeditated art and

[1] *1 Canongate*, i. 110 (Chapter V).

hasty workmanship. A particular device for which he censures Shakespeare, the use of a time-interval to bring about the happy ending,[1] must have seemed to him permissible in narration: he often avails himself of it—notably, in *Old Mortality*. And it was surely in Shakespeare's general practice that he found warrant for crowded, intricate plots, drawn together at the end by a lavish use of coincidence, change of heart in any character who could possibly be credited with it, and the sudden death of the intractable. *Cymbeline* yielded him few quotations, but he could have cited it in self-defence. He acknowledged with cordial praise the carefully laid plans of Fielding, but chose another way himself. 'Characters expand', he pleads, 'under my hand; incidents are multiplied; the story lingers, while the materials increase; my regular mansion turns out a Gothic anomaly, and the work is closed long before I have attained the point I proposed.'[2] Such admissions as this—and they are numerous—denote a sort of careless bounty, a crowding of the stage with characters, any one of whom may be summoned to put his shoulder to the wheel when the plot requires it. Now—to follow the metaphor a little further—Shakespeare and Scott may be said to pay these outriders in the same currency; they give them life out of all proportion to their intrinsic importance, and they give it by means of the words they put into their mouths. Surely we have all, at some time or other, been haunted by a Shakespearian quotation, challenged memory to produce the speaker, and been startled at getting for answer no more than *murderer* (a sizeable category this, among Shakespeare's professional characters), or gaoler, boatswain, constable—or merely lord, or gentleman. How sharply the utterance was individualized! 'I'll not meddle with [conscience]. . . It beggars any man that keeps it. It is turned out of towns and cities for a dangerous thing; and every man that means to live well endeavours to trust to himself and live without it'[3]— and yet this fellow has no title but 'second murderer', and was only required to kill Clarence and be done with it. Or the well-remembered words may be those of Perdita's foster-brother on gentility—and yet he is called simply 'clown'. Change the intonation of either passage but

---

[1] 'Essay on Drama' (*Miscellaneous Prose Works*, vi. 303).
[2] Introductory Epistle to *The Fortunes of Nigel*.   [3] *Richard III*, I. iv. 132.

a little, and it might be spoken by one of Scott's peripheral characters—but here my tongue takes fright, and I must leave it to you to recall his smugglers, gypsies, drovers, fishermen, crones—nameless, or named merely for the fun of it, like Mrs. Mucklewrath—and even slighter figures, lingering at cross-roads to be interrogated by his travellers: every one of them paid in this same coin of unforgettable words.

Of the acknowledged relationship between such characters as Davie Gellatley and Edie Ochiltree, and Shakespeare's fools and clowns, I shall say the less because Scott was here, as so often, not only the first but also his own best commentator. 'A strange guide this', thought Edward, 'and not much unlike one of Shakespeare's roynish clowns.'[1] And in the Magnum edition his encounter with Davie is followed by a circumstantial note on the practice of keeping fools in Scottish households. Edie Ochiltree calls forth a biographical account of his actual prototype, in the Preface to this edition, which includes the explicit comparison: 'He sung a good song, told a good story, and could crack a severe jest with all the acumen of Shakespeare's jesters, though without using, like them, the cloak of insanity.'[2] There is still room, however, for discrimination: their songs apart, Scott evidently preferred the more poetical fools, Feste above Touchstone, and Lear's fool beyond both. (He regretted his banishment from contemporary stage versions.)

Now, the inalienable heritage of these traditional characters was freedom: they could pass unchallenged between one group of persons and another; though they might be employed as messengers, they owed the plot no duty; their loyalties were an affair of instinct, not of contractual obligation, and they put no curb upon their tongues. What such characters could see, they saw clearly and told outright. Thus they are able to speak directly to us, whether in a passage of intuitive wisdom: 'Our riches will soon be equal',[3]—or of sly insight: 'The Baillie used sometimes gently to rally Mr. Rubrick, upbraiding him with the nicety of his scruples. Indeed, it must be owned, that he himself, though at heart a keen partisan of the exiled family, had kept pretty fair with all the different turns

---

[1] *Waverley*, i. 120 (Chapter IX).   [2] *The Antiquary*, 1829, i, p. xiv.
[3] *The Antiquary*, i. 160 (Chapter VII).

of state in his time; so that Davie Gellatley once described him as a particularly good man, who had a very quiet and peaceful conscience, *that never did him any harm.*[1] In a flash we see the pattern of affairs that Scott has been building up, throughout those leisurely opening chapters.

I believe that one condition governs this traffic in character-types between playwright and novelist: only where they have their counterparts within Scott's own experience is it altogether fruitful and happy. In these instances, the gesture with which he recalls their Shakespearian forebears signifies acknowledgement of kinship rather than indebtedness. Not that Scott's shoulders were ever bowed by this sort of debt; but he seems to me least felicitous when he is borrowing simply to fill a void. Does he ever succeed with his girls in disguise, or are they little better than an expedient? While they are still in the thick of adventures, the trick may pass—though there is a suspicion, even here, of Shakespeare's sun glimmering through the inferior stained glass of Beaumont and Fletcher, as though Scott were, for once, not fully awake to the difference between the real thing and the imitation; but he is evidently uneasy when the tale is told and he must restore these heroines to their proper station in life. The Elizabethan stage had afforded a convention which no one was expected to regard as life-like: boy-actor into heroine into page, returning to heroine for the happy ending, and boy-actor for the epilogue. Stripped of this make-believe, such characters are not easy to accommodate within a conclusion which, for Scott, always means a return to peaceful conditions and signifies the restoration of family life. He seems to hold uncertainly in reserve the prospect of retirement into some unspecified religious order. Was Diana Vernon *intended* to return and marry Frank? Has not the end of *Rob Roy* an air of shame-faced improvisation? I suspect that, if Scott had written *As You Like It*, Celia would have married Orlando, and Rosalind would have devoted herself to the care of a father whose health was found to have been impaired by his sojourn in the Forest.

Look now at the contrast between these shadowy persons and a group of characters whose counterparts were readily available. Both

[1] *Waverley*, i. 140 (Chapter XI).

SCOTT AND SHAKESPEARE

Scott and Shakespeare seem to have warmed to a pedant. Scott liked the company of men engrossed in their profession, to whom its very terms were meat and drink; and what is a pedant but a man who has carried this happy preoccupation over an ill-defined frontier into a region where his own values admit no question? For the military pedant, Shakespeare offered a precedent, and eighteenth-century Scotland examples: professional soldiers versed in 'the true disciplines of the wars' under famous commanders abroad and baffled by the methods of fighting among their own countrymen. Scott saluted Fluellen when he made Waverley borrow Henry V's tribute for his own eulogy of the Baron of Bradwardine[1]—whom it fits but loosely. Fluellen's true lineal descendant does not appear until he rides his old charger, Gustavus, into *The Legend of Montrose*, refers every decision to 'the articles of war', and puts all the other characters to flight (like ghosts at cock-crow) by his superior authenticity. And this is the heart of the matter: Scott had known the original Major Dalgetty for as long as he had known Fluellen.[2]

Here I mean—with your good will, I hope—to skirt the district that lies directly ahead: the high-road of my argument leads straight towards those novels in which Scott deliberately traced a parallel between the story of one of Shakespeare's plays and events related to him as having happened in his familiar world—*The Bride of Lammermoor* and *The Heart of Midlothian*; but I shall pass them by. The subject has been much canvassed already. Furthermore, *The Bride of Lammermoor* does not seem to me truly representative either of Scott, or of Shakespeare's influence upon him: not only was he a very sick man when he wrote it; he was oppressed by the crude opiates which were all that contemporary medicine had to offer, and *Romeo and Juliet* took possession of his imagination in much the same manner as a recent experience makes part of a feverish dream. True, the situation of Isabel in *Measure for Measure* and its likeness to the first part of Helen Walker's story worked upon his waking mind and liberated what was most characteristic, and most veracious, in his imagination; but I have elsewhere developed this comparison, and, like someone who has served as juryman on

[1] *Waverley*, ii. 356 (Chapter XLVI).
[2] Lockhart, i. 18 (see also *Journal*, 27 June 1830, p. 602).

a long-drawn-out case, would plead exemption.[1] Besides, another theme draws me strongly.

This therefore is the contention which must conclude my argument: that Shakespeare and Scott are comparable in virtue of an endowment they share—in what measure, we need not now inquire. Each can command more than one language. I do not mean that they can make shift to give appropriate speech to their several characters; this is the least we ask of dramatist or novelist. What I have in mind can be indicated, at the outset, by a bare reference to the interplay of verse and prose commanded by the one, of English and Scots by the other. Not that I would set out to establish a symmetrical *correspondence*—for example, of Shakespearian verse with the intrinsically poetic language of such characters as Meg Merrilies, on the one hand, of Scott's passages of humdrum English with Shakespeare's prose, on the other. It will never make sense. Some of the prose in the plays (Shylock's, Rosalind's, Falstaff's) sets up the very same response in us as the poetry, whereas some of the verse is merely a workmanlike means of accomplishing a journey—a good nag for the road. Hamlet is master of both languages, and uses them indifferently. Familiar assumptions are turned upside-down when Brutus, delivering a formal oration, uses prose, and Antony speaks in apparently informal verse. And by no means all of the snatches of song are poetry. Only this is certain: Shakespeare has the freedom of both realms, and the art of passing to and fro, not only between scene and scene but even within a passage of dialogue; and there is no telling on whom he will bestow the gift of poetic utterance.

We are a long way from the world of eighteenth-century drama, which (to my eye, at least) is a sad and shabby place: the servants (and there *are* no other persons in humble station) seem to wear their master's cast-off clothes, and speak a corresponding language. There is a passage in Sheridan's *Critic* which amused Scott.

Sneer—But, Mr. Puff, I think not only the Justice, but the clown seems to talk in as high a style as the first hero among them.

Puff—Heaven forbid they should not, in a free country!—Sir, I am not for making slavish distinctions, and giving all the fine language to the upper sort of people.[2]

[1] See Mary Lascelles, *Shakespeare's 'Measure for Measure'*, 1953.   [2] III. i.

Now, whereas Sheridan is laughing at the conventions of earlier poetic drama, Scott is laughing *with* the poets, and turning his broad back alike on their successors, and on such novelists as Horace Walpole. It has been alleged that his humble characters speak well, his ladies and gentlemen ill, and that this division corresponds with his use of the idiom that came naturally to his tongue and of an English that he had learnt from books, for the one and the other. But this is too simple an explanation altogether. Within each of the two broad categories there are numerous variations—most numerous, I am given to understand, in the Scots; and their interplay is unpredictable. Many, but not all, of the eloquent speeches and the quick turns of humour are in Scots—but then, so is the talk of those characters who are not only prosaic but downright prosy. The songs of his own making (all but a few) sing themselves alike to your ears and mine—while some of the popular snatches are no more lyrical than the doggerel of Lear's fool. The Judge's speech in *The Two Drovers* is proof of the eloquence he has at his call in formal English; many passages of reflection and sentiment (Oldbuck's, for example) will return a true echo if uttered in either intonation; and his descriptive prose when he is deeply stirred (when armed forces are mustering before his mind's eye, for example) is classic in the true sense—not bookish, but simply good. And whatever bounty may be in his gift is *at his free disposal*: he can, and does, bestow it where he pleases—or, perhaps, where his imagination is awake and exacts his utmost endeavour from him. That, very often, is where Shakespeare's benign and liberating influence is at work.

II. SCOTT AND THE SENSE OF TIME

Before I pass on to explore the sense of time that is peculiar to Scott's writings, I must try to measure an apparent contrast between *his* response to the flight of years, and Shakespeare's. Apparent—a difference certainly exists; but how deep does it strike, and what does it signify?

Both (I have suggested) were sensible of this motion of time in the historic past. Both, therefore, saw man as a creature subject to its power; but they recognized also a stubborn, intractable resolve in each one of us to leave his mark, a conviction that (whatever may have befallen others) he will be able to make it ineffaceable. In Shakespeare's Sonnets (virtually overlooked by Scott) this is a predominant theme. Time is arraigned as the implacable enemy of beauty. This was, admittedly, a poetic convention of the age, and there was unimpeachable precedent for it. 'Devouring time', in the nineteenth sonnet, was evidently intended to recall Ovid—and was not the only echo. Indeed, this very sonnet crowns a series of which the argument is the transience of personal beauty. But in those that follow, not only is there stronger insistence on the poet's defiance of 'tyrant time', there is also, accompanying this most ancient claim, a note of authority, 'a Horatian resonance', Mr. Leishman calls it,[1] powerful enough to transcend what is conventional in it. This is very clear in Sonnet 55:

> Not marble, nor the gilded monuments
> Of princes shall outlive this powerful rhyme,
> But you shall shine more bright in these contents
> Than unswept stone, besmeared with sluttish time.

Time as the destroyer not only of the man, but even of the object that was meant to preserve remembrance of him; great verse triumphantly outlasting mere material objects—here indeed is poetic authority issuing, as though from the royal mint, poetical commonplace—but is there not also something unique, distinct from the common currency of poetry on this traditional theme? I find neither convention nor make-believe in those words which convey dismay at the manner of destruction—'unswept stone, besmeared with sluttish time'. An image of remarkable particularity is offered to the mind's eye. For me, at least, the line evokes the experience of looking at a monumental inscription in a ruined building—the writing illegible through the sheer dirt that accumulates once the roof is gone. Moreover, in that other half of our experience which we receive from the spoken or the written word, it wakes an echo: travellers' descriptions of Iona, in the eighteenth and nineteenth centuries; in particular, Johnson's conclusion: 'The graves are very numerous, and some of them undoubtedly contain the

---

[1] J. B. Leishman, 'Variations on a Theme in Shakespeare's Sonnets', in *Elizabethan and Jacobean Studies presented to F. P. Wilson*, 1959, p. 118.

remains of men, who did not expect to be so soon forgotten.'[1] How are we to explain the equanimity with which Scott, surveying the same monuments, wrote to Joanna Baillie, 'The ruins are of a rude architecture but curious to the Antiquary'[2]—unless we suppose the antiquary to be a man happily conscious that the stuff in his cellar improves with keeping? Though it may well seem like reposing too much weight on a mere coincidence of phrase, I will yet affirm that Shakespeare's 'The noble ruin of her magic, Antony' is no more fortuitous than Scott's note on the Castle of Doune: 'This noble ruin is dear to my recollection.'[3] Shakespeare (who uses the word *ruin* so often for human decline, whether of life or fortunes) could no more have joined it to a favourable epithet *without* intending irony than Scott could have brought them together *with* ironical intention.

What was it that made Scott, as a boy, dwell delightedly on 'the ruins of an ancient Abbey—the more distant vestiges of Roxburgh Castle', as he confesses in the Ashestiel fragment of autobiography?[4] In one of those sadly undervalued Introductions to the Cantos of *Marmion* (the third), he records the enduring impress of his early delight in ruins: tells how the lame child scrambled over mounds of close cropped turf and weathered masonry to find the cranny where flowers had taken root; how, more than thirty years later, the man looked back—

> And still I thought that shatter'd tower
> The mightiest work of human power.

The child had peopled it with

> ... forayers who, with headlong force,
> Down from that strength had spurr'd their horse,
> Their southern rapine to renew,
> Far in the distant Cheviots blue. ...

The man is still bound by the 'viewless chain' of recollection.

If we are to understand this reaction to the sight of ruined buildings, we must take many factors into the reckoning. We shall have to recall some picture of Poussin, or Claude: the heroic monument,

[1] *A Journey to the Western Islands of Scotland*, 1775, p. 353.
[2] *Letters, 1808–1811*, p. 360.
[3] Note in Magnum *Waverley*, 1829, Chapter XXXVII.   [4] Lockhart, ch. 1.

tomb of the once mighty, the now helpless, dead; the shepherds, unimportant but alive, resting in its shade, some spelling out the inscription, some with their backs to it; the melancholy that pervades the scene but has nothing to do with grief. The poets had been at the same ploy. Painters and poets together had brought about a change in the seeing eye, in the total response to the thing seen.

There are, besides, to any observer, ruins—and ruins. Shakespeare must have known abbeys made over to the townspeople, who, hitherto pent up in a part of the building, vented their sense of ill-usage by pulling down what they reckoned superfluous—and letting the weather into what they kept. Tewkesbury he must have known, and its history partially corresponds with this common pattern. On the other hand, time and weather can be kind—at least aesthetically—to some human memorials, such as those 'grassy barrows of the happier dead', on which Tennyson's Tithonus looked longingly down from his celestial prison. These forces had worked a beneficent change on Dryburgh Abbey, as Scott knew it. Destruction no longer wore its harshest aspect. That he distinguished very sharply between one ruin and another is plain from his mordant description of the derelict house, in the Introductory to *Chronicles of the Canongate*: it is bad, not so much because the scars are still raw, as because it never was good. Newly built, it was merely 'a huge lumping four-square pile of freestone'.[1] Decay cannot give pathos to what never had dignity. 'I went up to the house', says Chrystal Croftangry, the returned spendthrift, who knows that, but for his folly, it would not have replaced his former home. 'It was in that state of desertion which is perhaps the most unpleasant to look on, for the place was going to decay, without having been inhabited. There were about the mansion, though deserted, none of the slow mouldering touches of time, which communicates to buildings, as to the human frame, a sort of reverence, while depriving them of beauty and strength. The disconcerted schemes of the Laird of Castle-Treddles had resembled fruit that becomes decayed without ever having ripened... Desolation, in short, was where enjoyment had never been.'[2] (I am sorry to say that the only other reference

[1] *1 Canongate*, i. 52 (Chapter III).   [2] Ibid. 53–4.

I can recollect, in all Scott's writings, to a decayed building unredeemed by traces of architectural merit is that in *Rob Roy* to the older Oxford colleges.)

Let none of these particular observations lead us to suppose that Scott was content with a sentimental or an aesthetic reaction to evidence of change. It could stir him deeply; and this graver response does not coincide with any difference in himself: it does not come as he passes from youth and unthinking delight to age and reflection; nor with a decline in his circumstances. Some of the saddest words he ever wrote about the kind of change that troubled his heart and conscience were written in 1806 and 1815, when the world went well with him. There are many factors to be taken into account, but his own circumstances rank low among them.

It is time, however, to set the argument on a base of common experience. We apprehend the passage of time and the changes it works as a sort of motion. We are therefore wakened to particular attention when the pace is altered, especially by acceleration. But we are all the while conscious of this motion in terms of loss and renewal. For most of us, the sense of renewal is bound up with the recurring pattern made by the seasons; if we grew up in the country, by husbandry and field sports. For a countryman, Scott has surprisingly little of this seasonal pattern in his writings—at least, in the novels; there is slightly more weather in the verse romances, much more in the letters and journal. What is the time of year in *Rob Roy*? The young Osbaldistons are fox-hunting when Frank arrives; but, after an interval which seems of no great duration, he walks out into the garden to enjoy the scent of July flowers. Within a few days of this, he sets out for Glasgow, leaves it presently on a 'harvest morning', is involved in a succession of wintry journeys; and yet, when he enters the MacGregor country, the crops (of barley and oats) are still standing, and by the time he returns to Glasgow the Earl of Mar has raised his standard. This happened on the sixth of September. In *Redgauntlet* there is indeed a pattern imposed on the story by the rhythm of the natural world: the pattern of the Solway tides. Darsie, ignorant of their action, is nearly drowned by one. Alan must make his way among the smugglers by passwords which refer to them: 'What age is the moon? A plague of all Aberdeen almanacks!'[1] Nanty Ewart's movements are, of course, controlled by the state of the tides—which will, in the final crisis, determine the plans of the fugitives. But these references seem designed to fix place rather than time, and the movement to and fro carries no suggestion of the revolution and renewal of the seasons.

There *is* a pattern of renewal which is very clear and strong in Scott's thought: that of the family. No need to call the witness of his life, or quote the letters in which it is documented. But a few intimations scattered amongst his imaginative writings may be worth drawing together. It is explicit in the Introduction to the sixth Canto of *Marmion*:

> ... Still, within our valleys here,
> We hold the kindred title dear,
> Even when, perchance, its far-fetch'd claim
> To Southron ears sounds empty name...

Guy Mannering is knit together by this theme: the restoration of the fallen house of Ellangowan can only be accomplished by the true heir who, stolen away as a child, has been rescued from its fall. And, characteristically, Scott rounds on himself and gives a humorous twist to this favourite notion, in *The Antiquary*: 'There was always some idle story', Oldbuck says, 'of the room being haunted by the spirit of Aldobrand Oldenbuck, my great-great-great-grandfather—it's a shame to the English language that we have not a less clumsy way of expressing a relationship, of which we have occasion to think and speak so frequently'.[2]

Nevertheless, it seems to me that change regarded as loss dominates change regarded as renewal, throughout Scott's writings. This would seem to argue a tragic vision of life, and no one familiar with the songs would deny his quality as a tragic poet. But the argument cannot be so simply stated. Loss touches us all through the death of friends. It is surely significant that the Ashestiel fragment and *Marmion* were written in the same year. Any attempt at autobiography stirs this deep pool, in the stream of recollection, and the Introductions to the several Cantos, all in some way retrospective,

[1] ii. 289–90 (Chapter XII). [2] i. 206 (Chapter IX).

SCOTT AND THE SENSE OF TIME

are many of them elegiac. Scott's response to such loss as this was wholehearted, and expressed without stint in the letters; but he was not the sort of man to dwell on sorrow: the living had claims on him, and life must go forward. Moreover, in the novels, he was chary of such a subject, approaching it almost bashfully.

There is, however, another kind of loss, in common life: that of which we are sensible within ourselves. This is an experience to which Scott frequently recurs. Oldbuck, instinctively warming to Lovel, refers to 'an early and unhappy attachment', and the power of a particular place to recall it. He continues: 'It is at such moments as these . . . that we feel the changes of time. The same objects are before us—those inanimate things which we have gazed on in wayward infancy and impetuous youth, in anxious and scheming manhood—they are permanent and the same; but when we look upon them in cold unfeeling old age, can we, changed in our temper, our pursuits, our feelings—changed in our form, our limbs, and our strength—can we be ourselves called the same? Or do we not rather look back with a sort of wonder upon our former selves, as beings separate and distinct from what we now are?'[1] In the opening to the last chapter of *Woodstock* (which is, like many of his endings, an epilogue following on a time-interval) Scott speaks in his own person: 'Years rush by us like the wind. We see not whence the eddy comes, nor whitherward it is tending, and we seem ourselves to witness their flight without a sense that we are changed; and yet Time is beguiling man of his strength, as the winds rob the woods of their foliage.' Now, in his review of Jane Austen's *Emma*,[2] Scott contrasts the sense of time as we experience it with conventional representation of it in the novel. The passage is long and the language perhaps too figurative for its purpose—Scott is, as so often, *writing himself in*—but the gist of the argument is this. The lives of ordinary people often end where they began: 'the individual grows old among the characters with whom he was born'. 'The man of mark and adventure', on the other hand, leaves behind as he makes his way through life those with whom circumstances have from

[1] i. 211 (Chapter X).
[2] *Quarterly Review*, Oct. 1815. This review was not included in the *Miscellaneous Prose Works*.

time to time associated him; his life forms a record of which he is himself the only connecting link. The symmetrically-built novel, however, falsifies this distinction: takes the outstanding man, but weaves a close pattern into which are gathered, at the end, all who have, in the course of the story, had anything to do with him. Yet this is surely Scott's own practice, except in the (nearly tragic) tale of Chrystal Croftangry? Was not the prevailing bias of his imagination, as distinct from his observation, towards conventional tragicomedy, whose waters, like those of a fountain, play for a while in the air, only to return, as clear as ever, to the basin from which they seemed to rise? To this I would answer: Scott's novels (in contrast to his short stories) are never all of a piece. At the formal centre, caught in that circle of strong, unflattering light by which Scott directs attention towards his plot, are his heroes, heroines, and villains. We can be sure that all these will meet their deserts in the timeless world of tragicomedy. Gathered in the surrounding half-light, whose play often lures the eye away from that centre, are characters variously compounded of imagination and observation; and, when these powers are happily conjoined, such characters feel poignantly, and convey disturbingly, a sense of the working of time, and the air is thick with unanswered questions. What had drawn Scott, in the first place, to fiction was a piece of unflinching observation. Something that he saw, and some of the conjectures to which it gave rise, fascinated and troubled his imagination; and the record of his life-long concern with these, chequered with hopes and fears, is woven into the tales, the letters, the Journal, and Lockhart's narrative.

We have hitherto been considering two matters: the impact on the imagination (Shakespeare's and Scott's, in particular) made by some relic of the past which conveys a reminder of what time has engulfed—not individuals only, but whole generations; and the impact of our recognition of its present power over our own individual selves, and others like us. We have now to seek Scott's reaction to the *present* force of time and change operating on a whole civilization. The experiences themselves are distinct—no matter (as yet) whether any question arises of transmuting either into the stuff of art. It is one thing to survey a prehistoric burial mound and

SCOTT AND THE SENSE OF TIME

wonder at the traces of human life which lie, layer below layer, under the turf the sheep are grazing; it is quite another, looking at regimental colours laid up in a cathedral, to wonder whether we shall be the last generation to whom they signify anything.

For an intent observer of change, Scott was, in one respect, favourably placed: acceleration was sufficient to catch his eye, not rapid enough to baffle vision. It was his lot, he says, in the last chapter of *Waverley* ('A Postscript, which should have been a Preface'), to pass his childhood and youth among Jacobites, people belonging to a vanished world. 'And now, for the purpose of preserving some idea of the ancient manners of which I have witnessed the almost total extinction, I have embodied in imaginary scenes, and ascribed to fictitious characters, a part of the incidents which I then received from those who were actors in them. Indeed, the most romantic parts of this narrative are precisely those which have a foundation in fact.' But the ambition was deeper rooted than this would imply; in the same year he wrote to Morritt: 'It was a very old attempt of mine to embody some traits of those characters and manners peculiar to Scotland the last remnants of which vanished during my own youth so that few or no traces remain.'[1] Moreover, when he came to write the *General Preface* to the Waverley Novels in 1829, he told the same tale:

> I had been a good deal in the Highlands at a time when they were much less accessible, and much less visited, than they have been of late years, and was acquainted with many of the old warriors of 1745, who were, like most veterans, easily induced to fight their battles over again, for the benefit of a willing listener like myself. It naturally occurred to me, that the ancient traditions and high spirit of a people, who, living in a civilised age and country, retained so strong a tincture of manners belonging to an early period of society, must afford a subject favourable for romance, if it should not prove a curious tale marred in the telling.[2]

These accounts of his initial and abiding interest in the vision of a world where the Jacobite, or Highlander, might be living in one century, the Whig, or Lowlander, in another, while they are remarkably consistent, have not the air of a tale repeated by rote: and

[1] *Letters, 1812–1814*, p. 457.   [2] i, p. x.

Lord Cockburn's comment on the Ashestiel fragment, when the first volume of Lockhart appeared, confirms this impression: 'Scott's own account of his early years is admirable. No man ever traced the sources of his own mental peculiarities more satisfactorily.'[1]

Does all this sound too detached, too coolly observant of the thing observed and of the observer's reaction to it? Remember the letter which Scott wrote in 1806 to Lord Dalkeith, comparing the decline of Highland life with changes that had already taken place on the Border. He fears that *this* process may be more rapid and destructive than the other, since he can see nothing 'to balance the Landlords natural desire to make the most he could of his property except the pride of some individuals & the compassion of others'. And the consequence will be a desolation like that in a Border valley, where, for a hundred former landowners, each with his dependents, 'I think . . . we cannot now find ten'.

I have often heard my Grandmother & other old people talk of the *waefu*' year when seven Lairds of the Forest (all Scotts) became bankrupt at once but how or why I know not. The farmers when they had got rid of the inactive retainers of the small proprietors seem to have gone on for a long time reducing the number of the people on their farms. The ruins of cottages about every farm-house in the country show that this last cause of depopulation continued to operate till a very late period & indeed within the memory of Man. I could name many farms where the old people remember twenty *smoking chimneys* & where there are now not two.[2]

The echo of that phrase some nine years later, in *Guy Mannering*, shows what it meant to Scott. Remember also the concluding passage in his review of *The Culloden Papers* for the January number of the *Quarterly*, 1816, which foreshadows David Stewart's *Sketches of the . . . Highlanders of Scotland*, a work he was to acclaim. For the first phase of the decline in the feudal system (as it obtained in the Highlands) he borrows a congenial poetic image:

                Time
Has mouldered into beauty many a tower,
Which, when it frown'd with all its battlements,
Was only terrible.

[1] Op. cit. i. 134.   [2] *Letters 1787–1807*, p. 333.

But the pace of change, he argues, increased too soon and too much. No time has been allowed for the assimilation of a primitive to a progressive society. Emigration has carried off, not the superfluous, but the total population. 'The Highlands may become the fairy ground for romance and poetry, or subject of experiment for the professors of speculation, political and economical. But if the hour of need should come—and it may not, perhaps, be far distant— the pibroch may sound through the deserted region, but the summons will remain unanswered.'[1]

This was not all. By analogy with changes he had seen and in some sort approved, beyond the Highland line, Scott came to fear change that he could not approve. Not every civilization, he discerned, is destroyed by sudden calamity and violence. There may be a process of assimilation. I cannot recollect an expression of this fear in his published writings. Perhaps he cared too much. That it more than once broke from him in speech, we have on Lockhart's authority.

To consider whether this apprehension was well grounded is beyond my province. I have neither the knowledge nor the historical training. I pass with relief to illustrate the influence which Scott's consciousness of time and change exercised on his art.

He recognized that we have a capacity for living in the past, emotionally: our own remembered past, and also (if that is the way we have grown up) in the past as it was handed down to us in childhood by the preceding generation. He himself knew the circumstances in which this was most likely to impinge on present consciousness. Those whose past contains an experience of greater significance than anything that is likely ever to happen to them again move to another rhythm than those who are wholly engrossed in the present. Now, in the first and last of the great Scottish novels, *Waverley* and *Redgauntlet*, he confronts us with a world in which the very motion of men's lives is differentiated, according as they estimate the significance of a particular past event. For some of the people in *Waverley*, happenings in 1715, had, so to speak, stopped the clock; for some of the people in *Redgauntlet*, it was stopped in 1745. What made this differentiation remarkable, and therefore

[1] *Miscellaneous Prose Works*, xx. 92–3.

good material for narrative art, was that, at least in England and the Lowlands, those who were thus divided in thought and feeling might be living together as neighbours, bound by varying degrees of mutual dependence and obligation. Moreover, the conflict had engaged some whom we are not accustomed to think of as combatants: it was not only the men of war who were liable to find themselves proscribed, withdrawn from the current of active life; among the learned professions, in the Law and the Church, the same proscription operated. In those two placid-seeming households of Sir Everard Waverley and the Baron of Bradwardine, a clerical figure without a cure of souls reminds us of unresolved differences. The Baron himself must squander his energies in abstruse and eccentric studies, and, as Flora stiffly observes, keep uncongenial company, for the sake of his principles.[1] How much more satisfactory an explanation of idiosyncrasy this affords than Jonathan Oldbuck's private sorrow! One is part of the very stuff of which the story is built, the other has to be diligently worked into the plot. Even Edward Waverley may not complete his education abroad, for fear of finding himself at the Court of Saint-Germain—which makes his subsequent political innocence the more surprising.

Now, in this respect *Redgauntlet* is even better built than *Waverley*. I admit that there is much unashamed improvisation. The device of the novel-in-letters is taken up, relinquished, resumed, at the mere whim of the narrator. (Jane Austen, a woman who certainly knew her own mind, gave the method a fair and thorough trial and then left it behind.) Moreover, these letters exchanged between Darsie and Alan are, as George Gordon pointed out,[2] some of the least plausible ever devised for a novelist's purpose: why (for example) should Darsie so frequently tell Alan, a boy born and bred in Edinburgh, what they call this or that little thing, north of the Border—but that Scott has an English reader in mind? Admit this, and much more. Something impressive remains.

First, consider the date at which the story is set. Scott is reduced to sleight of hand here: his plot requires that all this should happen

---

[1] *Waverley*, i. 352 (Chapter XXIII).
[2] '*Redgauntlet*', *Scott Centenary Articles*, 1932, p. 148, reprinted from *T.L.S.* 4 Sept. 1924.

SCOTT AND THE SENSE OF TIME 207

some twenty years after the Forty-five, for it is necessary that Darsie, a grown man, should not have known his father; but the latest recorded visit of the Prince would not allow this. Scott gets by with two or three carefully imprecise and mutually contradictory time-references. Thus, the story can open in a world which appears to the two young men to consist of a present and future independent of the past; and so carefully has Darsie's mother chosen his guardians that his acceptance of the Hanoverian succession as a thing of course is much more credible than Edward Waverley's. His romantic wanderings open to him (and to the reader, who is usually a step ahead) a world based on no such assumption, and Alan's adventures in pursuit of him repeat the tale more circumstantially. By means of a series of encounters, many of them less fortuitous than they seem, the two friends learn that men are still living on the eve of a crucial day which they themselves had forgotten, the day that will settle a disputed claim which they had never supposed to be still at issue.

Darsie's first notable encounter is that with the blind fiddler, Willie Steenson, who, as a child, was reared in the house of old Sir Redwald Redgauntlet—a reference which makes no immediate personal impact on the young man; the secret that he is himself Sir Redwald's grandson is well kept; but the reader begins to divine something, at least in the conclusion of Willie's tale: 'Mony a merry year was I wi' him! but waes me! he gaed out with other pretty men in the forty-five—I'll say nae mair about it—My head never settled weel since I lost him.'[1] For Willie, the clock stopped in that year—as it must, for many, in time of war. Presently, Darsie is kidnapped by a formidable stranger—or so he supposes. This man, Hugh Redgauntlet, his father's younger brother, has himself put out a hand to the clock: resolved that time shall stand still until Darsie is of an age to play the part for which he has cast him, and reverse that decision of 1745, he has decreed that his clock shall not be rewound before the appointed hour. He will live in a time-interval of his own making rather than come to terms with a world which has gone on its way since his brother's death.

Meanwhile, Alan's quest has brought him to the house of Provost Crosbie—a staunch and wary Whig, but married to a fourth cousin

[1] *Redgauntlet*, i. 263 (Letter XI).

of the house of Redgauntlet, and an old friend of Maxwell, Laird of Summertrees, whom he recommends to Alan as an intermediary between himself and the Jacobite gentry, and one who may (he will not commit himself) know what has become of Darsie.

'An old forty-five man, of course?' said Alan Fairford.

'Ye may swear that,' replied the Provost—'as black a Jacobite as the auld leaven can make him. . . . You would have thought, if he had had but his own way at Derby, he would have marched Charlie Stuart through between Wade and the Duke, as a thread goes through the needle's ee, and seated him in St. James's before you could have said haud your hand. But though he is a windy body when he gets on his auld warld stories, he has mair gumption in him than most people—knows business, Mr. Alan, being bred to the law; but never took the gown, because of the oaths, which kept more folk out then than they do now—the more's the pity.'[1]

So there is another way of keeping faith with the past by refusal to be reconciled to the present. Maxwell appears and, warmed by the Provost's punch and Mrs. Crosbie's tacit admission of Jacobite sympathies, needs little persuasion to tell again the tale of his escape in '45—and put his shoulder to the wheel of the plot by affording clues to Darsie's secret. Time remembered may now be likened to an atmosphere which some of the people of the story require, if they are to continue breathing. When the tale is done, Crosbie proposes the toast:

'Here is to your good health; and may you never put your neck in such a venture again.'

'Humph!—I do not know', answered Summertrees. 'I am not like to be tempted with another opportunity—Yet who knows?' And then he made a deep pause.[2]

Presently, the threads are drawn firmly together. Here, surely, *Waverley* is surpassed. To extricate his former hero from the predicament into which he had brought himself, Scott had used a train of accidents, coincidences, and characters summoned from Limbo for the purpose. But as, throughout *Redgauntlet*, we have been sensible of the action of time, so, at the climax, we come to recognize it as

[1] ii. 224 (Chapter X). [2] ii. 254 (Chapter XI).

the prime agent. For the conspirators, the long awaited hour strikes; but it is already too late. Darsie, who was to have joined them in reversing the decision of twenty years ago, is present merely as a reluctant witness. It begins to be evident that the Jacobite gentry whom Redgauntlet has assembled do not share his implacable mood. The stranger round whom they are gathered remains a stranger, even when he discloses himself: this is no longer the man they knew. And, at the crucial moment, General Campbell walks unarmed into their midst, and intimates that, if the unlawful assembly now dissolves, constituted authority will regard it as never having occurred. (What is an *act of oblivion* but agreement to write off the past?) Redgauntlet recognizes this clemency as a mortal stroke. To all appearances, the conspirators, who have been thwarted by dissension among themselves and the treachery of an agent, are the victims of a few hours' delay. But the long, shuddering sigh of relief which comes from all the rest betrays the truth: they are many years too late. Time has not waited on human will. Those who have chosen to live in the past are of the past—ghosts surprised by daylight. It is a ghostly company, that, with General Campbell's discreet connivance, makes its way to the shore, to the waiting boat, and the brig that—again at the General's bidding—is standing off for *one more tide.*

These same circumstances, and even more notably the gifts that enabled him to turn them to account, afforded Scott a further opportunity. As they had given depth through the gravity of historical reference—the sense of serious issues attending on the action —so they gave it through distance—the sense of time intervening between the events and the narrator. Many novelists have chosen to present a story through the mind of an imaginary character, as though by refraction in water. If the character is complex, the events gain interest; if he is simple or sly, we please ourselves with the notion that we discern more in them than he can tell, or is willing to admit. Scott seems to have wanted either the patience required for sustained impersonation or the imperturbable detachment which makes Maria Edgeworth's *Castle Rackrent* unique. In a short-breathed tale like Wandering Willie's, or a fragment of autobiography like Nanty Ewart's, or the incidental reminiscences of Chrystal Croftangry, he is hard to match. His employment of Frank Osbaldiston as narrator, however, must be reckoned a failure. Everything about this story cries out for the use of the third person—a kindly intermediary, of an older generation, who will distance the follies of his coxcomb hero, as those of Edward Waverley are distanced, and softened.

Nevertheless, it may fairly be claimed that all Scott's best stories, long and short alike, are tales of a grandfather. He likes to filter them through memory, sometimes of more than one person. He can try us high when he uses this process as a way of writing himself in. On the completion of *Old Mortality*, he wrote to Lady Louisa Stuart: 'There are noble subjects for narrative during that period full of the strongest light & shadow, all human passions stirr'd up & stimulated by the most powerful motives, & the contending parties as distinctly contrasted in manners & in modes of thinking as in political principles. I am complete master of the whole history of these strange times both of persecutors and persecuted so I trust I have come decently off for as Falstaff very reasonably asks is not the *truth* the *truth*.'[1] Why then did he not speak with the authority to which he had so clear a right? Why does he give us the dying schoolmaster, who has derived the tale from the dead stone-mason and leaves it to the lifeless Jedediah Cleishbotham? And what led him on, in telling the story of *The Highland Widow*, through Chrystal Croftangry to Mrs. Bethune Balliol, to her postilion Donald MacLeish, back to her papers, and so home to Chrystal—who must needs inflate a tale which the old lady would have told succinctly, and her postilion, pithily? What can be the purpose of these successive *extensions*, unless to distance the tales that follow?

Such an effect of distance Scott had aimed at, and achieved, in his first metrical romance, *The Lay of the Last Minstrel*, casting back, first, to that earlier Duchess of Buccleuch, then to the old man who brought her his tribute of memories and traditions. The impression of remoteness exactly suited the kind of tale that he was not prepared to tell on his own authority, one that ventures beyond the bounds of our familiar daylight world and (if it obtains its purpose)

[1] *Letters, 1815–1817*, p. 293.

wakes in us the child who cries for fear in the night. He triumphs, in this kind, with Wandering Willie's Tale.[1] This remoteness Scott achieves by his manner of distancing the tale—by other means also, but they are akin to this, and all work together to one end. It is told by Willie Steenson to Darsie Latimer, with the preamble that it is not merely one of his repertory of 'fearsome' stories, but something that happened to his grandfather, when his father was no more than a boy. Thus it is established in the mind of a man whose blindness throws him upon memory of the thing heard—whether tune or tale— alike for his livelihood and his own entertainment; but it is received by Darsie as a mere curiosity, and between teller and hearer there is a peculiar relationship. Willie has his own reserve, just short of slyness. He has refused, despite his anxious wife's entreaty, to make money by 'the gentleman'; but we may surmise that he would not mind making a fool of him. Thus, we are free to take his tale as we choose—until *it* takes hold of us. Darsie, in his pleasant, shallow way, suggests that all ended remarkably well; but Willie's account of the long shadow lying across the family silences him.

When I distinguished the kind of depth that is given to Scott's stories by historical references from that given by distance measured in terms of personal memory, I was using one of those indispensable pieces of critical make-believe. We must pretend that we can see the parts distinctly, though we know that they signify nothing, except in so far as they compose a whole. Take away the sense of personal loss which hangs heavily over Steenie's tale, and you have merely part of Willie's professional repertory. It is the conjunction of these forces in Scott's greatest work that makes him like no other novelist. Take away from Steenie Steenson's visit to Hell all recollection of the Cavaliers and Covenanters; assemble round Sir Robert's table any company of bad men—and what remains? A good story, still; but not a great one.

Scott's vision of a present understandable only in its relation to the past came to him early. In the fourth Canto of the *Lay of the Last Minstrel* he uses a river image contrasting Teviot with the stream of life:

[1] See 'Scott and the Art of Revision', below, pp. 213–29.

> Where'er thou wind'st, by dale or hill,
> All, all is peaceful, all is still,
> As if thy waves, since Time was born,
> Since first they roll'd upon the Tweed,
> Had only heard the shepherd's reed,
> Nor started at the bugle-horn.
> Unlike the tide of human time,
> Which, though it change in ceaseless flow,
> Retains each grief, retains each crime,
> Its earliest course was doom'd to know;
> And, darker as it downward bears,
> Is stain'd with past and present tears. . .

What was tragic in his vision of life came to be tempered by many constituents in his character: intellectual curiosity; a lively sense of the ridiculous; the sort of happiness that for him, as for Jane Austen, *harmonized* life. In both, it was independent of circumstances, even of mortal sickness. Living in any other age, he might well have enjoyed these natural gifts, but hardly this peculiar kind of historical insight. It was the conjunction of the man and the hour that mattered.

Our strongest convictions, in literary criticism, are usually least susceptible of proof. But, have not the novelists tried, and failed, to recapture this magic ever since? They have achieved many fine things, but this is not among them.

> Within that circle none durst walk but he.

SCOTT AND THE ART OF REVISION

(1968)

THERE are many possible motives for an author's hesitancy or negligence in polishing his work, or refusal to reconsider and revise, and a prudent reader will be prepared to distinguish all or any of these from such reasons as the author himself may choose to give. Fulke Greville offers this account of his own dealings with the tragedies he had formerly laid aside: 'self-love ... moved me to take this Bear-whelp up againe and licke it'; but, even while he was about this task, he reflected that whatever care he might spend on these writings would but draw attention to their short-comings. He resolved therefore to 'take away all opinion of seriousnesse' from them and the handling they had undergone, 'and to this end carelessly cast them into the hypocriticall figure *Ironia*, wherein men commonly (to keep above their workes) seeme to make toies of the utmost they can doe'.[1] This enigmatic passage advances two considerations: how the author will stand in the opinion of his fellows; how, in his own regard. *They* will judge an artefact the more severely in so far as it is seen to be carefully wrought; *he* is resolved, as a man, to 'keep above his work'. In order therefore to deprecate censorious judgement and satisfy the critic within, he will 'seem to make toies of the utmost he can do'.

If ever great novelist followed this practice in both its branches, that novelist was Scott. His disavowal of care and pains, particularly in revision, is notorious: that is, too well known and too little understood. He was already writing in this strain some six years before he published a novel: in the Ashestiel Fragment, and the Introductions to the third, fifth, and sixth Cantos of *Marmion*. Here he affects to expostulate with friends who urge him to respect orthodox literary method; but underneath the good humour and the obstinacy, the patient ear for advice, and the determination to go his own way notwithstanding, there runs, from 1800 to the last

[1] *Life of Sir Philip Sidney*, ed. Nowell Smith, Oxford 1907, pp. 153-4.

pages of the *Journal*, a continuous argument with himself. The best known, and the most easily misread, of Scott's expostulations with his critics is the Introductory Epistle to *The Fortunes of Nigel*—ostensibly an answer to adverse reviews of his recent novels and censure of himself as a too prolific and careless novelist. It has often been quoted piecemeal, never examined whole as a piece of forensic argument. For this neglect there is some excuse: unlike the *Marmion* Introductions, the Epistle wants candour. Scott is playing hide-and-seek. Whereas he could have met much of this censure by showing the novels to be a mere part of his literary output, the value he still set on his fancied anonymity forbade him to associate the author of *Waverley* with the editor and biographer of Dryden. Therefore the altercation between Captain Clutterbuck, fictitious counsel for the prosecution, and the semi-fictitious defendant who, as novelist and nothing besides, is no more than a simulacrum of Scott, follows a devious course: the defence alleges the importance of the popular book trade to the prosperity of Edinburgh, the importance of entertainment to the well-being of the common reader, the importance to the author of freedom to obey the promptings of his own genius, and to enjoy such rewards as the world offers for success in any profession. This is merely the main engagement; there are so many skirmishes on the flanks, and the marshalling of the forces is so erratic, that we may fairly wish for an opportunity to ask Scott himself: 'What would you think of a client who, challenged to produce an alibi, undertook to show that he had been in ten different places on the occasion in question?' *Qui prouve trop, ne prouve rien*. Surely Scott's practice as a novelist, in this matter of revision, is more revealing, and far worthier scrutiny, than his defence of it.

Revision I understand in this broad sense: the whole process by which a writer returns, and reconsiders, and makes his second thoughts effectual. I have said that this process may be hindered in a variety of ways, and for reasons other than those the author alleges. Negligent revision, insufficient or ill judged, can result from two quite different habits of work—indeed, these habits arise from contrary states of mind. There is the self-concerned, calculating resolve to take no further trouble with a piece of writing that will already pass muster. Scott has been accused of this kind of negligence, and sometimes with reason, but he was the killer of his own reputation: his disavowals made such negligence appear his constant practice, whereas it alternated with another, its very opposite. His carelessness is often the result of unconcern with himself, concern with the story he has to tell. When this engrosses his attention, he leaves too much to his transcriber, or to his proofreader, while he himself presses on, as though speed alone could capture the visionary impression. Thus he would, in a single passage, revise to an extent far beyond what is commonly supposed, yet allow errors to slip through the uneven mesh of his scrutiny. Indeed, they might well be particularly numerous in such passages, because, intent on his main purpose, he had overtaxed the powers of his willing slaves: his own imagination at white heat, he was able to recapture and even recreate that vision; but he left too much to theirs.

There are other questions to be reckoned with. An artist, or craftsman, must ask himself how much reworking the fabric will tolerate. Jane Austen's recognition that hers was tough shows uncommon boldness and insight. Scott seems to have been often in doubt as to the resilience of his. Fortunately, we are sometimes able to observe him in the very act of revision, both manuscript and author's proofs having survived. Their existence for *Redgauntlet* has long been known, but investigators have been hindered from taking full advantage of this. David MacRitchie wrote on the proofs but had not seen the manuscript; George Gordon, when he described the alterations in the manuscript, did not know the whereabouts of the proofs, and to the reprint of his article he could add only a footnote. Here, to clear the record, is the order of events: In 1890 David MacRitchie came into possession of those proof-sheets of *Redgauntlet* which bore Scott's corrections, and in 1891 lent them to Andrew Lang, who included some slight remarks on them in his Introduction.[1] In March 1900 MacRitchie gave a full and useful account of them in *Longman's Magazine*. A leading article in the *TLS* for 4 September 1924 [by George Gordon] recounted a number of changes in the manuscript, which had been given to the Faculty

---

[1] Border edition of the novels. This volume is dated 1894.

of Advocates the year before.[1] The *TLS* for 11 September contained a letter by MacRitchie, mentioning the proof-sheets, Lang's use of them, and his own article. In 1931 Greville Worthington published his *Bibliography of the Waverley Novels*,[2] noting four cancels in the 1824 text of *Redgauntlet*,[3] and in 1932 W. C. van Antwerp reproduced two of the cancelled pages in their original state;[4] he became in 1937 owner of the proof-sheets, which, with the rest of his collection, were presently acquired by the Pierpont Morgan Library. Gillian Dyson's valuable article, *The Manuscripts and Proof Sheets of Scott's Waverley Novels*,[5] relating *Redgauntlet* to the rest, and all to circumstances in the printing-house, noted the recent disappearance of another set of proof-sheets, those corrected in James Ballantyne's hand. From this tale it will appear that everyone writing on *Redgauntlet* has been concerned with manuscript, proof, or printed text, or with two of these, but none with all three. Comparison between those three must be my starting-point.

Despite the pace at which the later novels went through the press, Scott enjoyed peculiar opportunities for bringing his second thoughts to bear on what he had written. By his own account,[6] this was his practice, at least until 1827: in order to preserve his supposed anonymity regarding the novels, he insisted that his hand should never be visible in the printing-house; proofs were set up, not from his manuscript but from a copy,[7] made under James Ballantyne's supervision; one set of these he corrected himself, and it then became Ballantyne's task to transfer the corrections to the other set. On this showing, there were four distinct states of *copy* in existence for any novel, before the first edition was printed; three stages at which it was possible for Scott to intervene, whether on his own initiative or at Ballantyne's request, after the completion

[1] This leader was reprinted in *Scott Centenary Articles*, Oxford 1932.
[2] In *Bibliographia: Studies in Book History and Book Structure, 1750–1900*, ed. Michael Sadleir.
[3] My copy contains traces of a fifth: in Volume iii, S5 (pp. 281–2) pasted to a stub.
[4] *A Collector's Comment on his first editions of the Works of Sir Walter Scott*, Gelber, Lilienthal, Inc., San Francisco.
[5] *Edinburgh Bibliographical Society Transactions*, IV. i (1960), 15–42.
[6] General Preface to the 1829 edition of *Waverley*, pp. xx–xxi.
[7] Miss Dyson cites a letter to *The Times*, 15 July 1868, by George Huntly Gordon, claiming to have transcribed thirty-seven volumes.

SCOTT AND THE ART OF REVISION

of his original manuscript. Two more will need to be taken into the reckoning: further proofs, and cancels.

In order to test these possibilities, I have chosen those pages well known to have been revised—i. 225–61, Wandering Willie's Tale—for close examination in the three extant states (manuscript, Scott's corrected proofs,[1] first edition), and surveyed the rest of the manuscript cursorily, finding that the difference, as to amount of revision, has been a little exaggerated: some other passages in the novel show almost as much. The *Tale*, however, has been revised to better purpose than these, and therefore has more to tell, as to Scott's mastery in this art of revision. True, it is an outstanding, and may be an exceptional, example of such care and skill; but no one who has examined it will be persuaded that he is here using this delicate and dangerously sharp tool for the first time.

Although its excellence is generally acknowledged, and the story should be well known, yet it is so necessary to have its exact outline under the reader's eye that I must attempt a summary: Sir Robert Redgauntlet, though he had been a notorious persecutor of the south-western Whigs in the *killing times*, could, even after the Revolution, still command loyalty in his own household and among his tenants. One of these, Steenie Steenson, grandfather[2] of the narrator, was in some favour with the Laird, and with his butler Dougal MacCallum, on account of his piping. Being doubly behindhand with his rent at a certain Martinmas term-day, he was obliged to borrow from his neighbours, notably one Tod Lapraik. He carried the money to Redgauntlet Castle and was brought by Dougal into the presence of Sir Robert and his jackanape, nicknamed Major Weir; but Sir Robert, even as he was preparing to count the money, was taken with the pangs of death; and, in the tumult, Steenie left the Castle without a receipt for it.* While the body was lying in state, Dougal confided to another old serving-man, Hutcheon, that he still heard his master's whistle at nights, and entreated his fellow servant's company. As these two sat together in the adjoining room, the whistle sounded and, answering the summons, Dougal fell dead

[1] I owe the favour of photographs of these proof-sheets to the authorities of the Pierpont Morgan Library, and the opportunity of examining the manuscript to the National Library of Scotland.
[2] *Father* in the first draft. See pp. 220 and 226 below.

and Hutcheon lost consciousness.*¹ When the new Laird, Sir John, demanded the two terms' arrears of rent, Steenie could produce no witness to his transaction with Sir Robert. From a stormy encounter at the Castle he returned to Tod Lapraik, with whom he fared no better. Before entering the wood which lay across his homeward road he called at a change-house and, swallowing a pint of brandy, uttered two wishes: that Sir Robert might never lie quiet in his grave until he had done justice to his tenant, and that the devil would enable him to trace the lost money-bag. Riding through the wood, he was joined by a stranger who offered help and conducted him (seemingly) back to Redgauntlet Castle, where he found Sir Robert holding revel with his fellow persecutors. Dougal admitted him and warned him to accept nothing but the receipt due for his rent, which he succeeded in obtaining; and, when Sir Robert bade him return and do homage for this favour, he found himself able to utter the name of God. The phantom rout vanished, and he lay as though dead until morning, when he came to himself in Redgauntlet churchyard. Back he returned to Sir John, produced the receipt and delivered Sir Robert's direction to look for the money in a place which Hutcheon was able to identify. There the bag with much else was found, guarded by the jackanape, which attacked Sir John and was killed by him. He demanded that the whole affair should be dismissed as a trick of the thieving monkey; but he was induced to let Steenie tell his tale to the Minister, through whose wife it eventually got about—and then Steenie made known *his* version.

The manuscript of *Redgauntlet* (Adv. MS. 19. 2. 29, in the National Library of Scotland, formerly the Advocates' Library) is written on one side of quarto leaves, the *Tale* occupying ff. 53 (l. 19) to 60 (l. 33) of the first volume.² His close script forbidding any substantial alteration in the text, Scott used the blank pages on the left hand for purposes ranging from corrections, made *currente calamo*, to considerable afterthoughts. Although it is not usually possible to differentiate, a few can be cited to illustrate this diversity of purpose and character.³

¹ This episode [*. . .*] is the only part of the story not witnessed by Steenie. See p. 227 below.
² Although the three volumes are bound in one, the divisions between them are marked, and foliation is discontinuous.
³ See pp. 222–4 below: Dougal MacCallum and Laurie Lapraik.

Those proofs which comprise the *Tale*, numbered pp. 224-61, consist of two complete gatherings and parts of two others: O8 (1 leaf), P–Q⁸, R1–3 (3 leaves). Discontinuity between P and Q, Q and R, seems to reflect difficulties in the printing-house: the contents of P had been so much amplified that Q had to be set up afresh, with p. 240 renumbered 241; Scott's corrections were now incorporated in the text—but he added others. The overlap between Q and R is only half as great, and has not entailed fresh pagination.

The sheets had been ruthlessly trimmed, and much of the manuscript correction effaced, before they reached MacRitchie's hands; but comparison with the manuscript and the printed text allows all but a few of these marginalia to be made out. Ballantyne's 'Please to read this', which appears on the first page of each gathering, must be distinguished from the results of his own proof-reading: that is, from specific queries.

It is, I think, clear that these were not the final proofs. The text of every gathering except O (a mere fifteen lines) diverges occasionally from the version eventually published. Some of these variants are manifestly authorial, and one is of very curious interest.[1]

The two cancels in the *Tale* consist, as van Antwerp showed, of the addition of *Dougal* on p. 231 (P4ʳ), and the substitution of Sir *John* for Sir *Robert* on p. 239 (P8ʳ), after printing. Only the first is significant.[2]

A comparative view of these several states of Wandering Willie's Tale should throw some light on the transmission of the text, and the evolution of the *Tale* as a triumph of narrative art. The two processes cannot be presented separately, the first being ancillary to the second. Moreover, the sum of the alterations falls little short of a hundred and forty—two-thirds of these, on my reckoning, significant. A choice must be made and, seeking to condense rather than limit illustration, I shall prefer examples in which both can be seen at work.

The pattern of transmission seems to run: Scott—the transcriber—Ballantyne (and his printers)—and Scott again. Despite numerous small differences between his manuscript and the proofs, I am convinced that Scott did not intervene to correct the transcript of these

---

[1] See p. 227 below. [2] See pp. 220-1 below.

eight leaves. The alterations appear to me all of a piece, and such as might arise from the efforts of a faithful, and trusted, amanuensis working on this part of the manuscript, with its peculiar difficulties. I am inclined, moreover, to believe that these were the first proofs Scott saw, and that none of the differences between manuscript and proof need signify authorial intervention. The transcriber was expected to know his habits as well as his handwriting, to divine his intentions and take responsibility; and he was allowed a proportionate share of freedom. Where a sentence was manifestly incomplete, he might insert the obvious word; he might dovetail successive afterthoughts into one another, and the whole passage into the text, by means of small omissions and additions.[1] Ballantyne may have overseen the work at this stage.[2] He must have taken charge when proof was set up from transcript—and this indeed is where his hand appears. He noted sentences which required more to complete them than the transcriber had been able to supply, readings which betrayed conjecture, and invoked Scott's help: 'Is this the word? The copy is with the Author.'

It seems probable that Ballantyne was charged with such tasks as the silent removal of Willie's references to his *father*, which Scott had failed to carry through. Between them, they missed five—of which one survives into present-day reprints. His brief for dealing summarily with inconsistencies may have extended to the cancels. One (P8) was a necessary correction: Steenie was speaking to Sir *John*, but Scott had inadvertently written Sir *Robert*, and the mistake had eluded both his proof-reading and Ballantyne's. The other is not an improvement: when Steenie brought his rent to the Castle, he was dismayed to find himself alone with Sir Robert. Scott recaptured that moment, and saw its horror heightened by the presence of the uncanny jackanape. He added, in proof, 'and the Major'. Surely it was Ballantyne who, in the P4 cancel, supplied Dougal MacCallum?[3] True, Dougal was there—or near by, but that

[1] Some two or three variants appear to be slips, for which the manuscript affords excuse.
[2] It was transcribed 'under Mr. Ballantyne's eye', according to the *Waverley* Preface (above, p. 216, n. 6), p. xxi.
[3] Misspelled, but that signifies nothing. The spelling of this and other names is erratic throughout.

would *lower* the tension, for Steenie; and this addition makes nonsense of the parenthesis: 'a thing that hadna chanced to him before.' I suspect that Ballantyne mistook Scott's purpose, supposing him to be attending to circumstantial detail, and tried to follow suit.

Greville Worthington reports that 'the leaves P4 and P8 in Vol. I are found in two states after cancellation', and that in the (presumed) later state of p. 232 *would* has been changed to *wad*.[1] Ballantyne may have been responsible for observing the convention as to Scottish spellings for certain common words. Scott undoubtedly *heard* the words in his own tongue, but he seldom troubled to mark the distinction in the first draft. His revision tends in this direction, but fitfully.

Spelling apart, the transcriber, whether of the manuscript or of the corrections in these proofs, was stiffly tested. He must use initiative, but could not always hope to supply deficiencies by casting about for the obvious word. When Scott wrote: 'The like o' Steenie wasna the wood that they made Whigs o' . . . ', someone stumbled, and the proof ran: 'wasna the *worst* that . . . An appeal to the author brought a marginal correction: 'wasna the *sort* that. . .'. Either he had not returned to his own manuscript, or the blunder had warned him that his metaphor was too bold.

A similar misreading seems to have yielded a happier result. Scott's *a* and *u* are often indistinguishable. In the 1824 text, the wood through which Steenie rides at night is called, on that occasion, Pitmarkie, but Sir John presently calls it Pitmurkie. In 1827,[2] the first occurrence is altered to agree with the second—no mere mechanical correction. In the manuscript, Sir John, anxious to discredit Steenie's tale, had proposed that they should 'lay the hail dirdum on that ill-deedie creature, Major Weir, and say naething about your dream in the wood at a' —'. This 'a' —', in the proofs, became a blank, such as Scott's forgetfulness of names often entailed. A hand which I believe to be Ballantyne's inserted the name of the wood—in a margin so mutilated that the spelling can only be inferred from the printed text. And so one of Scott's finest place-names was rescued from oblivion by Ballantyne's blunder.

[1] Op. cit., p. 132.
[2] *Tales and Romances by the Author of Waverley*, Edinburgh 1827, vols. III, IV.

Ballantyne has become a figure of fun for anyone writing on Scott's revision, but he surely deserved some of the confidence which Scott expressed in a letter written just after delivery of the last sheets of the transcript,[1] asking him to read the proofs carefully because his corrections are valued—and a little of the credit allowed him in the *Waverley* Preface.[2] Much was required of him.

There was besides a bias in Scott which might make his afterthoughts hard to follow: he would not discard. It is impossible to imagine him sacrificing that tenth chapter of *Persuasion*. Thus, if he discovered an inconsistency or repetition, he would, as it were, darn or patch, even though it might have been better to go back and begin afresh. He confesses to this habitual practice in many of his retrospective introductions, alike to poems and novels, and the *Tale* affords a small instance of it. Sir Robert's horse-shoe frown, devised to link Redgauntlets past and present, tale with novel, is not in the manuscript; it was added in proof: 'Ye maun ken he had a way of bending his brows that men saw the visible mark of a horseshoe in his forehead deep-dinted as if it had been stamped there.' When the same grimace is attributed to Sir John, in the body of the manuscript text, it is described as though for the first time. Scott then notices the discrepancy, and adds in proof: 'that self-same fearsome shape.'

These are trifles, and although 'we must confess the faults of our favourite, to gain credit to our praise of his excellencies',[3] I am glad to have done with cavilling. Again and again, in these thirty-seven pages, Scott's revision bears witness to his imaginative insight. Thus, Dougal MacCallum is much more than a serviceable piece of the story's mechanism; he carries a share of its meaning, which is in accord with that of the novel. 'Though death breaks service,' said MacCallum, 'it shall never break my service to Sir Robert.' It is his master's death he has in mind, but his own which will renew his servitude: he answers the familiar summons, and is found 'lying

---

[1] Dated 3 June 1824 by Grierson, who quotes from a letter of Cadell's: 'The printer got the last portion of MS. on the 2d', *Letters*, 1823–1825 pp. 290, 310.

[2] p. xx. If Scott is, as usual, too generous, the balance may have been too roughly redressed.

[3] Johnson writing to Charles Burney about Shakespeare. *Letters*, no. 177.

dead within twa steps of the bed where his master's coffin was placed'. It is well known that those who support a tyranny have no choice but to perish in its fall. This platitude does not tell us, however, what happens when they meet their fellow reprobates in Hell, as Dougal meets Steenie—and warns him how he must act to escape. Loyalty, being an instinctive principle of association, was something Scott understood—and he did not insist that its object, whether man or cause, should be beyond reproach. (This theme runs through *Redgauntlet*.) So intrinsic does Dougal's significance prove, in the story as we know it, that to surprise Scott himself in the act of discovering it is a strange experience. He had written: 'Weel Dougal died and as weel he did before the Revolution for its like it would have broke the auld carles heart.' He struck this out and substituted (on the left-hand page): 'Weel—round came the Revolution and it had like to have broken the hearts baith of Dougald and his master. But the change was not altogether sae great as they feard and other folk thought for.'

Laurie Lapraik, the time-server, is another afterthought, woven into the story gradually—with less certainty than Dougal. He first appears on the left-hand page of the manuscript, when Steenie borrows the money to pay his rent: 'The maist of it was from a neighbour they caad Laurie Lapraik—a sly tod Laurie had wealth o' gear—could hunt wi the hound & rin wi the hare & be Whig or Tory saint or sinner as the wind stood. He was a professor at this time but he liked an orra sound and a tune on the pipes weel eneugh at a byetime And abune a' he thought he had good security for the siller he lent my father over the stocking at Primrose Know.' When Steenie retreats worsted from Sir John, the manuscript merely carries him to 'his chief creditor', and while these two are at odds a blank is left for the name, which seems to have registered faintly. But the character was indispensable, and Scott assiduously worked Laurie into the proofs in preparation for the moment when he was to provoke Steenie into abusing his doctrine. Here Ballantyne, having lost the thread, inquired in the margin: 'What doctrine?'— and Scott wrote, below the question: 'Laurie was a professor and had just used the cant of his sect'. Ballantyne, in his capacity of common reader, should not have overlooked those two words:

professor[1] and *doctrine*. Laurie was not indeed one of the 'puir hill-folk' whose blood was on Sir Robert's hands when he went to his 'appointed place'; it was not for him to read the great roll-call of those dead persecutors by whom Sir Robert is there surrounded. Yet, as one sort of Whig, he serves not only to reduce Steenie to brandy, blasphemy, and despair by recalling his part in the persecution, but also to make us understand that the revellers in the ghostly castle are not the idle phantoms of fashionable fiction but historical figures—in a country where history reverberates a long while.

At its best, Scott's revision furthers his artistic purpose at more levels than one: grappling us to his story and giving that story significance. On such occasions it is itself an art.

How is purpose to be divined, in an author who chose to give so misleading an account of himself? A full answer demands the scope of a book; but something may be provisionally attempted, by close attention to this closely revised *Tale*. Scott has to master certain problems, here as elsewhere; but here they are seen with peculiar clarity, and his success is beyond question. These problems can be summarily indicated in one word: equilibrium. He has to maintain a balance between conflicting claims: rights and wrongs in the historical conflict of interests; formal symmetry and naturalism in the pattern of events; supernatural and natural interpretations of what happened.

Our vantage-point for a survey of the first two will be a simple anecdote which Scott read in Joseph Train's notes to his *Strains of the Mountain Muse*.[2] His response to this little volume was the beginning of a lifelong friendship and literary association between the two men. Train's anecdote gives: the persecutor, Sir Robert Grierson of Lagg; the tenant who was deprived of the receipt for his rent by Sir Robert's sudden death; the encounter with a stranger in a wood on his homeward road; the castle and the *long dead* porter;[3] a legendary fiddler tuning up to play for the revellers; the strange

[1] *Professor* 'any person who pretended to uncommon sanctity of faith and manner' —*Waverley*, ii. 118 (Chapter XXIX).
[2] Printed in Edinburgh for the Author (1814), pp. 191–5.
[3] Hence (I conjecture) Scott's first draft, in which Dougal dies before the Revolution.

receipt obtained, presented—and accepted by the hitherto incredulous new Laird. We cannot, however, be sure what it gave Scott; for it was never his way to reply, when offered information: 'I know that—tell me something else'. Only after cordial thanks and a request for further particulars would he admit, quietly, that he already had some knowledge of the matter. He had, indeed, accumulated a great deal of information about the suppression of the south-western Whigs, so far back as 1803, when he was preparing to amplify the *Minstrelsy*: it furnished introductions and notes to those additional ballads, from *Lesley's March* to *The Battle of Bothwellbridge*, which compose a consecutive passage of Scottish history. Moreover, his correspondence with Charles Kirkpatrick Sharpe of the year before shows his familiarity with the legends that had gathered round this conflict, and attached themselves indifferently to one and another of the persecutors, from famous names down to those remembered only in Galloway, or in Cameronian literature. Thus, he was doing no violence to tradition when he mounted Sir Robert Redgauntlet on the horse which the devil had given to Claverhouse, and (in *Old Mortality*) made Claverhouse himself tell Morton that he was popularly supposed to drink blood—as Sir Robert Grierson, among others, was said to have done. These and other superstitions—such as the devil's failure to protect his own against a silver bullet—had been known to him ever since he first looked into John Howie's *Scots Worthies*;[1] and he was at his best when his knowledge had undergone the process which H. J. C. Grierson happily calls *incubation*. In October 1802 he had written to Sharpe: 'I have Lagg's elegy & am acquainted with the traditions of the period respecting most of the persecutors and persecuted saints'.[2] He repeated this claim when he wrote to Lady Louisa Stuart after the completion of *Old Mortality*.[3] He read the tale with his usual compassionate insight: 'The Covenanters deny to their governors that toleration, which was iniquitously refused to themselves'.[4] This is a characteristic observation—which offended both sides.

[1] *Biographia Scoticana . . . Scots Worthies*, 2nd edn., Glasgow 1781, with Appendix, *The Judgement and Justice of God*, 1782.
[2] *Letters*, 1787–1807 p. 161. [3] Ibid. 1815–17 p. 292.
[4] *Minstrelsy of the Scottish Border*, Edinburgh 1803, iii. 210.

Scott's recognition of the irresistible hold upon his imagination which this knowledge retained, and its consequent value to himself, is evident from the risks he accepted for its sake. The time of *Redgauntlet* is fixed by Darsie's age at some twenty years after the '45—which raises historical difficulties of its own, but that is another story. Willie, now a man of sixty-two, had a father—presently changed to grandfather—who had been active before the Revolution. He himself was brought up in the household of Sir Redwald Redgauntlet—presumably Darsie's grandfather—who, he says, perished in the '45; but Maxwell of Summertrees testifies to Willie's fidelity at Harry Redgauntlet's end, in the aftermath of Culloden—and Sir Henry was Darsie's father. The fall of the Grierson fortunes in the '15—rather than the '45—would give an easier time-scheme for the *Tale*—and one impossible for the novel. But this game is not worth playing, unless it serves to show with what bold—surely deliberate and certainly successful—imprecision of reference Scott can set the *Tale* where he pleases, in the past, adjusting the generations in the Steenson family—and overlooking those of the Redgauntlets—while he realizes the asset he has thus created by introducing Laurie and developing the character of the new Laird, with his assured command of all the lawful means of oppression. Sir John allows Steenie to consult their own minister, because 'he is a douce man, regards the honour of our family, and *the mair that* he may look for some patronage from me'. The words I have italicized were added in proof, and, like much other revision, drive the nail home.

Of the reconciliation of formal symmetry with naturalism much might be said, but this must serve. Scott had, in the tale of the tenant, his landlords, and the phantom company,[1] a single train of events, the visits to the old and new Laird alternating as in a simple rhymed quatrain. By his elaboration of circumstantial detail and development of character he built, as it were, a more intricate stanza, whose virtue is that it can at once surprise and satisfy. Here are some of the afterthoughts by which this elaboration and de-

---

[1] Alexander Fergusson says that this story was 'current in Nithsdale', and that it had been given to Joseph Train by James Dennistoun (*The Laird of Lag: a Life Sketch*, Edinburgh 1886, pp. 216, 217). Scott confused the issue by his note on the *Tale* in 1832. The strain of negligence, caprice, even mischief in those retrospective notes requires investigation, but not here.

velopment were accomplished: the rental-book, on which Steenie kept his eye 'as if it were a mastiff-dog that he was afraid would spring up and bite him', links his two interviews, with father and son; the cryptic message, to look for the money in the Cat's Cradle, has to be interpreted by Hutcheon, because, as Steenie says, such matters are known only to him and 'another serving-man that is now gane and that I wad not like to name'. Such echoes are fewer and less resonant in the first draft.

The equilibrium between natural and supernatural interpretations of the *Tale* lies at the heart of the impression it leaves. Some readers have been content with a facile resolution of their conflicting claims. A. W. Verrall saw nothing but a trick, turning on a trivial discrepancy between the two accounts of Sir Robert's death, which would allow us to suppose that Steenie had got his receipt in the ordinary course, and dreamed up the rest. 'Scott's own view of the facts, the rationalistic view, is implied clearly enough in the final paragraph of the story, and indeed throughout.'[1] To this there are two objections. The first relates to that final paragraph: its second sentence was added after the correction of the extant proofs. It runs: 'Indeed ye'll no hinder some to threap, that it was nane o' the Auld Enemy that Dougal and my gudesire saw in the Laird's room, but only that wanchancy creature, the Major, capering on the coffin; and that, as to the blawing on the Laird's whistle that was heard after he was dead, the filthy brute could do that as weel as the Laird himself, if no better.' Hearsay set against hearsay does not disturb the equilibrium of doubt. The conclusion—'But Heaven kens the truth'—is no mere pious formula. Nor can the further emphasis thus given to it be fortuitous.

That inserted sentence must be part of Scott's final revision, in his last proofs. Yet it contains a very curious error. It was not 'my gudesire', but Hutcheon, who ventured into the Laird's room with Dougal that night. How did Scott come to admit this discrepancy? Did he take the bold, Shakespearian, and apparently successful[2] way of sacrificing some lesser good—probability, consistency—to

[1] 'The Prose of Walter Scott' (*Quarterly Review*, 1910), reprinted in *Collected Literary Essays*, ed. Bayfield and Duff, Cambridge 1913, p. 268.
[2] It seems to have escaped notice.

imaginative coherence? (This is not the moment for reminding us that Steenie, eyewitness to the rest of the *Tale*, was not there.) Was he simply careless? This, the time-honoured explanation, would be plausible, if it were not for the delicate tissue of revision by which he had enhanced the imaginative effect of Steenie's 'dream'. That is my second objection to the merely naturalistic interpretation of the *Tale*. It is well known that he added 'the Bluidy Advocate Mac-Kenyie' to the ghostly company in proof, but not that he had reworked the whole passage in manuscript, adding not only circumstantial detail but also this development of one circumstance —the monkey's absence: 'for he heard them say as he came forward, "Is not Major Weir come yet" & another answered "The Jackanape will be here betimes the morn".' What is more, one further alteration seems to have been made in the final proofs, for the version of the printed text— ' "Is not the Major come yet?" '—differs from manuscript and extant proofs by that uncanny touch of familiarity. So it is after all the jackanape which holds the key to both interpretations. True, he was a thieving brute—but he too had his hour, and his appointed place.[1] The very waking, whether from dream or vision, has been revised with the same mastery: Steenie had originally found himself lying 'in the middle of the forest the birds were singing the sun was shining and his horse was feeding quietly beside him'. But after revision of the proofs he lay in the 'auld kirkyard of Redgauntlet parishine just at the door of the family aisle & the scutcheon of the auld knight Sir Robert hanging over his head—There was a deep morning fog on grass & gravestone around him and his horse was quietly feeding beside the minister's twa cows'.

How are we to understand the expense of such care as this on a story of supernatural happenings?[2] *Not* for the sake of condoning

---

[1] In *My Aunt Margaret's Mirror* Scott characterizes a supernatural tale as one in which the narrator, having professed general disbelief in its assumptions, confesses to 'something . . . which he has been always obliged to give up as inexplicable'. *Chronicles of the Canongate, First Series*, in the collected (1829–33) edition, Edinburgh 1832, p. 306.

[2] I find myself unable to accept Dr. C. O. Parsons' conclusions, or even, within the space available, to canvass our differences regarding Scott's attitude to the supernatural. See *Witchcraft and Demonology in Scott's Fiction*, Edinburgh and London 1964, also earlier studies.

'that horrid belief in witchcraft, which cost many innocent persons, and crazy imposters, their lives, for the supposed commission of impossible crimes'.[1] Scott's gentleness of heart made the history of that belief abhorrent to him. It is not to credulity that he speaks. We are sometimes assailed by a more pervasive fear, an enfolding darkness different from those several shadows projected by doubts of our own sufficiency, or the all too sufficient power of particular adversaries. I cannot associate this visitation with belief, for it is at variance with religion; and it enjoys too little acquaintance with either intellect or will to be called voluntary suspension of disbelief. Scott understood this experience: the fear of unknown powers, and of the force inherent in the spoken word for invoking them—as Steenie invokes the dead and the devil. He understood also the countervailing hope, that means may be found of revoking this too potent word, even that an ally within the enemy's stronghold may direct us to those means—as Dougal directs Steenie. Such fear and hope may be conveniently assigned to the persons of a tale; and this will be easier if one of them is telling it. Scott shows elsewhere that he can dispense with this latter condition, relying on dialogue alone to convey Meg Merrilies' faith in the effect of her curse and in her power to call it home and take the evil to herself. (Kipling, in *The Wish House*, chose the safer way.) These differences of method do not signify. Whatever the means by which a writer attributes such fear and hope to imaginary persons, he does not thereby disencumber himself of every burden which possession of the imaginative faculty has laid upon us.

These are unsounded waters—but no deeper than we must expect to reach if we bring to a great novelist our whole attention. Has Scott ever been read with the care which he himself deprecated— but which his art invites?[2]

[1] *Letters on Demonology and Witchcraft*, 1830, p. 172.
[2] I acknowledge gratefully the help of Dr. Ian Jack and Dr. J. D. Fleeman in revising this essay. Any remaining errors are of course my own.

JANE AUSTEN AND WALTER SCOTT
A MINOR POINT OF COMPARISON
(1971)

IN a crucial episode of *The Bride of Lammermoor*, the wily Lord Keeper, Sir William Ashton, sets about obtaining young Ravenswood's confidence, and his assent to the proposition that the law has, effectually and rightly, superseded the sword wherever men contend for advantage or security. The irruption at this point of the swashbuckler Craigengelt—a happy illustration of Scott's command of punctuation—lends colour to his argument. A master of appearances, he candidly and humorously admits the law's shortcomings, but presents 'the civil polity' as protector of the people of Scotland, and himself as its true servant. Ravenswood falls under his spell and is caught in the toils. Here Scott, as so often, conveys his sense of social change in an encounter between two men: Sir William's ascendancy is not merely a personal triumph; law is the armament of the future.[1]

It was not, however, in society alone that Scott remarked this change. Always sensitive to the moods and conventions of the novel, he had, in the first (or 'introductory') chapter of *Waverley*, contrasted the substitution of predatory law-suits for armed assault in current fiction.[2] He might indeed have maintained that law, whether realistically presented or subjected to the demands of the plot, is a principal agent of the eighteenth-century novelist.[3] Even in the nineteenth century, with commerce for rival, it held its ground, and questionable wills contended with closed banks for the ruin of the heroine.

Novelists who employ the law in the furtherance of their designs fall into several groups. There are those who write from the inside

[1] ii. 44, 59 (Chapters XVI, XVII).   [2] i. 10, 11.
[3] When Nassau Senior protested at the elimination, by sudden death, of every one of the Osbaldistons standing between Frank and the estate, it was with the rider that 'an ordinary novelist . . . would have made out some story of an old entail, or a forged will, or have tried to find some other expedient' with more 'resemblance to the common course of events'. *Quarterly Review*, xxvi (Oct. 1821), p. iii.

—chief among them, Scott; those who write, as it were, from underneath—sensible, like Dickens, of its pressures; those who turn an observant and quizzical eye on its anomalies—Trollope, for example; those who, like Galt, master that knowledge of its workings which their story requires; and one who accepts it with inscrutable detachment: Jane Austen.

Only in so far as the law concerns itself with inheritance is Jane Austen concerned with the law; and even this degree of concernment is less than it appears. What she gives us is seldom more than the *expectation* of inheritance; and this may not rest on any legal claim. Wickham's expectations are the most illusory, being fabricated for the purpose of ingratiating himself with those who do not know his past history. Others are plausible only to the characters who entertain them, since they rest on calculations we may not share: Willoughby's, on mere kinship to a cousin whom he has given no cause to love him; Frank Churchill's, on the indulgence of an uncle and aunt to whom his secret engagement is an affront. Neither could claim to be heir-at-law; yet their heir-apparent pretensions obtain credit where they seek it. Marianne takes Allenham for granted as part of the future she expects to share with Willoughby. Emma, warned of impending bad news, conjectures that Frank has been ousted from an inheritance to which he could lay claim only by favour.[1] What Jane Austen herself thought of such expectations as these may be inferred from their effect on the *expectant*: they hinder both men from acting honourably. I surmise that the full force of her censure may be felt in the final blow she administers to Willoughby: he might have enjoyed both Allenham and Marianne, since Mrs. Smith required only that he should marry 'a woman of character'. This is inconsistent with her former stipulation that he should marry the woman he had seduced; and such inconsistency is rare in Jane Austen's novels. Here it serves to establish Mrs. Smith's freedom to punish or reward a presumptuously expectant cousin.

By a nice and very characteristic turn of irony, the one indisputable claim to legal inheritance in the six novels is treated in a vein of hilarious comedy:

[1] *Emma*, p. 393 (Chapter XLVI).

'Indeed, Mr. Bennet,' said she, 'it is very hard to think that Charlotte Lucas should ever be mistress of this house, that *I* should ever be forced to make way for *her*, and live to see her take my place in it!'

'My dear, do not give way to such gloomy thoughts. Let us hope for better things. Let us flatter ourselves that *I* may be the survivor.'

This was not very consoling to Mrs. Bennet, and, therefore, instead of making any answer, she went on as before,

'I cannot bear to think that they should have all this estate. If it were not for the entail I should not mind it.'

'What should you not mind?'

'I should not mind any thing at all.'

'Let us be thankful that you are preserved from a state of such insensibility.'

'I never can be thankful, Mr. Bennet, for any thing about the entail. How any one could have the conscience to entail away an estate from one's own daughters I cannot understand; and all for the sake of Mr. Collins too!—Why shoud *he* have it more than anybody else?'

'I leave it to yourself to determine,' said Mr. Bennet.[1]

And by this time we are ready to cry 'Why indeed?'

What Walter Scott would have made of the entail on Longbourn is a matter of idle speculation. It is tempting to surmise how he might have involved Uncle Phillips—his own sort of frugality, quite different from Jane Austen's, would not have wasted a brother of Mrs. Bennet practising as an attorney in Meryton, and with a clerk in his office who is to marry Mary Bennet. But these thoughts must be resisted. In the context which Jane Austen has framed for it, this entail is operative only in terms of Mrs. Bennet and her nerves, Mr. Collins and his proposal of expiation.

At this point, Jane Austen's engagement with the law may be seen to diminish still further. If inheritance, in her plots, is more likely to signify expectations than valid claims, these very expectations often affect the lives of those concerned, in a circumscribed context. The point at issue is *eligibility*. Amongst people who seem to us indelicately knowledgeable about one another's financial assets, the two-edged question is frequently asked: are this man's

[1] *Pride and Prejudice*, p. 130 (Chapter XXIII).

expectations such that he can afford to marry a portionless girl? Mr. Collins points this predicament when, offering his expectations and himself to Elizabeth, he enjoins her to consider 'that in spite of your manifold attractions, it is by no means certain that another offer of marriage may ever be made you. Your portion is unhappily so small that it will in all likelihood undo the effect of your loveliness and amiable qualifications.'[1]

The girl whose portion is so small as to leave her future in doubt is evidently Jane Austen's counterpart to those romantic heroines who, as she and Scott alike noticed, require extraordinary circumstances to make us wonder what will become of them. (They are, moreover, obligingly ready to encounter such hazards: those of Ann Radcliffe 'voluntarily expose themselves to situations, which in nature a lonely female would certainly have avoided'.[2]) The Dashwoods, Bennets, and Watsons, on the other hand, suffer only those vicissitudes which common experience of life in their day would warrant: by no fault of their own, nor even because of any heroic virtue, they are slenderly provided. In *Sense and Sensibility* three of the four characters with whom we are invited to feel sympathy are at the mercy, not of a villain nursing guilty secrets and illicit designs, but of members of their several families to whom the law has allowed command of the family purse. The whim of an old gentleman has left Mrs. Dashwood and her daughters dependent on the meanest man in English fiction. By an equally unfortunate disposal of property, Mrs. Ferrars's two sons depend on her illiberality; and poor Edward, having been bred to no profession, is in much the same position as a portionless daughter. The harsh reality of such dependence is sharpened for Emma Watson by natural disappointment: she had reason to suppose that the aunt and uncle who brought her up would provide for her; but her aunt, on being left a widow, chose instead to provide for an Irish captain, and Emma found herself dependent on her own needy and ill-assorted family. 'You know we must marry', her sister Elizabeth explains. 'I could do very well single for my own part—A little Company, & a pleasant Ball now & then, would be enough for me, if one could be

[1] p. 108 (Chapter XIX).
[2] Scott, 'Mrs. Ann Radcliffe' (*Collected Prose Works*, 1834, iii. 368–9).

young for ever, but my Father cannot provide for us, & it is very bad to grow old & be poor & laughed at.'[1]

The Dashwoods, like the Bennets and the Watsons, are unprovided daughters, and their tacit acceptance of this condition may fairly be called the centre of gravity in the novel. The airy passage of heritable property to and fro, in *Sense and Sensibility*, does not imply social satire: Jane Austen is not asking why power to give or withhold livelihood should be thus assigned; she is content to depict the exercise of such power by liberal and illiberal persons. She recognized that the law relating to inheritance did not put it beyond the power of one member of a family to beggar another. Her question—which of those standing to gain by it would forgo this advantage?—is one proper to comedy of character—whose scope no one ever estimated more justly. From the whole transaction of Mrs. Ferrars's disinheritance and reinstatement (with a difference) of her two sons, Robert emerges effortlessly enriched by Edward's expectations. In comedy of intrigue, he would have been at the pains of forging a will—and John Dashwood of exerting undue pressure on a testator. Yet both are in lawful possession—one, of the fortune his sisters might have looked to share, the other of that which his brother had reason to hope for. There is a kind of sublimity in John's conviction of his own merit; in Robert's, of his irresistible charm; in the faith of both, that the world must be well governed, since wealth rests in the right hands.

What their author thought of this dispensation may be inferred from her care for those whom it would leave empty-handed. She draws on no subterfuge, whether romantic—mistaken identity; or sentimental—change of heart. The problem that has been set in terms of character must be solved in those terms: what is to be reckoned with remains constant. The law gives Mrs. Ferrars power; her temperament, the will to misuse it. The marvel is that these factors together should yield high comedy—the comedy that has always some hilarity in its vigilance. It proceeds from Jane Austen's peculiar treatment of the law. In the crisis of disinheritance, whereas a passing reference to Mrs. Ferrars's lawyer reminds us that this is supposed to be a legal transaction, the narrative is

[1] *The Watsons*, in *Minor Works*, ed. R. W. Chapman, 1954, p. 317.

taken up with her demands on her physician. Moreover, that same temperament will bring her eventually to a position so preposterous that only a legal fiction can represent it:

> Her family had of late been exceedingly fluctuating. For many years of her life she had had two sons; but the crime and annihilation of Edward a few weeks ago had robbed her of one; the similar annihilation of Robert had left her for a fortnight without any; and now, by the resuscitation of Edward, she had one again.[1]

His hold is indeed precarious; but his mother's disposition will expose her to the wiles of Lucy and the effrontery of Robert; and, while they contend for the spoils, over which Fanny and Lucy will presently fall out, he will slip easily into a daughter's place, with the promise of such a portion as 'had been given with Fanny'.

This is told in the dry, frosty manner which Jane Austen keeps for the final chapters; but the crisis itself has broken upon us hilariously in dialogue. It is recounted three times—and not once too often: first, by the downright, uncomprehending Mrs. Jennings; then by John Dashwood, in a version on which he has imposed his own extravagant interpretation; last by Robert Ferrars, more obtuse than Mrs. Jennings, more flamboyant than John. The shimmer of absurdity which plays over all three accounts surely promises a happy outcome: the resolution of discords in marriage which will be accomplished through Colonel Brandon's liberality.

From their constant predicament, Jane Austen's heroines are rescued by marriage[2]—so invariably that we are almost lulled into acceptance of the ironically grave proposition which opens *Mansfield Park*: when Miss Maria Ward married Sir Thomas Bertram, 'all Huntingdon exclaimed on the greatness of the match, and her uncle, the lawyer, himself, allowed her to be at least three thousand pounds short of any equitable claim to it'. Her two sisters were expected to do equally well for themselves. 'But there are not so many men of large fortune in the world, as there are pretty women to deserve them.'[3]

---

[1] *Sense and Sensibility*, p. 373 (Chapter L).
[2] Cassandra Austen told 'some of her nieces' that Emma Watson was to marry Mr. Howard (*The Watsons*, p. 363).
[3] p. 8 (Chapter I).

The bland demeanour which Jane Austen chooses to wear *as novelist* can be deceptive. 'Single women', she warns a too fastidious niece, 'have a dreadful propensity for being poor.'[1] The novels themselves sometimes betray a latent concern. Jane Fairfax has been brought up, not in expectation of wealth, but in familiarity with its agreeable consequences; and now she must face the condition of an unprovided girl in a society which has but one use for her. Elizabeth Watson expresses her view of this situation plainly, when her sister Emma, not yet familiar with the genteel poverty in which the family is steeped, protests that she would rather teach in a school than marry a man she did not like: 'I would rather do any thing than be Teacher at a school. . . . *I* have been at school, Emma, & know what a Life they lead; *you* never have,—I should not like marrying a disagreeable Man any more than yourself,—but I do not think there *are* many very disagreeable Men; I think I could like any good humoured Man with a comfortable Income.—I suppose my Aunt brought you up to be rather refined.'[2] Although Mrs. Elton claims that a post in any family of her recommending is quite another matter, no one even pretends to believe her. There is an odd turn in the discussion of Jane's predicament which I consider revealing. When Mrs. Weston pleads that Jane's 'one great deviation from the strict rule of right' is to be forgiven in view of her comfortless prospect, Emma is quick to concur: 'If a woman can ever be excused for thinking only of herself, it is in a situation like Jane Fairfax's. Of such, one may almost say that "the world is not theirs, nor the world's law."'[3] Her intention is so clear that we are likely to jump the apparent misprint and assume that Emma is quoting from *Rambler* 107: 'The world is not their friend, nor the world's law'.[4] But that was an adaptation of a line from *Romeo and Juliet*[5]—applied to the case of unhappy prostitutes, and oddly inappropriate. There can be no question of a deliberately garbled quotation, in Mrs. Elton's vein. Emma speaks from the heart, and her author surely speaks through her. For an explanation of this

---

[1] Letter 141. [2] *Emma*, p. 318. [3] p. 400 (Chapter XLVI).
[4] This part of *Rambler* 107 was contributed by Johnson's former schoolfellow, Joseph Simpson. See Yale *Johnson*, iv. 207, n.
[5] Romeo to the Apothecary: 'The world is not thy friend, nor the world's law' (v. i. 72).

A MINOR POINT OF COMPARISON 237

incongruity, I would appeal to common experience. It is not when we chatter, and (as it were) improvise, that the mind races and the tongue somersaults. It is when we utter a conviction deeply felt and long held that we are betrayed to verbal slips, misquotations, or quotations misapplied. It was, I believe, the duration and depth of Jane Austen's concern with the Jane Fairfaxes of her world that here tripped even so circumspect a writer.

Marriage rescues her heroines from one or another sort of irksome dependence or insecurity.[1] Moreover, a good marriage—and this means something quite different from the 'establishment' for which Charlotte Lucas is willing to endure Mr. Collins—a *good* marriage diffuses its benefits. Mrs. Smith has been left in straitened circumstances by the refusal of Mr. Elliot to act as her husband's executor. His legal right to refuse is not in dispute, though Anne and her friend are agreed as to his want of justice and compassion. Something may yet be retrieved, but it is not in the power of either woman to effect this. Anne's marriage affords a natural remedy. 'Captain Wentworth, by putting [Mrs. Smith] in the way of recovering her husband's property in the West Indies; by writing for her, acting for her, and seeing her through all the petty difficulties of the case, with the activity and exertion of a fearless man and a determined friend, fully requited the services which she had rendered, or ever meant to render, to his wife.'[2]

The final resolution of all difficulties by marriage will perhaps be dismissed with the reflection that this, after all, was the kind of story Jane Austen was writing; but that would fall short of the full explanation. Whereas other novelists were then looking for the exceptional, she chose to write about the *rule*, the regular and probable; and, in the world she knew, marriage was by far the likeliest provision for a woman's future.

Scott's decided preference was for the exceptional, for events and persons so far removed from the rule that he often felt impelled to insist: this, or something like it, really happened. He can besides be very circumstantial about the means to these remarkable ends—

[1] Emma's confidence that financial security will be enough for her is merely one of her illusions.
[2] *Persuasion*, pp. 251–2 (Chapter XXIV).

notably when this calls for the employment of a man of law. The lawyers of other novelists may be mere token figures, presiding over the final distribution of property as friars preside over marriages in Shakespearian romantic comedy. If Scott ever dallies with this convention, it is certainly not in *Guy Mannering*. I choose Lucy Bertram's story to illustrate my argument.

This strand in the densely crowded narrative has been little noticed—partly because Lucy herself is not very interesting. But I believe that the best ground for comparison between two writers will often lie just where there are many superficial resemblances, and one fundamental difference; and that is what this tale of a portionless heroine offers. The faint lineaments of Lucy's portrait need not trouble us if we recognize that what matters is her function. Persons of this sort—I shall take leave to call them *occasion-giving* characters— are plentiful and serviceable in our novels of the prime: say, from Fielding to Dickens.[1] They have come down from the romantic tales whose traces are discernible in these ample, unfastidious novels. The principal function of these characters is to range others in opposed ranks, according as they are (or would be) preservers or destroyers, and to bring out the full significance of that opposition. Although they are not cyphers, they need not be intrinsically interesting—some of them were children, in an age which took a simple view of childhood. What they contribute is the fact of helplessness, and the contrary responses it evokes.

Harry Bertram is not, of course, helpless; but, so long as he remains ignorant of his own identity, he is in an indefensible position, and his enemies are strong, unscrupulous, and closely bound to one another. He attracts to himself, in the proper romantic manner, defenders from worlds far stranger than that to which he, as an eighteenth-century gentleman, belongs. There is the faithful dog, Dandie Dinmont, and the uncanny and unpredictable protectress, Meg Merrilies. Only when the course of his story begins to join his sister's will he gain adherents of a more commonplace sort, armed with knowledge of the world, and the law. Lucy is indeed helpless: her spendthrift and broken father has died, leaving

---

[1] For the development of this argument in relation to Dickens see Kathleen Tillotson, *Novels of the Eighteen-forties* (1954), pp. 174–5.

A MINOR POINT OF COMPARISON 239

nothing but an embarrassed estate which, in default of heirs male, can be sold up to pay his debts. Her hope of marriage to Charles Hazlewood is blighted by his parents' objection to a portionless daughter-in-law. So far, she might be the heroine of any nineteenth-century novel. But, by her helplessness, and Scott's reaction to it, she brings into play the operations of the law, for good and ill, and gives occasion, not only for conflict, but also for the development of its significance.

Glossin's part in the encounter is framed with a nice irony. Harry Bertram stands in his way. So long as any question of the boy's survival remains, it is to his interest to hurry on the apparently legal transaction which will give him possession of the Ellangowan estate. Our suspicions, confusedly aroused by the hubbub of local tradition and gossip, are confirmed and clarified by the explanation which Mr. Mac-Morlan offers to Colonel Mannering.[1] When Glossin finds, however, that he has a living Bertram to reckon with, he resorts to violence—but that is Harry's story, and in Lucy's he plays the part of a shady but plausible lawyer, with a reputation to maintain. Lucy is not in his way—except in so far as public opinion condemns him for forcing on the sale, over her head. He will therefore conciliate public opinion by bringing to the notice of the influential Colonel Mannering Lucy's claim on Margaret Bertram's estate. This, he reckons, will cost him nothing, and will gain him credit where he most needs it. He underestimates the antagonism he has aroused. He produces with a flourish the will he formerly drew up for Margaret Bertram, leaving Singleside to Lucy.[2] He says nothing of his own doubts as to the supersession of this will; but Mannering, refusing to negotiate with him, consults Mac-Morlan, who at once raises the issue; and, when the Colonel proposes to look after Lucy's interests himself, furnishes him with an introduction to Pleydell in Edinburgh.

This is a favourite device with Scott: conscious of having at his command a capital scene or episode, he carries his titular hero—

[1] i. 207–8 (Chapter XII).
[2] ii. 244–5 (Chapter XXXV). Glossin says that the will was made while Margaret Bertram was living at Ellangowan. Has Scott been careless here? Margaret had been glad to make her home with the Bertrams in Mrs. Bertram's lifetime (i. 303–4 (Chapter XIX)); that is, before Lucy was born.

Waverley, Mannering, Oldbuck—into the midst; and, by keeping him in motion, masks the slenderness of his motive for intervening. Here he obtains, not only the effect of an eyewitness at the Wilkie-like scenes of Pleydell's *High Jinks* and the reading of Margaret Bertram's will, but also a larger purpose. By establishing an alliance and developing a friendship between Lucy's two principal protectors, he does not merely recruit the powerful adherents whom Harry Bertram will ultimately need, and connect the stories of brother and sister; he gains an opportunity, in the talk of these congenial associates, for a shrewd and lively commentary on the workings of the law. And we are made free of a world he knows and enjoys.

Here, then, are the lawyers in *Guy Mannering*, like portraits hanging round a college hall. There is Mac-Morlan—a pendant to Glossin; not only an honest man and good neighbour, but also—for Mannering's benefit, and (it goes without saying) for ours—an untainted source of truth, about the Bertram family, past and present. There is Protocol, whose devious course Pleydell is able to interpret. Protocol runs his eye over the will in Lucy's favour. 'Too cool . . . too cool by half', Pleydell whispers to Mannering;

'He has another deed in his pocket still.'
'Why does he not show it then, and be d—d to him?' . . .
'Why, how should I know?' answered the barrister,—'why does a cat not kill a mouse when she takes him?—the love of power, and of teasing I suppose.'[1]

And, when Protocol announces that Margaret Bertram has made him trustee for the young Bertram whom everyone present believes to be dead, Pleydell remarks to Mannering:

'Protocol is not worse than other people, I believe; but this old lady has determined that if he do not turn rogue, it shall not be for want of temptation.'[2]

There is Pleydell himself, with his *humour*—delightful to Scott and to those who could likewise recognize the portrayal of an *original*; Pleydell, with his broad culture and capacity for philosophical reflection: 'A lawyer without history or literature is a

[1] ii. 309 (Chapter XXXVIII).   [2] ii. 314-15 (Chapter XXXVIII).

A MINOR POINT OF COMPARISON 241

mere mechanic, a mere working mason; if he possesses some knowledge of these, he may call himself an architect.'[1] 'I have now satisfied myself,' he tells Mannering, when he has been worsted by Dandie's insatiable thirst for law,

'that if our profession sees more of human folly and human roguery than others, it is as affording the only channel through which they can vent themselves. In civilized society, law is the chimney through which all that smoke discharges itself that used to circulate through the whole house, and put every one's eyes out—no wonder, therefore, that the vent itself should sometimes get a little sooty.'[2]

It is in the exchanges between Pleydell and Mannering that Glossin becomes an almost credible figure. They dispute whether he or Hatteraick be the greater rogue, and Pleydell concludes:

'Very natural, Colonel, that you should be interested in the ruffian and I in the knave—that's all professional taste—but I can tell you Glossin would have been a pretty lawyer, had he not had such a turn for the roguish part of the profession.' 'Scandal would say, he might not be the worse lawyer for that.' 'Scandal would tell a lie, then, as she usually does. Law's like laudanum; it's much more easy to use it as a quack does, than to learn to apply it like a physician.'[3]

Learning of these hopes and endeavours on her behalf, Lucy responds as a heroine should: she wonders how they will affect her prospect of marriage with Charles Hazlewood—though, in the event, it is not to legal right that she will owe this happy consummation, but to her brother's generosity, when the case has gone in his favour.

It was only to be expected that the framework of law within which most of Scott's characters contend for advantage should be much more substantial than that to which Jane Austen pays a sort of ironical deference; that it should engage the attention and offer sustenance to the speculative imagination. But, in his reaction to the theme, he shows another and perhaps surprising aspect of his large and many-sided genius.

Fiction, at least from the Middle Ages, witnesses to a peculiar imaginative hunger: the desire to envisage a social order other than that which we acknowledge, and on the whole accept. I am not

[1] ii. 290 (Chapter XXXVII).   [2] ii. 326 (Chapter XXXIX).
[3] iii. 335–6 (Chapter LVI).

referring to the comic reign of topsy-turvydom, nor the reversals of satire and burlesque. What I have in mind is not disorder, but an alternative order. It is discernible at least so far back as the *Tale of Gamelyn*, which lies behind Lodge's *Rosalynde* and *As You Like It*.

> 'Yonge men,' sayde Gamelyn · 'by your lewte,
> What man is your maister · that ye with be?'
> Alle they answerde · withoute lesing,
> 'Oure maister is y-crouned · of outlawes king.'
>
> Gamelyn and Adam · wente forth in-feere,
> And they grette the maister · that they founde there.
> Than seide the maister · king of outlawes,
> 'What seeke ye, yonge men · under woode-schawes?'
> Gamelyn answerde · the king with his croune,
> 'He moste needes walke in woode · that may not walke in towne. . . .'[1]

And Gameyln is duly elected into the outlaw polity, where he will eventually hold office. This is not the pastoral world; that may at any time be invaded by violence, but this contains the violent opposition between oppression and rough justice. This is not the ideal world excogitated by philosophers, a concept of the reason. It is a world framed to satisfy a hunger of the popular imagination.

Scott's own imagination was, evidently, drawn to this outlaw polity, but he confuses the issue by his large protestations. 'I . . . have an unfortunate propensity', he wrote to Morritt, 'for the dubious characters of Borderers Buccanneers highland robbers and all others of a Robin-Hood description. . . . I suppose the blood of the old cattle-drivers of Teviotdale continues to stir in my veins.'[2] This is but one of many such vaunting apologies, which confound together all sorts of ruffians, rebels, and outlaws, and it fails to do justice to his own fine discrimination, between—and even within— these categories. He makes use of the Robin Hood legend in *Ivanhoe*, and the verse heading which he invented for Chapter XXXIII is a friendly salute to the English tradition of an outlaw polity. Nevertheless, his dismissal of Locksley/Robin Hood as someone who dies

---

[1] *The Tale of Gamelyn* in Chaucer's *Works*, ed. Skeat (1900), iv. 661, Appendix to *Canterbury Tales*. I apologize for bringing forward again an illustration I have used in 'Shakespeare's Pastoral Comedy' (see p. 38 above); it is the most apposite I know.

[2] Scott to Morritt, 28 July 1814 (*Letters, 1811–1814*, p. 479).

in a black-letter garland prized by antiquaries shows his incomplete understanding of it.[1] As a good magistrate, Scott is, of course, cognizant of those who have fallen outside the law. As a sagacious historian, he can enter into the position of those who must appeal from it, to another law: Hugh Redgauntlet, in whose eyes the reigning sovereign is a usurper; Joshuah Geddes, who believes that the State has usurped the function of the individual conscience; above all, Jeanie Deans, on whose fidelity to that other law persuasion and force exert themselves in vain. But there is still a distinction to be made between these insights and a pattern of thought, or dream, which had been laid down in Scott's childhood. *Guy Mannering* proves that this vision of an order, outside society yet not merely unsocial, preceded his acquaintance with the law.

His anonymous contribution to *Blackwood's Edinburgh Magazine* in 1817, 'Notices Concerning the Scottish Gypsies',[2] carries evidence of his early sympathy with Jean Gordon. Her story, as he had heard it, and the appearance of her granddaughter, Madge, whom he had seen, were lodged in his memory and imagination. He retells the tale several times,[3] and always the emphasis falls on Jean's insistence that those over whom she rules should refrain from robbing their benefactors, and on her own reparation when they break this law.[4] Moreover, he is not (I am convinced) busy with mere testimony to likelihood, for he retains a certain singularity in the central figure—as a man will do, who builds a story on a strange dream, and cannot be persuaded to relinquish the initial improbability. For reasons lying beyond the scope of my present argument, fiction seldom represents a woman as ruler in the outlaw polity. She is more likely to appear as a solitary rebel, or—if she commands the allegiance of men—as merely lawless and destructive, like Helen MacGregor. Perhaps this is why Scott insists on Meg Merrilies's masculine stature and hardihood. He does not appear to recognize the gypsy

---

[1] iii. 281–2 (Chapter XLII).
[2] i (Apr. 1817), pp. 43–58; (May), pp. 154–61; (Sept.), pp. 615–20.
[3] In the anonymous review of *Tales of my Landlord* (*First Series*) in the *Quarterly Review*, xvi (Jan. 1817), pp. 430–80, referring to the *Blackwood* 'Notices' as though already published; and in the Magnum edition of *Guy Mannering*, 1829, claiming nearly all those 'Notices'.
[4] The stratagem by which she preserved the Gudeman of Lochside from her unruly followers is used by Meg Merrilies (ii. 88–105 (Chapters XXVII, XXVIII)).

community as matriarchal. But, 'When a child, and among the scenes which she frequented, I have often heard these stories, and cried piteously for poor Jean Gordon'.[1] And so a woman it had to be.

From Meg Merrilies to any character in Jane Austen's novels is indeed a very far cry. Nevertheless, I believe that, if these diverse products of the imagination can be brought into focus *together*, we may discover that pattern of superficial likeness and fundamental difference between the two novelists which has been obscured by a more obvious contrast.

In Lucy Bertram's part of *Guy Mannering*—and it is a part which, though secondary, cannot be spared—Scott is telling a conventional tale of the distressed heroine; and Lucy's distress appears to be of a conventional kind: her poverty stands in the way of the marriage on which she has set her heart. It must be admitted that he was drawn to this tale—probably at the outset—by something other than the availability of a popular convention. His heart and his imagination, never far apart, had been captured by the anecdote of the woman left destitute at her father's death and preserved from want by the faithful dominie;[2] but, having embarked on it, he was lured into making the dominie even more helpless than his charge, and so had to bring in law and authority, Pleydell and Mannering, to rescue them both. Thus Lucy's predicament, and the eventual solution of her problem, agree well enough with current convention in the naturalistic novel. This was a convention within which Jane Austen habitually worked. For her, however, the legal aspect of this predicament—the testamentary dispositions which leave her women unprovided—is merely the thing without which there would have been no story: the wall (so to speak) between Pyramus and Thisbe.[3] She owes it no more than such civil attention as she might pay to a tale, however tedious or absurd, received in social intercourse; and, in her own transmission of it, a due regard for probability. The lovers, not the wall, engage her interest. Scott is content to take their love for granted, as something already there.

---

[1] *Blackwood*, i. 56. He did not forget her. See, e.g., *Letters, 1825–26*, pp. 474 and 506.
[2] Scott recounts the anecdote in his Introduction to the Magnum edition of *Guy Mannering*.
[3] The actual obstacle was ill will between the parents, but the wall is a very convenient symbol.

It is the wall that interests him: how is it built and how has it weathered? Can it be circumvented—or penetrated? He relishes the *business of the obstacle*. He frames it in human terms, a trial of skill, and will, between lawyers. He grounds it in social and historical probability: thus, even had Mrs. Godfrey Bertram survived the (supposed) death of her son, and lived to bring up her daughter, it is impossible to imagine her denouncing the entail on Ellangowan as Mrs. Bennet denounces that on Longbourn.[1]

So far, these two are separated by diversity of experience and circumstances: by what they know, and what (as novelists) they choose not to know. Another separation comes with Scott's historical vision, and his choice of the past as setting even for this tale of domestic distress—since he is thereby enabled to couple it with another, of outright lawlessness. Yet I doubt whether even here we reach the fundamental divergence between them. Whether they envisage their characters and events within the framework of the law, or outside it, they are still united by a belief in its reality; for both, it exists as part of the social order. But for Scott this is not the only order—as Meg Merrilies here bears witness.

To all appearance, Meg belongs in Harry Bertram's story alone, but her intervention in Lucy's is required to bring about a junction of the two, and the final resolution. By inducing Margaret Bertram to change her will, she sets up a train of events: Mannering and Pleydell, learning from the dead woman's maid how this came about, begin piecing together their recollections of Meg, and of her part in the vicissitudes of the Bertram family; and so at last the long coil is unwound. In the event, Meg Merrilies and what she signifies may be seen to pervade, even to dominate, the whole novel.

At a deeper level than that of simple experience; at the level of a strange sense of reality which can subsist, independent of rational conviction, by virtue of that 'licentious and vagrant faculty',[2] the imagination—Scott and Jane Austen diverge. I suspect that many of us—perhaps all in whom the imagination took its impress early— will recognize this duality in ourselves, and yet be startled to meet

---

[1] 'We are a poor people and in families of consideration our estates are almost uniformly settled on heirs male' (Scott, *Letters*, 1825–26, p. 396).
[2] *Rambler* 125.

it in a mind of such strong and settled rationality as Scott's. For it is evident that his imagination accepted that other order, that polity outside society, of which Meg Merrilies is here the symbol. His mind was a denizen of two worlds; Jane Austen's, of one. For her there was no *alternative order*.

ROBERT WILLIAM CHAPMAN
1881–1960

(1961)

ROBERT WILLIAM CHAPMAN was born at Eskbank, near Dalkeith, on 5 October 1881. Both his parents were English. His father, Edward Chapman, after teaching for some years in Dundee, took orders in the Episcopal Church of Scotland. His mother, Hannah Cannon, came of a Yorkshire family lately settled in Dundee. Robert was the youngest of their six children. His father's death, when he was three years old, left the family poorly provided, except as to intellectual endowments. Mrs. Chapman settled at Carnoustie, and sent the children to Dundee High School. Her bereavement deepened her concern with the grave, precocious, delicate youngest son. He, after taking prizes at school, obtained the first bursary at St. Andrews, where he became an outstanding pupil of Professor Burnet, and, at twenty-one, proceeded, with first-class classical honours and the Guthrie and Adam de Brome scholarships, to Oxford. At Oriel, enduring friendships were formed: with Maynard Fletcher, who died young, in India; with Rupert Smith, who spent much of his life abroad; with George Gordon, later to become Merton Professor of English Literature in Oxford and President of Magdalen; and Wilfrid Normand, later Lord Normand, Lord President of the Court of Session. Although the labours and loyalties of his working life were thereafter given to Oxford, Robert Chapman kept a place apart in his affections for the north, and for the friends of his youth, in whose company he delighted to revisit the hills and moors to which he remained constant.

Teaching in vacations, to supplement his scholarships, he took Firsts in Classical Moderations and Literae Humaniores, and won the Gaisford Prize for Greek Prose. Shortly after taking his degree he was appointed assistant to Charles Cannan, Secretary to the Delegates of the Clarendon Press. Here his initial concern and life-long interest was lexicography: he had much to do with forwarding the progress of the *New English Dictionary* and the revised Liddell and Scott: also with Greek texts. From this exclusive devotion to traditional scholarship he was first drawn by the work of Miss Katharine Marion Metcalfe, who, after taking a First in the Honour School of English Language and Literature, had come from Lady Margaret Hall to be assistant English tutor at Somerville. Speaking nearly thirty years later, on Book Collecting, he was to recall that 'my career as a conscious collector began when I married a lady who had bought an *Arcadia* in folio while yet a schoolgirl'. Miss Metcalfe, having possessed herself of a first edition of *Pride and Prejudice* (which was more than every great library could then claim), proposed to edit the novel from the original text—a project eagerly recommended to the Press by Walter Raleigh. Her edition was published in 1912. Robert Chapman and Katharine Metcalfe were married in 1913, and together planned that complete edition of Jane Austen's novels from authoritative texts which should supersede almost eighty years of casual reprinting. This intended partnership was thwarted by many circumstances—separation in time of war and family cares (three sons and a daughter were born to them); but the original inspiration was to yield abundant fruit, and Mrs. Chapman continued to be consulted, in this as in subsequent literary projects.

The outbreak of war changed the course of their lives. Robert Chapman served as a volunteer with the Royal Garrison Artillery in Salonika. So it came about that a volume of essays by Captain Chapman, R.G.A., carried a reference on its title-page to Macedonia; and, even more strangely, that the Preface to an edition of Johnson's *Journey* and Boswell's *Tour* was to open with these words: 'This edition was planned, and in part executed, in Macedonia, in the summer of 1918. I had a camp behind Smol Hill, on the left bank of the Vardar, and a six-inch gun (Mark XI, a naval piece, on an improvised carriage; "very rare in this state"), with which I made a demonstration in aid of the French and Greek armies, when they stormed the heights beyond the river.' Service in this campaign entailed tedium, discomfort, and the undermining of physical vitality. George Gordon, who had survived a more dangerous war than his friend, wrote, after visiting the Dardanelles in 1919: 'There is no doubt that you fellows out there, though you had more chance of living, had a much worse time'. But no material circumstances could sap Robert Chapman's intellectual vitality. He had taken books with him, among them Boswell's *Life of Johnson*, and what he found in it led him to ask that early editions of the *Journey* and the *Tour* might be sent out to him. 'To handle a first edition would be like walking down Duke Humphrey again', he wrote in 1916. Thus, to quote from the Preface once more, 'a temporary gunner . . . might have been found collating the three editions of the *Tour to the Hebrides*, or re-reading *A Journey to the Western Islands* in the hope of finding a corruption in the text'. Perhaps it was in these conditions that he acquired his capacity for abstraction and concentration: as his *Portrait of a Scholar and Other Essays Written in Macedonia 1916–1918* was the product of 'camps and dug-outs and troop-trains', so, in later years, he would employ the leisure hours of visits or the intervals of journeys on whatever work he had in hand. His friends can recall some intricate piece of index-making (to his editions of Jane Austen or Johnson) as an evening task, carried serenely to completion through the current of talk. He claimed, of his valedictory to the Society for Pure English, that it had been written in trains between Basingstoke and Edenbridge.

The war over, he returned to Oxford and the Clarendon Press. In December of 1919 Charles Cannan died; and on 15 January 1920 Robert Chapman succeeded him as Secretary to the Delegates. Thenceforth, he was engaged in three complementary activities: administration, the promotion of others' books, and the making of his own. It will not always be possible to draw lines between these three, but the division may help to show the range of his impact on the world of letters.

In his administrative capacity he had to carry the Press through a period of steeply rising costs in the publishing trade. A fine Greek scholar, whom more than one college would have welcomed as a Fellow, he might not seem the obvious man to shoulder this responsibility; and indeed it lay heavy at the last on one who discerned what sort of future impended. But Robert Chapman inherited business aptitudes from his father, who had excelled in administrative work for the Central Office of the Scottish Church. This was not his sole resource. The secretaryship asks a nice regard for the equilibrium between powers (which are, in the last resort, persons), within and without the Press and the University. Unclouded friendship made the Secretary and the Publisher (Sir Humphrey Milford) happy partners, and kept the Clarendon Press and Amen House in constant touch. Mr. Kenneth Sisam, who had succeeded to the assistant secretaryship, was likewise a good friend, and complementary in temperament to Robert Chapman, whose carefulness and subtlety would occasionally lead him to frame a network of evidence for and against some proposal, when the case called for decision. In those who worked for him he inspired unostentatious but steady devotion.

Among publications furthered or promoted by Robert Chapman, or brought to completion in his secretaryship, the *New English Dictionary* must stand first, because of its magnitude. For the same reason, however, it is a monument that speaks for itself. He tells something of the work in progress, the methods and aims of its editors, in his (anonymous) *Account of the Oxford University Press 1468-1921*; and looks back towards the completed undertaking, and his own share in the *Supplement*, in his lecture on *Lexicography*. The University signalized his contribution by the conferment of the degree of Honorary D.Litt., in 1928.

Important books published during—and largely by reason of—Robert Chapman's reign are so numerous that it is necessary to single out one here, one there, for mention; and I hope I may be allowed to choose those of which I have a little knowledge: notably, the great texts of English authors. His years of activity are broadly spanned by Grierson's Donne, with which he had been concerned as assistant secretary and which was brought to completion in 1912, and Professor George Sherburn's edition of Pope's correspondence, with which he continued to give help for some while after his retirement in 1942, though it was not published until 1956. In the midst, Dr. L. F. Powell's Boswell occupies a dominant position. Circumstances had made it necessary to revise Birbeck Hill's edition of Boswell's *Life of Johnson*, and desirable to add the *Tour to the Hebrides*. Of this work, the greatest of all that Robert Chapman projected, the first volume appeared in 1934, and the last (the single, comprehensive index) in 1950. There is, besides, the Gray *Letters* of Paget Toynbee and Leonard Whibley. Ancillary to such stately vessels as these, a tug-boat in the tide-way, came the little *Annals of English Literature 1475–1925*, with its simple but ingenious pattern of double reference.

The progress of these works through the Press illustrates some of Robert Chapman's distinctive qualities—for example, his gifts as mediator. To an author demanding yet one more opportunity for reconsideration, he would reply, not with any reference to rules or conditions, but with the remonstrance that to ask it now would 'take the heart out of the printers'. Mediation between an editor, eminent in his own world, and the owner of the manuscripts he sought to edit, required a very delicate intimation of the degree of ceremony that might well be used in approaching someone to whom these manuscripts were simply family possessions—and, where this failed, a greater measure of patience than personal disappointment calls for. His capacity for drawing others in to contribute their peculiar skills and resources was of Johnsonian proportions; and his practice recalled the sociability of eighteenth-century scholarship at its happiest. Dining often in other colleges besides his own (Magdalen made him a Fellow in 1931), he knew *who* was working on *what*: where a good book might be looked for, and by whose assistance it might be made better. Of his own wide and various stores of knowledge, author and editor alike were made free. (How many of us realized the full worth of what was so lightly placed at our disposal?) Yet, knowing so much, and holding strong opinions of his own, he never overbore theirs. Dr. Powell relates how—a difference arising over the method of indexing his Boswell—the Secretary accepted the editor's choice, though it ran counter to his own, saying: 'It's your book'. To a young author[1] he wrote, conveying suggestions as to his manuscript, but concluding: 'If you don't feel like doing anything more to it, I'll publish it as it stands'. When the circumstances of publication made it necessary that a decision should be his own, he was quick to avow it in face of adverse criticism.

Robert Chapman was building up a tradition as to the treatment of 'English Classics'—that treatment which he had prefigured in

[1] Geoffrey Tillotson.

his first volume of essays—and himself leading the way: applying the discipline of classical studies to authors hitherto reprinted without systematic textual scrutiny. Although it is impossible to confine his own books to categories, it will nevertheless be convenient to set foremost (as those by which he will be chiefly remembered) his editions of Jane Austen and Johnson. Chronologically, they interweave. Thus, in January 1914 he is planning to edit the six novels, jointly with Mrs. Chapman; but the chances of war presently bring the tale of the Hebridean travellers to the fore, and so one edition follows closely upon the other: *The Novels of Jane Austen*, 1923; *Johnson's Journey to the Western Islands of Scotland and Boswell's Journal of a Tour to the Hebrides with Samuel Johnson*, 1924. Many little volumes of Jane Austen's unpublished writings, and the *Memoir* by her nephew, succeed in the late twenties, with *Rasselas* intervening in 1927. The climax, though not the conclusion, of the Austenian studies comes with *Jane Austen's Letters to her Sister Cassandra and Others* in 1932; and, although some minor pieces are to appear severally as the manuscripts become available, the field is now clear for Johnson. Reports of progress in the periodical literature of the thirties and forties—lists of autograph letters, investigations of Mrs. Piozzi's dealings with those that she published—all these lead up to the crowning achievement: *The Letters of Samuel Johnson with Mrs. Thrale's Genuine Letters to Him*, 1952.

The business of editing was not quite over: the text of his little anthology, *Selections from Samuel Johnson*, 1955, was scrutinized as carefully as ever; but most of the labours of the last years went to complete the tale, already considerable, of critical and biographical writing on the authors of his choice.

It is easy to forget, now, what an innovation it was to handle the text of an English novelist with a solicitude hitherto reserved for major poets. In claiming to have collated the early editions—its proper degree of authority assigned to each—the editor tells less than the whole story: Jane Austen was not a practised proof-reader, and had been served no more than moderately well by her publishers; there was mending to be done. All the persons and events of her novels were present to him with such distinctness and precision that he could detect the small misprints which had long passed muster, and the bigger blunders which had been dismissed or ignored as beyond cure. At the end, one sole crux in *Mansfield Park* remained—and there her own pen may have stumbled. Not every novelist will endure this scrutiny and reward this care; we shall not now know how the text of Trollope, on which R. W. C. was working desultorily in his latter years, would have stood up to it. Scott, an early favourite, whom he could quote with sudden felicity, would have asked another life-time, at least.

The text of the letters made further demands: notably, the tracing and deciphering of manuscripts. The tale has been told elsewhere[1] of a meeting on the high seas between Robert Chapman and Pierpont Morgan, resulting in permission to transcribe the collection of Jane Austen's letters in his possession. Johnson's were, of course, more widely dispersed: the big collections were on the further side of the Atlantic, where R. W. C. was always made welcome, whether he came charged with the business of the Press or on his own affairs; but pockets of ore were still being discovered— at the eleventh hour and afterwards, to his chagrin. Transcription, here, was no light undertaking. 'I think I know Johnson's rather deceptive hand better than anyone', was as near as he ever came to boasting; and years of attention to Johnson's published work— emerging, for example, in his study of revision in the *Rambler*, *Rasselas*, and the *Idler*—had taught him what was to be looked for. We may, in sum, discern behind the editions, alike of Jane Austen's and Johnson's letters and her 'minor works', a campaign of many years' duration, and the patient, indefatigable strategy by which manuscripts were located, borrowed, copied—and elucidated. For the quotation with which R. W. C. opens his Preface to Jane Austen's novels applies equally well to the letters of both authors: 'Dr. Johnson "observed, that all works which describe manners, require notes in sixty or seventy years."' (What would we not give for such notes, from him, on Henry James—another favourite of long standing?) This social commentary on Johnson's letters was necessarily of bookish origin—though authorities to whom the problems were living issues might be called in to interpret; but for

[1] Margaret Lane, 'Dr. R. W. Chapman', in *The Times Literary Supplement*, 6 Aug. 1954.

Jane Austen it was sometimes possible to draw on the spoken word. Admirals were still living who had served in sail; so was a descendant of the firm that could have made Jane Fairfax's piano; Bath was less changed than London; above all, the Austen family was not extinct. In the edition of the novels, these notes on contemporary manners did more than elucidate; they testified to Jane Austen's fidelity—a virtue which could sometimes seduce her editor from his self-imposed rule against appreciative criticism. He was willing to demonstrate her method of work so long as the argument proceeded from verifiable facts, and he took much pleasure in showing what use she had made of an almanac in constructing the time-scheme of this or that novel, and to what purpose. This was a ploy begun with Mr. (later Sir Frank) MacKinnon: besides illustrating her exact workmanship, it was of use in establishing the chronology of novels she was known to have revised. The indexes to these editions were like nobody else's. R. W. C. disapproved of an undifferentiated index—the 'Unitarian heresy', he called it—and devised an intricate system of categories. There are seven distinct indexes to Johnson's *Letters*. Once mastered, they are invaluable to the reader, not merely for reference but also as a conspectus of Johnson's mental landscape.

These were labours of love, in a sense not always recognized by those who assumed that such a learned editor must value niceties for their own sake, and never divined the quality of the regard which this editor felt towards these two authors. He did indeed consider precise documentation the sole approach to biography, but never lost sight of the goal: his aim was not merely to present the facts in due order, but also to remove hindrances to true vision —those with which shallowness and ignorance had tarnished the portrait. He must have been badly hurt by the reception of Jane Austen's letters: towards her he cherished a protective tenderness, and it was about the time when reviewers were announcing their triumphant discovery that the writer of the celebrated novels was no better than anyone else and rather less likeable than most that he mentioned his wish to write a book about her, for the sake of banishing misconceptions. In 1952, when Johnson's letters were ready to appear, he wrote to reassure a friend who had asked him whether a projected piece of work on Johnson would be trespass, ending: 'If I can help—who have sometimes dreamed of a short life —command me.' That dream should not have surprised anyone familiar with the appendixes and indexes to his edition of the Hebridean travels. The framework of his book on Jane Austen is discernible in his Clark lectures; but the short life of Johnson remained unwritten.

The tale of Robert Chapman's own writings begins with the *Portrait of a Scholar*—that collection of essays of which Walter Raleigh said: 'I like these. They have pluck, which is what makes literature as distinct from cultured writing.' They anticipate later developments, not only in their occasional bearing on his favourite authors, but also in an elegiac tone which is not confined to the portrait of Bywater. Those who knew him, in Oxford, as the author of many obituary notices remarked his skill in this sort of writing; but there went more than skill to some of these memorials. To turn to him in distress under the burden of a similar task was to learn what it had cost him to write one of them. He cared deeply that his friends should be esteemed at their true worth, and had had poignant experience of the transience of reputation. His *S.P.E. Retrospect* (from which his own notable share in the enterprise is not apparent) reads like the obituary of a generation.

Of his own literary career he once wrote: 'He is sometimes reproached, by his family and friends, for devoting to the niceties of scholarship talents that, they kindly hint, are worthy of a loftier flight. His reply is that, if he has not "known genius familiarly", he has known dozens of people who could write, say, readable essays, and some who could write very good ones. He has known few whom he could trust to make the best use of the delicate tools of editorial scholarship.' This is a little misleading: the volume in which it appears (*Johnsonian and Other Essays*) proves it an understatement; his writings, though brief, were numerous. Many bore only his initials—which he liked his younger friends to use, in referring to him; many appeared anonymously. A complete list is much to be desired. It would, for example, set in perspective alike the occasional, single lectures and those given at Trinity College, Cambridge, in 1948: the Clark Lectures—by the courtesy of the

Cambridge University Press, published in Oxford: *Jane Austen, Facts and Problems*. But his whole impact on the world of letters has been most happily summed up by Mr. H. W. Liebert: 'Almost everyone working on English Literature of the Eighteenth Century soon comes to borrow (if he does not steal) from the extensive and precise labours of Dr. R. W. Chapman.'[1]

In the true eighteenth-century tradition, this massive knowledge was grounded in book-collecting. His was not a rich man's collection, and he would warn others against mere fastidiousness (as in his lecture on *The Sense of the Past*); but he took delight in the treasures of richer friends, and, when obliged to part with his own, said nothing about it. The Bodleian benefited by his constant watchfulness.

This tale of books and bookish cares represents only the life he led within doors: the scholar familiar to the world of scholarship. His life-long friends knew another Robert Chapman: a lover of the Highlands, the Border—of Cairngorms, Lammermuirs, Cheviots, Cuillins—and a tireless walker. He loved beauty and solitude; he enjoyed companionship, from which a younger generation was not excluded. He had decided likes and dislikes: rich and well tilled arable gave him little pleasure; rooks in a windy sky were his music. He might perhaps be called an eclectic naturalist: of the birds, beasts, and plants belonging to his favourite terrain he had a sound working knowledge—with something to spare for less favoured creatures. These expeditions lightened the burdens of the between-war years. The second war, bringing back memories of loss in the first and new anxieties on behalf of his sons, bore hardly on a man whose health, never robust, had once been undermined: he became very ill and, on 31 July 1942, retired from the secretaryship. Some measure of recovery brought further years of fruitful work, but in 1956 a crippling illness confined him within an ever narrowing circle. He never complained, either of deprivation or of hardship, and in hospital was a source of comfort to fellow patients. To the end, his mind was not dimmed: he could detect a faulty accent in a quotation from Theocritus, and recommend the best edition.

[1] Herman W. Liebert, 'This Harmless Drudge', in *The New Colophon* (vol. I, part ii, 1948).

Strength slowly ebbed, and he died in Oxford on 20 April 1960. He had been a Member of the Council of Friends of the Bodleian and the Oxford Bibliographical Society, and Lamont Lecturer at Yale University (1950). The honours conferred on him included the LL.D. of his own first University, St. Andrews, and the C.B.E. (1955).

In person, Robert Chapman was uncommonly tall, with a straggling gait which, like his famous bicycle, covered a lot of ground. His countenance was melancholy, except when lit by a smile. His letters were a delight and a torment: their mingled ceremony and idiosyncrasy were always fresh; but his hand was not easy, his ink seemed fugitive, he wrote on the backs of expendable sheets of the thinnest paper, and the kernel of an important sentence would often be a Greek or Latin phrase—not written out in full. There were those who professed to find him formidable, and it is possible to see why without thinking them right. He was not always and everywhere approachable, and he probably knew the tactical value of his own silences. Only his family and his oldest friends could be aware of the strength and tenderness of feeling that underlay his habitual reserve; but it was given to some few others to recognize that the benignity with which he regarded Jane Austen's least wise and witty heroine had its counterpart in common life. He was scrupulously considerate: though naturally fastidious, he could reduce his wants to a very few, and even these he would forgo, rather than give trouble. Neither his critical discrimination nor his keen-edged wit ever betrayed him into speaking ill of anyone.

When Johnson died, a friend wrote: 'He has made a chasm, which not only nothing can fill up, but which nothing has a tendency to fill up.—Johnson is dead.—Let us go to the next best;—there is nobody;—no man can be said to put you in mind of Johnson.' Only the name needs changing.

NOTE. I am grateful for permission to read among the files at the Clarendon Press. Of my debts to those who knew R. W. C. longest and most closely, I particularly wish to acknowledge that to Lord Normand, for a portrait in favour of which I would gladly have given up this faint impression.

INDEX

Abu Bakr Ibn al Tufail, 106, 121.
Addison, Joseph, 19, 61, 100 n., 105, 109.
Agostini, Nicolo delli, 11, 12.
Alciati, Andrea, 20.
Ames, Joseph, 82 n., 84 n.
Amyot, Jaques, 17.
Ariosto, Ludovico, 13.
Aristotle, pseudo-, 15–16.
Arthur, King, 82–90.
Ascham, Roger, 82–3.
Ashwell, George, 106 n.
Austen, Cassandra, 235 n.
Austen, Jane, 117, 201, 206, 215, 222, 231–46 *passim*, 248–9, 252–7.

Bailey, John, 92.
Baillie, Joanna, 197.
Balderston, Katharine C., 173.
Ballantyne, James, 219–23.
Barclay, Alexander, 18.
Beaumont, Francis, 86, 192.
Bellerophon, 1–28 *passim*.
Bennet, James, 82, 83 n.
Bethell, S. L., 76.
Bible, the, 20, 24, 27, 48, 69, 73, 76, 77, 79, 89, 175.
Bion, Lament for, 4.
Blackwood, Adam, 131–5.
Blackwood's Edinburgh Magazine, 243, 244 n.
Boccaccio, Giovanni, 9, 10, 14–16, 17–19, 20, 24, 26.
Boethius, 6.
Boiardo, Matteo Maria, 1, 11, 33, 34.
Boisguillebert, Pierre le Pesant, Sieur de, 133–5.
Boswell, James, 91, 92, 93, 94, 103, 104, 126, 155–68, 170, 172, 174, 177, 248, 249, 250, 251.
Boswell, Margaret, Mrs., 168.
Brewer, Wilmon, 180.
Brooks, Harold, 49, 54, 139 n.
Browne, Sir Thomas, 153.
Bunyan, John, 127, 128.
Burney, Charles, 222 n.
Burney, Frances, Mme d'Arblay, 108.
Burton, Robert, 15, 153.

Butler, Samuel, 8.
Bywater, Ingram, 255.

Cairncross, A. S., 66, 67.
Cannan, Charles, 247, 249.
Carter, Elizabeth, 102, 106 n.
Catullus, 3.
Caussin, Nicolas, 133–4.
Caxton, William, 82.
Chambers, Sir Edmund, 66.
Chambers, Robert, 173.
Chapman, Edward, 247, 249.
Chapman, Hannah, Mrs. Edward, 247.
Chapman, Katharine, Mrs. Robert, 248, 252.
Chapman, Robert William, 131, 168, 169, 170–8, 247–57.
Chapone, Hester Mulso, Mrs., 95, 102–3, 104 n.
Charles Stuart, Prince, 188, 208.
Charles XII of Sweden, 147, 148.
Chatham, William Pitt, Earl of, 51.
Chaucer, Geoffrey, 5, 10 n., 38, 40, 56, 147, 183, 242 n.
Cicero, 15, 147, 150.
Claude Lorraine, 197.
Claverhouse, John Graham, Viscount Dundee, 225.
Clifford, J. L., 173.
Cockburn, Henry, Lord, 187–8, 204.
Coghill, Nevill, 56–7.
'Col', Donald Maclean, 'Young Col', 160.
Coleridge, Samuel Taylor, 31, 42, 57.
Collins, William, 107, 125.
Comes, i.e. Natale Conti, and lesser mythographers, 14–20, 26.
Conant, M. P., 109.
Corbett, Richard, 8.
Corson, J. C., 179.
Cowl, R. P., 85.
Cowley, Abraham, 97 n.
Curtius, E. R., 5 n., 6.

Dalkeith, Charles Scott, Earl of Dalkeith, later Duke of Buccleuch, 204.
Dalrymple, Sir David, 92.
Daniel, P. A., 65.

INDEX

Dante Alighieri, 9, 10.
Daphnis and Chloe, 33.
Day Lewis, C., 25.
Dekker, Thomas, 42.
de la Mare, Walter, 119.
Demosthenes, 147, 150.
Dennistoun, James, 226 n.
Dick, Sir Alexander, 163.
Dickens, Charles, 231, 238.
Diodati, Charles, 13, 26.
Domenichi, Ludovico, 12.
Domitian, 138.
Donne, John, 41, 250.
Doran, Madeleine, 66, 68.
Douce, Francis, 85.
Douglas, Gavin, 6.
Dover Wilson, J., 65.
Drummond, William, 13.
Dryden, John, 97 n., 116, 131, 140–3, 146, 149, 151, 152, 181, 212.
Dunbabin, T. J., 3 n.
Duthie, G. I., 65–71, 76 n.
Dyson, Gillian, 216.

Edgeworth, Maria, 209.
'E. K.', 22.
Elizabeth I, 143.
Elton, William R., 77 n.
Emin, Joseph, 106.
Estienne, Charles, 16 n.

Farnham, Willard, 55.
Fergusson, Adam, 226 n.
Fielding, Henry, 190, 238.
Fischer, H. A., 3 n.
Fleeman, J. D., 166 n., 229 n.
Fletcher, John, 192.
Fletcher, Maynard, 247.
Forbes, Sir William, 160.
Freebairn, James, 133 n., 134–5.

Galt, John, 231.
Gamelyn, the Tale of, 38–9, 242
Gardner, Dame Helen, 30.
Gesta Romanorum, 69.
Gibbon, Edward, 106.
Gifford, Henry, 137 n.
Goldsmith, Oliver, 93, 108 n.
Gordon, George, 179, 206, 215, 247.
Gordon, George Huntly, 216 n.
Gordon, Jean, 243–4.
Gordon, Madge, 243.

Gordon, R. K., 180.
Granville Barker, Harley, 68, 69.
Gray, Thomas, 96 n., 251.
Greene, Robert, 43, 51.
Greg, Sir Walter, 65, 66, 68.
Greville, Fulke, Lord Brooke, 213.
Grierson, Sir Herbert, 222 n., 225, 250.
Grierson, Sir Robert, of Lagg, 224, 226.

Hadrian, 138.
Hailes, David Dalrymple, Lord, 163.
Halle, Edward, 19.
Hamilton, John, Archbishop of St. Andrews, 131, 132, 134, 135.
Hannibal, 147, 148.
Hardy, J. P., 120, 124, 126.
Harvey, Gabriel, 13.
Hawes, Stephen, 18–19.
Hawkesworth, John, 104, 117.
Haywood, Eliza, Mrs., 134–5.
Hazlitt, William, 29–30, 103.
Hector, Edmund, 174.
Henderson, Isobel, 25.
Henry VIII, 19.
Henryson, Robert, 18.
Herodotus, 147.
Hesiod, 3.
Heywood, Thomas, 83.
Hill, George Birkbeck, 131, 170, 171, 174, 175, 250.
Hilles, Frederick W., 120, 122, 123.
Hogarth, William, 125.
Holland, Philemon, 17.
Holyday, Barten, 141.
Homer, 3, 15, 17.
Horace, 3 n., 4, 21, 138, 139, 151.
Howie, John, 225.
Hubbard, Margaret, 25.
Humphreys, A. R., 49, 61, 85 n.
Hyde, Mary, Mrs. Donald, and the Hyde Collection, 149 n., 174 n.

Jack, Ian, 179 n., 229 n.
James, D. G., 74 n., 79 n.
James, Henry, 253.
James, Sir Walter James, 164.
Jenkins, Harold, 29 n.
Jenyns, Soame, 112 n.
Johnson, Elizabeth, Mrs. Samuel, 135 n., 177.
Johnson, Michael, 111, 155.

INDEX

Johnson, Samuel, references to particular works:
Adventurer, 69, 72–3, 75, 92, 93, 94, 97, 100, 113.
Bravery of the English Common Soldier, On the, 93.
Dictionary, 111, 131, 158 n., 175.
Fountains, The, 115.
Idler, 110 n., 165.
Irene, 137.
Journey to the Western Islands of Scotland, 130, 155–69, 196–7.
Letters, 81, 121, 131, 136, 155–60, 164 n., 166, 170–8, 222.
Lives of the Poets, 19, 96 n., 97, 98, 100, 105 n., 107, 113, 118, 140, 151, 172.
London, 137, 140, 142–6.
Rambler, 1, 50, 73 n., 93, 96 n., 98, 99, 109, 110, 111, 114, 115 n., 116, 127, 137, 236.
Rasselas, 95, 96, 100, 102–29, 169.
Review of William Tytler's Inquiry, 130.
Shakespeare:
Preface, 50, 52, 54, 97.
Notes, 58, 61, 63, 71, 73–4, 78, 83, 85, 96, 98, 182.
Vanity of Human Wishes, 101, 104, 124, 137–8, 139, 140, 146–54.
Vision of Theodore, 109, 128.
mentioned, 32, 84, 86.
Johnson, Sarah, Mrs. Michael, 104, 111.
Johnsonian Miscellanies, 171.
Jones, Emrys, 120, 123, 124.
Jonson, Ben, 52, 55, 63, 85, 86, 138, 187.
Juvenal, 137–53.

Keith, George, 106 n.
Ker, W. P., 120, 122.
Kipling, Rudyard, 229.
Kirkby, John, 106, 107.
Knight, Ellis Cornelia, 103.
Knight, Lady (mother of Ellis Cornelia Knight), 115 n.
Knights, L. C., 70.
Knox, John, 70, 79.
Kolb, Gwyn J., 120, 122, 123.

Labowsky, L., 25.
Lamb, Charles, 125.
Lane, Margaret, the Countess of Huntingdon, 253.
Lang, Andrew, 215, 216.

Laud, William, Archbishop of Canterbury, 150–1.
Lawrie, John, 161.
Lefèvre, Raoul, 17 n.
Leishman, J. B., 196.
Lennox, Charlotte Ramsay, Mrs., 175.
Liebert, H. W., 256.
Lisburne, Wilmot Vaughan, Visc., 161.
Livingston Lowes, J., 10 n.
Lobo, Jerome, 105, 107.
Lochbuy, John Maclean, Laird of, 161.
Lockhart, J. G., 104 n., 180, 202, 205.
Lodge, Thomas, 39, 242.
Lydgate, John, 6, 7, 18.
Lyly, John, 51.

Macdonald, Sir Alexander, 156, 160.
Mackenzie, George, 132, 135.
MacKinnon, Sir Frank, 254.
Macleod, John, of Raasay, 157–9.
Macleod, Norman, of Dunvegan, 157.
MacRitchie, David, 215, 216, 219.
Malherbe, François de, 7.
Malone, Edmond, 84, 94, 164, 189.
Malory, Sir Thomas, 82–90.
Mansfield, William Murray, Earl of, 161.
Mantuan, Baptista Spagnolo, 32.
Mar, John Erskine, Earl of, 199.
Martin, Martin, 155.
Marvell, Andrew, 20–1.
Mary Stuart, Queen of Scots, 130–6.
Maxwell, J. C., 77.
Maynard, François de, 7.
Meredith, George, 25.
Milford, Sir Humphrey, 250.
Milton, John, 1, 2, 3, 13, 14, 24–8, 32, 81, 118, 186.
Montemayor, Jorge de, 33–4, 36.
Morgan, Pierpont, 253.
Morgann, Maurice, 88, 126.
Morritt, John, 203, 242.
Muir, Kenneth, 66, 79.
Mulcaster, Richard, 84, 85.
Murphy, Arthur, 103, 104 n.
Murray, Sir David, 13.

Nashe, Thomas, 87 n.
Nero, 140.
Nichol Smith, D., 82, 116 n., 120, 144, 175, 179.
Nichols, John, 172.
Noble, Richmond, 76.
Normand, Wilfred, Lord, 247, 257 n.

INDEX

Ockley, Simon, 106, 107.
Oldham, John, 138, 139, 140, 142, 143, 145, 146.

Palmer, Samuel, 186.
Parallel, A, of Shakespeare and Scott, 180, 185.
Parsons, C. O., 228 n.
Pausanias, 4, 17.
Pegasus, 1–28, *passim*.
Pennant, Thomas, 155, 168.
Percy, Thomas, Bishop, 83, 84, 86.
Persius, 4, 5, 6, 12, 141.
Pétis de la Croix, 105.
Petrarch, Francesco Petrarca, 15.
Philips, Ambrose, 105.
Pindar, 3.
Piozzi, Gabriel, 131.
Piozzi, Mrs., *see* Thrale.
Plato, 64.
Plautus, 54.
Plutarch, 17.
Pococke, Edward, 106.
Pococke, Edward, the younger, 106, 107.
Pope, Alexander, 54, 98, 113, 121, 126, 168, 169, 250.
Porter, Lucy, 104, 121.
Pottle, Frederick A., 164.
Poussin, Nicolas, 197.
Powell, L. F., 163 n., 169 n., 170, 171, 172, 250, 251.
Pringle, Sir John, 162.
Prior, Matthew, 148 n.
Propertius, 3 n., 4.
Pyramus and Thisbe, the story of, 244.

Quarterly Review, 180, 184 n., 201–2, 204–5, 230 n., 243 n.

Radcliffe, Ann, Mrs., 186, 233.
Raleigh, Sir Walter, 41.
Raleigh, Sir Walter Alexander, 103, 120, 122, 125, 179, 248, 255.
Ramsay, James, 169.
Randolph, Thomas, 8.
Reade, A. L., 170.
Reinach, S., 1 n., 11.
Renwick, W. L., 23 n., 179 n.
Reynolds, Frances, 162, 173.
Reynolds, Sir Joshua, 107, 162, 173.
Richardson, Samuel, 75.
Richelieu, Cardinal, 7.

Richmond, George, 186.
Roaf, Christina, 25.
Robin Hood, 37–9, 242.
Robinson, Richard, 85.
Rochester, John Wilmot, Earl of, 139.
Roscommon, Wentworth Dillon, Earl of, 138.
Rossiter, A. P., 52.

Saintsbury, George, 58.
Sandys, E., 5 n.
Sandys, George, 20 n.
Savage, Richard, 144.
Scott, John, 132, 133.
Scott, Sir Walter, references to particular works:
  The Abbot, 132 n.
  The Antiquary, 179, 187, 191, 195, 200, 201, 240.
  Ashestiel fragment, 197, 200, 204, 213.
  The Bride of Lammermoor, 193, 230.
  Chronicles of the Canongate, 189, 198, 202, 210, 228 n.
  Count Robert of Paris, 181.
  Demonology and Witchcraft, Letters on, 229.
  Drama, Essay on, 189–90.
  The Fortunes of Nigel, 190, 214.
  Guy Mannering, 194, 200, 229, 238–41, 243–6.
  The Heart of Midlothian, 179, 181, 187, 193, 243.
  Ivanhoe, 242–3.
  Journal, 181, 184, 202, 214.
  The Lay of the Last Minstrel, 33, 210, 211–12.
  A Legend of Montrose, 193.
  Letters, 188, 197, 203, 204, 210, 225, 244 n., 245 n.
  'Lives of the Novelists', 103–4, 233.
  Marmion, 183, 197, 200, 213, 214.
  Minstrelsy of the Scottish Border, 225.
  The Monastery, 186.
  My Aunt Margaret's Mirror, 228 n.
  Notices concerning Scottish Gypsies, 243, 244 n.
  Old Mortality, 182, 190, 210, 225.
  Redgauntlet, 182, 199–200, 205–9, 211, 215–29, 243.
  Reviews in the *Quarterly*, 180, 184 n., 201–2, 204–5, 243.
  Rob Roy, 185, 192, 199, 210.
  The Two Drovers, 195.

INDEX

Waverley, 179, 185, 188, 191, 192, 193, 197, 203, 205–8, 210, 214, 222, 240.
Woodstock, 201.
mentioned, 253.
Scottish historians, 131.
Sejanus, 140, 147, 148, 149.
Senior, Nassau, 230 n.
Seward, William, 51.
Seznec, J., 14 n.
Shakespeare, William, references to particular plays and poems:
All's Well that Ends Well, 63.
Antony and Cleopatra, 151–2, 197.
As You Like It, 36, 43, 54, 191, 192, 194, 242.
The Comedy of Errors, 49, 54.
Coriolanus, 53.
Cymbeline, 43, 53.
Hamlet, 51, 53, 184, 194.
Henry IV, 1 and 2, 30, 47, 49, 51, 56–62, 83–90, 180 n., 181–2, 183, 189, 194, 210.
Henry V, 46, 51, 53, 61, 63, 89–90, 182, 193.
Henry VIII, 148–9.
Julius Caesar, 194.
King John, 52–3, 187.
King Lear, 54, 65–80 passim, 182, 183, 191, 195.
Love's Labour's Lost, 49, 54, 55, 57, 63.
Lucrece, 53.
Measure for Measure, 51, 53, 55, 181, 184, 193.
The Merchant of Venice, 194.
The Merry Wives of Windsor, 62, 182, 184.
A Midsummer Night's Dream, 31–2, 61.
Much Ado about Nothing, 49, 63, 183–4.
Pericles, 53.
Richard III, 187, 190.
Romeo and Juliet, 193, 236.
Sonnets, 196.
The Taming of the Shrew, 57.
The Tempest, 43, 77, 181, 183.
Twelfth Night, 29, 36, 57–8, 191.
The Two Gentlemen of Verona, 37, 38.
The Winter's Tale, 37, 43–6, 190.
mentioned, 8, 172, 202.
Sharpe, Charles Kirkpatrick, 225.
Shaw, George Bernard, 47, 49.
Shelley, Percy Bysshe, 64.
Sherbo, Arthur, 84 n.

Sherburn, George, 250.
Sheridan, Richard Brinsley, 180, 194–5.
Sidney, Mary, Countess of Pembroke, 24, 33.
Sidney, Sir Philip, 12, 22, 23, 24, 25, 33–4, 39, 70, 71, 73, 213 n., 248.
Sisam, Kenneth, 250.
Smart, Christopher, 125.
Smith, Rupert, 247.
Spens, Janet, 179.
Spenser, Edmund, 1, 13 n., 22, 23, 24, 81, 82.
Spon, Jacob, 164.
Starnes, D. T., 14 n.
Stewart, Colonel David, 204.
Strahan, Andrew, 158, 166.
Strahan, William, 104, 158, 159, 160, 162, 163, 166.
Stuart, Lady Louisa, 210, 225.
Surtees, Robert, 188.
Swift, Jonathan, 126, 148 n.
Syfret, Rosemary, 25.

Talbert, E. W., 14 n.
Talbot, Catharine, 106.
Taylor, John, 159.
Temple, William Johnson, 160, 162, 163.
Tennyson, Alfred Lord, 58, 198.
Theobald, Lewis, 83.
Theocritus, 256.
Thrale, Henry, 155, 159, 177.
Thrale, Hester Lynch Salusbury, Mrs. Thrale, afterwards Mrs. Piozzi, 91, 93–4, 99, 104 n., 131, 137, 155, 156, 157, 158 n., 159, 170–8, 252.
Thrale, Hester Maria, 'Queeney', 173.
Thurber, James, 47–8.
Tillotson, Geoffrey, 105, 251 n.
Tillotson, Kathleen Constable, Mrs., 238.
Tinker, C. B., 163 n.
Todd, W. B., 160 n., 166 n.
Toynbee, Paget, 251.
Train, Joseph, 224, 226 n.
Trollope, Anthony, 231, 253.
Tuve, Rosemond, 26 n.
Tyers, Thomas, 94.
Tytler, William, 130.

Upton, James, 82, 83 n.

van Antwerp, W. C., 216.
Verrall, A. W., 227.

Vinaver, Eugène, 86–8.
Virgil, 6, 131.
Voltaire, François Marie Arouet de, 105, 112.

Walker, Alice, 66, 67.
Walpole, Horace, 195.
Walton, John, 6.
Warburton, William, Bishop, 98.
Warton, Thomas, 81–4, 85 n., 86, 170.
Watkins, W. B. C., 84 n.
Welsford, Enid, 62.
Wheler, Sir George, 164.

Whibley, Leonard, 251.
White, Gilbert, 165.
Whitley, Alvin, 120, 122, 123, 128 n.
Williams, Anna, 115 n.
Wolsey, Thomas, Cardinal, 147, 148, 149.
Wordsworth, William, 54.
Worthington, Greville, 216, 221.

Xerxes, 147.

Young, Bartholomew, 34.

PENSACOLA JUNIOR COLLEGE LIBRARY
PR99 .L33
Lascelles, Mary.   000
Notions and facts: collec   210101

3 5101 00046649 5

PR   73-18885
99   Lascelles, Mary.
.L33
          Notions and facts:
             collected criticism
             and research.

WITHDRAWN

Pensacola Junior College Library